NAME YOUR BABY

by the same author

ENGLISH HOUSE NAMES

THE GUINNESS BOOK OF NAMES

FIRST NAMES FIRST

WHAT'S IN A NAME?

SCOTTISH CHRISTIAN NAMES

OUR SECRET NAMES

EVERYMAN'S DICTIONARY OF FIRST NAMES
(with William Gosling)

A DICTIONARY OF PUB NAMES
(with Gordon Wright)

A DICTIONARY OF DAYS

NAME YOUR BABY

Leslie Alan Dunkling

ff

faber and faber

LONDON BOSTON

First published in 1987
by Faber and Faber Limited
3 Queen Square London WCIN 3AU
This updated edition first published in 1993

Printed in Great Britain by
Clays Ltd, St Ives Plc

A CIP record for this book is
available from the British Library

ISBN 0–571–17119–2

Contents

101 INTERESTING IDEAS

3 Automobile names – *Try auto-suggestion*
3 Alcoholic names – *Make a spirited effort*
4 'Peace' names – *Be a pacifist*
4 Animal names – *Create a menagerie*
5 Royal names – *Be a royal family*
7 'Silent' names – *Tell her to be quiet*
7 Fruity names – *Look at the fruit bowl*
8 Initial names – *Initiate a name*
8 Month names – *March in time*
9 Film star names – *Do some star gazing*
10 'Girl' names – *Give her a maiden name*
10 'Beautiful' names – *Tell her she's beautiful*
10 Country names – *Join the country club*
11 Sporty names – *Be a sport*
12 Letter names – *Stick to the letter*
13 Smelly names – *Get on the right scent*
13 Adam's Rib names – *Put an end to it*
14 Colourful names – *Use a colour scheme*
14 Risky names – *Run a risk*
15 'Treasure' names – *Treasure her*
16 Junior names – *Repeat yourself*
17 Link names – *Forge a link*
17 Literary names – *Make a novel choice*
18 Shakespearean names – *Consult the Bard*
19 Mysterious names – *Be mysterious*
19 Money names – *Pay cash on delivery*
20 Diminutive names – *Call them names*
21 Invented names – *Be inventive*
22 Hyphenated names – *Hyphenate*
22 'Doctor' names – *Remember the deliveryman*
23 Difficult names – *Make short work of it*
23 'Sweet' names – *Use a sweetener*
24 Palindromic names – *Look both ways*

25 Speculative names – *Speculate*
25 Street names – *Be streets ahead*
26 Battle names – *Battle it out*
26 Woody names – *Turn over a new leaf*
26 Sea names – *Put to sea*
27 Noble names – *Confer nobility*
28 Tough names – *Toughen him up*
29 Weapon names – *Have a babe in arms*
29 Happy names – *Make your child happy*
30 Incident names – *Wait and see*
31 Boys named Sue – *Name him Sue*
32 Girls named George – *Name her George*
33 'Wanted' names – *Make no mistake*
33 Biblical names – *Try the family Bible*
34 Musical names – *Scale new heights*
35 Funny names – *Humour them*
36 Name spells – *Spell it out*
37 Mythological names – *Be mythological*
37 'Love' names – *Have a love affair*
38 Place names – *Put them in their place*
38 Family names – *Protect the family name*
39 Pronounceable names – *Pronounce judgement*
40 Clothing names – *Give a name that wears well*
40 Song names – *Sing her praises*
41 Fancy names – *Make it plain*
41 Patterned names – *Be consistent*
42 Number names – *Keep count*
43 Ordered names – *Order things differently*
44 Seasonal names – *Add a touch of seasoning*
45 'Church' names – *Go to church*
45 Pure names – *Be a purist*
46 Hat names – *Keep it under your hat*
47 Heavenly names – *Praise her to the skies*
48 'Bright' names – *Look on the bright side*
48 Victorious names – *Send her victorious*
48 Slogan names – *Get the message*
49 Classy names – *Give a classy name*

50 Day names – *Name the day*
51 Time of day names – *Bide your time*
52 Stored names – *Take it out of store*
52 University names – *Study the subject*
52 'Boy' names – *Be a bit of a lad*
53 Middle names – *Take the middle road*
53 Flower names – *Lead her up the garden path*
54 Insect names – *Join the in-sect*
55 Black and white names – *Put it in black and white*
56 Christian names – *Use a Christian name*
56 Saints' names – *Consult the calendar*
57 Reversed names – *Turn it around*
58 Weather names – *Listen to the weather forecast*
59 River names – *Brook no arguments*
60 Bird names – *Take a bird's eye view*
62 'Virtue' names – *Be virtuous*
63 Economical names – *Be economical*
64 Poetical names – *Be poetical*
65 Fishy names – *Try a new angle*
66 Vegetable names – *Be a vegetarian*
66 Lucky names – *Try your luck*
67 Remark names – *Use a remarkable name*
68 Alphabetic names – *Be alphabetical*
68 Irish names – *Put a smile in their eyes*
69 Scottish names – *Take the low road*
70 Welsh names – *Make them welcome in the hillsides*
71 Twinned names – *Pair them off*
72 Sibling's choice of names – *Get them interested*
73 Fashionable names – *Fashion a name*
73 Compromise names – *Compromise*
74 Individual names – *Do your own thing*
75 DICTIONARY AND INDEX
253 Top fifties
267 Final Quiz

Introduction

I became a Leslie by accident. My mother really wanted to name me Alan, because she admired the American actor Alan Ladd. Then she realized that if she made Alan my middle name and gave me a first name beginning with L, my initials would be L.A.D. Leslie happened to be the commonest suitable name at the time: a generation or so later I would no doubt have become Lee or Luke. As it was I became Leslie Alan Dunkling as far as the world was concerned, though for my mother I was a kind of reproduction Alan Lad(d).

You'll find some other examples of film star influence on naming in the 'ideas' section of this book. If you can't decide how to choose a name for your child, the anecdotes about how other parents have solved the problem will stimulate you in one way or another. The first part of the book is all about 'naming', as an aspect of human behaviour. You'll find the tales of what others have done as surprising, curious, amusing and odd as stories about other people's behaviour always are. What we do ourselves, of course, is 'normal'.

The second main section of this book concerns the names themselves. Names are fascinating in their own right, having come to us from many different sources and languages at different times. I give their original meanings whenever it is possible to do so.

Young parents also need to know which names are currently being well used, which are going out of fashion, which are being neglected, and so on. I have provided popularity charts for different years so that you can see the trends for yourself.

Then there's the Final Quiz at the end of the book. The questions there are meant to make you aware of any hidden traps which may be associated with a particular name, especially when coupled with your family name.

I think it's a wonderful privilege to have to name a baby. For the baby's sake it's important to get it right, so it's worth taking care. It's possible to do that and to enjoy yourself at the same time, as you narrow down the search for that one name which is just right. I wish you both enjoyment and success as you set about the task.

Leslie Dunkling
St Valentine's Day, 1987

101 INTERESTING IDEAS

If you can't decide on a name perhaps you could . . .

Try auto-suggestion

Jaguar Ferrari Tonniges of Nebraska has a brother who is Aston Martin Tonniges and a sister named Lancia LeMans. The family could justifiably be described as car-freaks. Jaguar himself now has two sons named Ferrari and Austin Healey.

The names of people and automobiles have more in common than you might think. Mercedes was a girl's name before it was given to the car. Bentley, Ford, Austin, Morgan, Morris, Riley, Lincoln, Stanley and Packard were also transferred from people, and can easily be transferred back.

An American family whose last name is Carr named their son Henry Ford. Another couple, the husband fond of his sports car, the wife a lawyer, found the ideal name for their daughter in Portia. To the wife she is the clever lady barrister in Shakespeare's *Merchant of Venice*. The husband thinks of his daughter as a Porsche, sleek, luxurious and fast-moving.

Make a spirited effort

Alcoholic names seem to be on the increase. Sherry is now more common, perhaps inspired by Sherry Lansing, the former actress who became a senior executive with 20th Century Fox.

Perry is really a form of Peregrine, though in Perry Como's case it was based on his original last name, Perido. Perry is also the name of a pleasant pear- based drink.

In North Carolina there are men who bear the first name Macon. They are named in honour of a locally born statesman, Nathaniel Macon, rather than for the French white wine of the same name. Margaux Hemingway, on the other hand, says that she was conceived after her parents had drunk a bottle of

Château Margaux. They named her Margot, but she herself changed the spelling of her name when she discovered the reason for it.

Brandy is becoming a fairly popular girl's name in the US. It is also found as Brandi, Brandie, Brandee. More recently Tequila, the name of the Mexican liquor, has appeared as a girl's name.

An individual example of an alcoholic name is borne by the tennis player Carling Bassett, named for the brewery established by her family.

Be a pacifist

Most parents hope that their child will have a peaceful life. That cannot be guaranteed, but one can at least give a child a peaceful name. A girl can be named Irene or Salome, for instance, the Greek and Hebrew forms of 'peace'. A Welsh family chose to use Heddus, based on *heddw*, the Welsh word for 'peace', to name a daughter born during the peace celebrations of 1918. Olive or Olivia might also be used, since the olive branch has long been a symbol of peace.

A Frederick is a 'peaceful ruler', while a Solomon is a 'man of peace'. 'Peace' is also an element in the names Humphrey, Wilfred, Manfred and Winfred. Peace itself has been used as a first name, and the Puritans used Peaceable. One of my favourite names in this group belonged to the writer William Makepeace Thackeray. Another is borne by that fine singer Placido Domingo, whose name means 'peaceful Sunday'.

Create a menagerie

Animal lovers have plenty of names to choose from, though some are less appealing than others, and some are not what they seem. The character called Ratty in

Samuel Lover's novel *Handy Andy* is officially Horatio, and named in honour of Lord Nelson. There is, however at least one American girl who really is named Mousie. She has an older sister, named Kitty.

Other animal-based first names include:

Sheep – Rachel
Dog – Caleb
Gazelle – Dorcas, Tabitha
Bear – Orson, Björn, Arthur, Bernard, Ursula
Lion – Leo, Leonard, Lionel
Wolf – Adolf, Lovell, Phelan, Ulrick, Rudolph, Ralph, Randolph, Wolf
Horse – Philip, Philippa, Hippolyta
Boar – Averil, Everard
Beaver – Beverley
Goat – Giles
Antelope – Jael
Stag – Hartley
Weasel – Huldah
Fox – Todd
Mouse – Achbor

Creature was sometimes used as a first name in the sixteenth century. It was given before the child was born, and before its sex was known, when it was feared that it would not survive. If it did survive, then the name was retained. In 1579, for instance, a man called John Haffynden married Creature Cheseman.

Be a royal family

There are plenty of names to use which can help to create a 'royal' family. King, for instance, has been borne by such well-known men as King Vidor, the film director, and King Gillette, who invented the disposable razor-blade. It is sometimes given with a middle name such as George, and I once came across an American student called King Solomon Jones.

The French, *roi*, 'king', which in an older form of French was *roy*, has given rise to names like Leroy, Leroi, Fitzroy, Elroy, Roy. Rex as a name derives directly from the Latin, *rex*, 'king'. The Hebrew equivalent Melech occurs in the Bible, and Basil belongs to this group. It derives from a Greek word which means 'kingly'.

Most of these 'king' names have a 'queen' which matches them. Leroy has a feminine equivalent in Laraine, which is probably based on the French, *la reine*, 'the queen'. Reine itself occurs as a first name, but far more popular has been the Latin, Regina. The countless statues of Victoria Regina, 'Victoria the queen', must have helped spread this name. The French and Russian forms, Regine and Raina, are also used, while the Bible supplies us with the Hebrew, Milcah, 'queen'.

Queen itself, usually in its pet form Queenie, was popular before 1930. Both forms are still found, together with modern variants such as Queena and Queenette.

In *Bleak House* by Charles Dickens, Caddy explains that young Mr Turveydrop's first name is Prince, in honour of the Prince Regent. 'I wish it wasn't,' she says, 'because it sounds like a dog.' This long-standing canine association has restricted the use of the name to a large extent, though it occurs in some black American families.

Princess is rare as a name, but Sarah, which means 'princess' in Hebrew, has been by far the most popular of all 'royal' names. Sara is another form of Sarah, but Zara has a different origin. Zara was used to name the daughter of Princess Anne in 1981, which caused many people to assume that the name would become more popular. There's plenty of evidence, however, to show that parents do not automatically take up names used by the British royal family. If the names are thought to be old-fashioned or unsuitable for other reasons, then the reaction tends to be: 'All right for them perhaps but not for us'. One other royal name must be mentioned – Royal itself, which has been regularly used for at least a century. Royal Doud, for instance, was the grandfather of Mrs Mamie Geneva Eisenhower. The name has recently appeared in the US in a feminine form. Be prepared in future to meet a Royalyn or Royalene.

Tell her to be quiet

In the words of St Paul, 'Let the women learn in silence, with all subjection.' The Puritans of the seventeenth century sometimes took this statement to their hearts and named their daughters Silence. The name was meant to be a constant reminder that they were to be seen and not heard.

In a curious way, the name lives on, based on the Latin, *tace*, Be silent! often written as Tacy or Tacey to match its pronunciation. The name is still given in those forms, so there are still girls around whose name means 'Shut up!'

Look at the fruit bowl

The Bible refers to children as the 'fruit of the womb', and perhaps a fruity name is appropriate. Some parents obviously think so, since they bestow names like Cherry (also Cerise, its French form) and Berry. I have a letter in my files from Mr Mark Lemmon of Bristol. His father, who died in the 1930s at the age of ninety-one, was named Orange Lemmon.

Anona, the Latin word for 'pineapple', has been used as a first name, as has the rare Pomona, Latin for 'apple'. Pomona was also the name of the Roman goddess of fruit.

I have heard of one girl who is a Peach (in every sense, I'm sure). I also wonder whether in real life there are any namesakes of Mark Twain's Huckleberry Finn.

Initiate a name

Arjay Miller, President of the Ford Motor Company, had a father whose initials were R.J. His name must have caused a few minor misunderstandings, just as ladies named Elsie occasionally receive letters addressed to someone with the initials L.C.

I see from a computer read-out of names being used in the US at the moment that other parents have initialled their children rather than named them. In a single year I find examples of boys named J.B., E.J. and J.W.

When initial letters are used to form a word or name, it is called an acronym. There is a famous example in literature of a first name of that type. Kim Ravenal, in Edna Ferber's *Showboat*, is born on the Mississippi, at the point where Kentucky, Illinois and Missouri meet. This is the origin of the girl's name, though the boy's name Kim has more to do with Kimball O'Hara, in Rudyard Kipling's novel, *Kim*.

March in time

The month in which a baby is born may suggest a name. Marcia, Mark or Marcus would do very well for a March baby, for instance. Those names, and the name of the month, are all connected with Mars, the Roman god of war.

April has been very popular. It is frequently found in its French form Avril, and also occurs as Apryl. May and June are also well established.

July suggests Julie or Juliet, though a lady of the latter name, who received it because she was born in that month, tells me that she has been plagued with Romeo jokes all her life. An August child could become Augustus or Augusta, though either would probably be known as Gus or Gussie.

The other months are rather more difficult. Nova for a November girl perhaps; Octavia for October. I also came across a girl called Janet, as I thought, but she revealed that she was really Januetta.

Do some star gazing

In the 1920s and 1930s film stars often provided the inspiration for parents who needed a name. By far the most successful star in this respect was Shirley Temple, who made her first film appearance as an engaging child in 1934. Shirley immediately rocketed up the names' popularity chart. Other stars, with names like Carol, Maureen, Marlene, Ingrid, Myrna, Merle and Lana, had varying degrees of influence.

By 1939, when *Gone With The Wind* was released, there had been a shift away from the names of the stars themselves to the names of the characters they portrayed. The stars of that film included Leslie Howard, Clark Gable, Vivien Leigh and Olivia de Havilland. Leslie was well past its peak as a male name by that time, and was revived only when Leslie Caron came along to give it a new image as a girl's name. Clark was virtually ignored by parents, and Vivien and Olivia enjoyed a very limited success. It was the names of Margaret Mitchell's characters – Melanie, Ashley and the like – which were taken up in force.

More recent films have shown a similar trend. Grace Kelly was Tracy Samantha Lord in *High Society*, causing Tracy and Samantha to be well used rather than Grace. When Dustin Hoffman played Benjamin in *The Graduate*, Benjamin became popular. A rare modern exception to this rule is provided by Hayley Mills. Hayley was unknown as a first name until Miss Mills appeared as a child star. She now has several thousand namesakes, proof that stardom can still work its magic.

Give her a maiden name

One way of naming a girl is to call her 'girl'. That is the meaning of the name borne by the Australian writer Colleen McCullough and the Canadian actress Colleen Dewhurst. Colleen is thought of as a typically Irish name, but it is more widely used outside Ireland than by Irish parents.

Cora is based on the Greek word for 'maiden'. This could be translated into Welsh as Rhiain or Rhian, while the nearest Latin equivalent is probably Virginia. Aramaic, one of the languages of the Bible, has given us Talitha, 'little girl'. I have seen Maidie, 'little maid', used as a name. It looks and sounds pleasant enough, but there is a danger that later in life she will become an 'old Maidie'.

Tell her she's beautiful

In a biblical context, Cain refers to the first murderer. In Wales Cain is a girl's name based on the word for 'beautiful'. The biblical name with the same meaning, in Persian, is Vashti. A girl can also become the French Belle, or Latin Bella. The Old Norse name Astrid means 'divinely beautiful'.

Linda has been used by many parents in recent years because it is a Spanish word meaning 'pretty'. Bonita is a similar name, and recalls the Scottish Bonnie. The latter name manages to suggest a girl who is both pretty and healthy-looking, a very pleasant combination.

Join the country club

America was named in honour of an Italian, Amerigo Vespucci, at the suggestion of a German. Just as countries can be named for people, so the names of countries can be used as first names. Girls are called

America from time to time, for instance, and further north one occasionally finds a girl called Canada.

English parents may use Albion, Briton or Britannia. Wallace would be suitable for a Welshman, since it means precisely that, though it is associated far more strongly with Scotland. A Scottish name would be Scott, while the Irish could return to a former name of Ireland itself, Erin.

Other possibilities in this area include India, used by the Mountbatten family as a first name, Lord Mountbatten having been the last British Viceroy of India, and Asia. Israel and Jordan are used for boys. Kenya has been much used in recent years by black American families, who have also experimented with Jamaica. Clearly, when it comes to naming the baby, there are many parents who like to see how the land lies.

Be a sport

When the father takes over the job of naming the baby the result can sometimes be disastrous. He ends up naming the child after all the players of the local football team, or all the heavyweight boxing champions. Not that sporting names cannot be used successfully. Chelsea and Charlton, for instance, are perfectly suitable first names in current use which have a strong football flavour. It was reported some years ago that two supporters of Stoke City decided to name their son after whoever scored the first goal on the following Saturday. It turned out to be Terry Conroy and the boy was duly named Terence.

Wembley Stadium has special associations for many sports fans, and Wembley has been given as a name on at least two occasions. The Fulham goalkeeper Peter Mellor gave it to his son, born shortly before Fulham were due to appear at Wembley in the

Cup Final. Earlier the name had been used by a young German couple who attended an England–Germany international. The excitement caused by Gerd Müller's goal proved too much for the wife. She was rushed off to the maternity ward of a nearby hospital and gave birth to Georg Wembley Hesse.

An Australian who admired the athlete Herb Elliott was determined to name a son in his honour, but his wife presented him with three daughters. All three were given 'herb' names – Rosemary, Thyme and Marjoram.

Stick to the letter

One of my correspondents tells me that A has been used as a first name in his family for several generations. In a similar way the former American President was Harry S Truman, S being his middle name, not an initial. The President's two grandfathers had first names beginning with S, and using that letter as a middle name managed to flatter them both.

I know a Beatrice whose friends call her Bea, and a Deanna who is known as Dee. The American writer Dee Brown bears that as his first name, presumably linking with his father's name, Daniel. When Ethel and Euphemia were common names, the bearers were frequently addressed as Eff.

Jay is often a letter name, chosen because both parents have names beginning with J. Kay was once a pet form of Kathleen but became a name in its own right. Emmas and Emilys are often known as Em, and so it goes on. There's a character called X Billings in *To Kill A Mockingbird* by Harper Lee, while Sinclair Lewis gives us Zed Wintergeist in *Bethel Merriday*. Fiction is rarely stranger than fact. The Registrar General's records show that a British Zee Smith was named in 1971.

Get on the right scent

According to Sophy Moody, who wrote a book about a hundred years ago called *What Is Your Name?*, Naiogabui is a name used by the Fiji islanders which means 'one who smells sweetly'. Women have always been concerned with smelling sweetly, and perhaps it is surprising that so few names reflect that fact.

Juliet remarked that a rose by any other name would smell as sweet, reminding us that most of the flower names used for girls conjure up an aromatic as well as a visual image. The Greek names Myra and Myron refer to a 'sweet-smelling oil', and Keturah is related to 'incense'. One of Job's daughters was named Keziah, 'cassia'. It was the custom in biblical times for ladies in the Middle East to carry a twig of a sweet-smelling plant, such as cassia, at all times.

Black American families have turned to the names of well-known perfumes. Chanel has recently had great success, spelt either like that or as Channel, Shanel, Shanell, Shannel, Shannell. Madame Chanel herself bore the names Gabrielle Bonheur but was known to her friends as Coco.

Put an end to it

You can usually arrive at a name for a girl by taking a male name and adding a feminine ending to it. Such names – Roberta, Georgina, Josephine, etc. – are often called Adam's rib names. It doesn't work in reverse, by the way. Male names can't be derived from girls' names by a similar process.

Feminists tend to object to such names, and one can see their point. After all, Eve may have been formed from Adam's rib, but her name certainly wasn't based on his. It is only in modern times that you find names like Adamette and Adamine.

Use a colour scheme

I know someone who sees a particular colour when any name is mentioned. For her, Bob and Barbara are a kind of transparent blue, Philip is a light green, Ruth is maroon, Sue is pink, Ronald is lilac, Margaret crimson, Christina scarlet, and so on. That is a rather special reaction to names, but many first names suggest colours in other ways.

Scarlett O'Hara is one of the more colourful characters in literature. There have been few Scarletts or Scarlets in real life, though redness is the underlying meaning of names like Adam, Clancy, Ormonde, Rowan, Roy, Rory, Russell, Rufus, Ruby, Ginger and Cherry.

Here are some other colour names:

White – Laban, Alban, Candida, Blanche, Bianca, Wynne, Fiona, Ivory
Black – Melanie, Blake, Dougal, Kieran, Gethin, Kerwin, Maurice, Nigel, Ebony
Yellow (blond) – Boyd, Xanthe, Flavia
Brown – Auburn, Amber, Electra, Duncan, Hazel
Green – Oran, Jade, Olive, Emerald, Beryl
Blue – Azure, Sapphire, Violet, Ianthe
Gold – Aurelius, Aurelia

Aurelia conjures up an image of a dignified lady dressed in a magnificent gown. When the name is turned into English it seems absolutely right for that scatterbrained blonde, Goldie Hawn.

Run a risk

Charles Dickens was fascinated by names, and makes many comments on them throughout his novels. Sometimes he chose to remind parents of the risk they run when they name a child. Will it grow up to justify its name? He made the point rather savagely with a character called Pleasant. We meet her when she is twenty-four, 'possessed of what is colloquially termed a swivel eye, anxious, meagre, of a muddy complexion, and looking as old again as she really was.' Elsewhere he describes the Pecksniff sisters. Charity is a hypocritical shrew, and Mercy is little better. He returned to the attack again in one of his short stories, where he says of another woman, 'Her name was Mercy, though she had none on me.'

Helen can also be a risky name. It was the classic beauty of the original Helen which 'launched a thousand ships, And burnt the topless towers of Ilium'. 'Helen, so ridiculously not of Troy,' wrote G. B. Stern of a girl who failed to achieve such standards. Her parents, if you like, had taken a risk and lost. Things do occasionally go wrong in this way when a child is named, but it would be a dull world if all parents played it absolutely safe.

Treasure her

Hester Prynne's daughter, in Hawthorne's famous story *The Scarlet Letter*, is named Pearl because she is 'her mother's only treasure, purchased with all she had'. Margaret also means 'pearl' and is used by some parents because of its meaning.

Jewel names were decidedly fashionable sixty years ago. Beryl and Ruby were especially popular, but Coral, Opal, Amethyst and the like were also found. In modern times these have become Gemma (Italian, 'gem'), Crystal and Amber. Mick and Bianca Jagger named their daughter Jade, and Esmeralda would be another possibility. It's the Spanish word for 'emerald'.

Precious has been used for both sexes. There's the West Indian weightlifter Precious Mackenzie, and the singer Precious Wilson. The latter, about to star in her own television show, explained that her mother 'wanted one child, preferably a girl, so when I arrived she was overjoyed.'

I'm not sure I can believe the report I read about a boy named Onyx. It is not so much the name as the reason the parents gave for choosing it – they said he was onyx-pected.

Repeat yourself

Sometimes a girl, often at the father's insistence, is given the same name as her mother. This seems a pleasant compliment, though it may create practical problems. Sometimes a boy, also at the father's insistence, is named in exactly the same way as the father. He becomes a Junior, and is sometimes addressed in that way. (Junior even has a pet form. Before I realized this I was convinced that some American men were called June.) Psychiatrists have been attacking this practice for many years, pointing out the possible consequences of placing a son firmly in his father's shadow. Others have talked of the complacency or conceit that such fathers reveal, though the fathers themselves would speak of justifiable family pride. Naming in this way remains an option for all parents. One can only say that it is now far less common than it used to be.

Some Juniors have certainly emerged from any paternal shadow. Marlon Brando is the son of Marlon Brando, the American baseball pitcher Vida Blue's father was Vida Rochelle Meschach Abednego Blue. Before he became Clint Eastwood, the actor was known as Clinton Eastwood Junior.

Forge a link

Some parents like to link the name of their child to

one of their own names. Mrs Gaskell gives the example of a mother named Hyacinth and her daughter Cynthia in *Wives and Daughters*. There's a similar sound link in Thackeray's Isabella and Belinda, described by the proud husband/father as his 'two Bells'.

The writer Enid Bagnold had an interesting middle name, Algerine, which linked with her mother's maiden name, Alger. There is also a link between Artemis Cooper and her grandmother, the late Lady Diana Cooper. The goddess who was Artemis to the Greeks was known as Diana to the Romans.

Make a novel choice

Someone once said that pregnant women should not be allowed to read novels. Romantic novelists, in particular, have a reputation for inventing fanciful names for their characters, and those names are there in the minds of mothers-to-be at a critical time. Some husbands therefore find themselves in the position of Goldsmith's Vicar of Wakefield: 'I intended to call my daughter after Aunt Grissel, but my wife, who had been reading romances, insisted upon her being called Olivia.' In this instance it was probably just as well that the mother had been reading romances, though the daughter would have become Griselda on her birth certificate, not Grissel. Another pet form of this name was Grizzle. It would be a crying shame to impose that on a baby.

Jancis Robinson, the British journalist, was named from a character in *Precious Bane*, a novel by Mary Webb. Stanley Baldwin praised this book in the House of Commons in 1925 and helped turn it into a major bestseller. The name appears to be a blend of Jane and Francis.

Correspondents tell me of being named 'Vanessa

because my mother thought the character in Hugh Walpole's Herries books such a nice girl', and 'Ursula from D. H. Lawrence's *The Rainbow*'. Such examples do not instantly reveal themselves to be 'novel names'. Lorna belongs firmly in that class, since it was probably invented by R. D. Blackmore for his novel *Lorna Doone*.

Other names, such as Catriona, Melanie and Emma have very strong literary associations, though it was probably the film version of *Gone With The Wind* that made Melanie popular, rather than the book. As for Emma, there is little doubt that Mrs Emma Peel of the television series *The Avengers* had more to do with its widespread modern use than Jane Austen's character of that name.

Consult the Bard

The works of Shakespeare suggest a number of interesting names, especially for girls: Beatrice, Celia, Charmian, Cordelia, Emilia, Helena, Imogen, Isabella, Juliet, Katharine, Marina, Miranda, Olivia, Ophelia, Phoebe, Portia, Rosalind, Viola. Those have been amongst the most popular, though examples of Cressida, Perdita, Regan and the like are found.

It is more difficult to name a boy from a Shakespearian character. A Hamlet, Romeo, Othello, Macbeth or Lear might be a little out of place in the suburbs. Laurence Olivier showed that it could be done, however, by naming his son Tarquin, a name which is mentioned in five different plays.

Ferdinand, a character in *The Tempest*, inspired many parents in the nineteenth century, but the name seems less suitable for modern times. It was Ferdinand who found the perfect way to ask a young lady her name: 'I do beseech you, Chiefly that I might set it in my prayers, What is your name?'

Be mysterious

'All beautiful women should have an air of mystery,' says a character in *Fenella Phizackerley* by Margaret Forster. He is suggesting that his daughter's name needs to be mysterious as well. He proposes Anastasia, which has 'mystery as well as originality'. It's a Greek name, in fact, and means 'resurrection'. It is often shortened to Stacy. Dickens' candidate as a mysterious female name is Sophronia. In *The Old Curiosity Shop* he describes it 'as being euphonious and genteel, and furthermore indicative of mystery'. Once again it's a Greek name, meaning 'prudent, self-controlled'. I suppose a girl who bore the name today would be known as Sophy, which happens to be rather fashionable.

Marie Corelli managed to convince many parents of the 1920s and 1930s that Thelma was a mysteriously feminine name. In her novel *Thelma* (1887) she makes one of the male characters say, 'There is something mysteriously suggestive about the sound of it; like a chord of music played softly in the distance.'

I have personally met only one young lady who had a truly mysterious name. She was actually a Teresa, but liked to be known as Terri. I speak about her in the past tense because she decided to get married. Unfortunately that meant that she was a Miss Terri no longer.

Pay cash on delivery

I met a Penny recently, though I assume that she was Penelope on her birth certificate. When I thought about it I realized that certain other money names have gained currency.

There is Bob, for instance, a 'bob' being a shilling when I was young, or five pence as it is now. Then there is Sterling, which has been reasonably well used as a first name. One of its meanings is 'British money'.

Dollar does not seem to have been used to name a child, but its slang form Buck certainly has. The golfer Lee Buck Trevino is one well-known bearer of it. As for a Bill, he's worth ten Bucks, of course.

I see that Dinero, Spanish for 'money', was used to name a boy in Detroit in 1981. It was in that year that Welthy Fisher died. Her first name was a deliberate variant of 'wealthy'. She became a missionary, and lived to the ripe old age of 101.

Call them names

It is worth remembering that there can be a difference between what you call your child and what you name it. You may want to call her Katie or him Bob, but you'd be well advised to use Katharine or Robert as the official name. There may come a time when they will wish to use the more formal name. At least you will have given them the option.

Most names have pet forms, 'titles of endearment' as the essayist William Hazlitt once called them, which will be used by friends and relations. Professor Ninian Smart, the British theologian, says that his name was frequently shortened to Ninny, which caused him to become involved in many fights when he was a boy. His parents could perhaps have guessed which pet form would be used; sometimes it's difficult to tell. This point was made by a correspondent to a magazine, relating what happened to her three daughters, Abigail, Rebecca and Shoshanna. Their 'titles of endearment' at school quickly became Biggy, Ecky and Slosh.

Be inventive

In *Nicholas Nickleby*, by Charles Dickens, we are introduced to Miss Morleena Kenwigs, 'regarding whose uncommon Christian name it may be here remarked that it had been invented and composed by Mrs Kenwigs previous to her lying-in, for the special distinction of her eldest child, in case it should prove a daughter.'

I have often wondered whether it was by design or accident that when Monica Dickens, the great-granddaughter of Charles Dickens and a novelist in her own right, needed to mention an invented name in *Kate and Emma* she came very close to Morleena: ' "You'd rather live somewhere else, Arleena?" He pronounced it carefully, as seriously as if it were Joan. A few years in the juvenile court, and you can tackle any name.'

These two quotations usefully put forward the arguments for and against newly invented names. It is tempting for parents to think of creating a unique name for their child. The problem, as Monica Dickens implies, is that other people may react negatively to the name. If it is unfamiliar it may be considered odd rather than unusual. As far as the namebearer is concerned, there is a world of difference between those two judgements.

My correspondents sometimes explain to me how their own names have been formed. Tanga was a blend of tango and rumba used by parents who were dance enthusiasts; Jenniphine was a mixture of Jennifer and Josephine. 'My father liked Patricia, my mother Tina,' wrote Mrs Read of Dorset. 'They compromised and my name became Patina.' By chance, Mrs Read's parents ensured that she would always be 'dishy', for there is a word patina which means dish.

The British singer Petula Clark bears a name which was invented by her father. Its resemblance to the Latin, *petulantia*, 'sauciness, pertness', is perhaps accidental. Similarly, the American model/actress sensation of the 1970s, Farrah Fawcett-Majors, has said that her mother made up Farrah to go with Fawcett. There was, however, already a Persian name Farah meaning 'joy'.

Clearly there is endless scope for the invention of names, but it is perhaps a dangerous game to play. Perhaps it's better to invent a name for oneself, but not impose it on a child.

Hyphenate

It seems to have been the French who introduced the idea of hyphenating two names in order to form a new unit. We're all familiar with names of the Jean-Paul type, and American families have experimented with them to some extent, but they have never been really well used. If you cannot decide between two names, see what they look like with a hyphen placed between them. Together they may give you the name you need.

Remember the deliveryman

Doctor used to be given as a first name to the seventh son of a seventh son, it being believed that such a person would have special powers. The name has also been used as a compliment to the doctor who assisted at the birth. Still more frequently, the doctor's own first name is used for the child, adapted slightly if the sex is different. Carson McCullers describes a doctor named Benedict Mady Copeland. Many boys become Benedict in his honour, while girls become Benny Mae, Madyben, Benedine, Madine and so on.

Midwives and nurses are also honoured in this way, for understandable reasons. They help to bring the child safely into the world and parents are glad to show their gratitude.

Make short work of it

In George Eliot's story *Silas Marner*, Silas proposes to call the child he adopts Hephzibah, after his mother. 'Eh, that's a hard name,' says another character. The parish registers of the nineteenth century make it clear that she had a point. The name appears as Hephsibah, Hephzabah, Hephzebah, Hepzabah, Hepzibah, Hepseba and so on. I don't think this means that such names should be avoided in favour of the short and simple. Those who cannot spell very well will manage to make a mess of even the simplest name, and for daily use a long name will always take on a short form. Hephzibah itself, a Hebrew name meaning 'My delight is in her' and borne by the late pianist sister of Yehudi Menuhin, commonly became Eppie, Epsie, Hepsie, Hepsey or Hep when it was regularly used.

A long name may be more difficult for others to remember at first, but once they fix it in their minds they will remember both the name and the person who bears it. For a while, it's true, a young child who bears a 'hard' name may have difficulty coping with it, but that will pass. One thinks of the four-year-old on her first day at school, who was asked by the teacher how she spelt her name. 'Mummy helps me,' was the reply.

Use a sweetener

Little girls, as we all know, are made of 'sugar and spice and all things nice' and they grow to be sweet sixteen. For centuries they have also been given 'sweet' names.

The Latin word *dulcis*, 'sweet', led to Dulcie, a name which was fashionable in the 1920s and 1930s. Much earlier girls had been named Dulcibella, from the Latin, 'sweetly beautiful', though this became Dowsabel in ordinary speech.

Another group of names is based on the idea of 'honey', from the Greek, *meli*, *melitos*, and the Latin, *mel*, *mellis*. Melita, Melinda and Melina are examples, the last of these being associated with the Greek actress Melina Mercouri. Melissa, 'honey-bee', has been popular recently. It was still rare when Dickens used it to name Miss Melissa Waekles in *The Old Curiosity Shop*. She is one of the sisters who runs a ladies' seminary, teaching English grammar, composition, geography and the use of the dumb-bells. Dickens says that 'Miss Melissa might have been five-and-thirty summers or thereabouts, and verged on the autumnal.' This did not encourage nineteenth-century parents to make use of the name.

A more famous literary name, meaning 'all honey', is Pamela. Any girls bearing this name should certainly read Samuel Richardson's novel *Pamela*, about an eighteenth-century servant girl.

Perhaps the most modern 'sweet' name is Candy, often spelt Candi. It is probably a pet form of Candace or Candice, but the name does manage to suggest a young lady who is attractively packaged and good enough to eat.

Look both ways

A word or name which reads the same whether it is spelt forwards or backwards is called a palindrome. Some first names are palindromes in themselves – Hannah, Anna, Ada, Otto, Aziza and the like. These are sometimes deliberately chosen by families whose last names are also palindromes. Elsdon C. Smith, in his *Treasury of Name Lore*, cites Otto Rentner of Chicago and Anna Laval of Evansville, Indiana. Elsdon also mentions those who have formed a first name for a child by spelling the family name backwards, so that the whole name becomes a palindrome. Revilo Oliver was formerly a classics professor at the University of Illinois. Opal Lapo, Marba Abram and Ronnoc Connor were others named in this way.

Speculate

You can always name a child after a rich relation. The hope is that the compliment will ultimately be repaid in gifts or a bequest to the child concerned. Ian Hay once described such naming as the use of a 'sprat to catch a testamentary whale'.

Be streets ahead

There's an American girl called Chlorine and thereby hangs a tale. Her father was sent to register the birth (and the name Valerie) but stopped on the way to celebrate with friends. This made him forget the intended name so he used the name of the street in which he lived. It happened to be on an estate where all the streets had chemical names, such as Sulphide Street.

Maybe a street could inspire a name in other ways. After all, a street can also be called a road, avenue, close, etc. In the area where I live we also have a Dale, Dell, Garth, Glen, Grove, Lea and Orchard. Maybe such names would start children on the road to success?

Battle it out

First names like Alma, Kimberley and Ladysmith came into use because of battles fought at those places. Often the fathers did not return to see the children who bore them. 'Battle' is also the meaning of the Slavonic Boris, Welsh Cadel and German Hilda. Matilda is 'mighty in battle', Louis, Louise and Louisa are 'famous in battle', Imelda is 'all-embracing battle'.

The late Westray Battle Boyce was Director of the American Women's Army Corps. Battle was her maiden name, and several other members of her family had military careers. Battles, it is to be hoped, will not inspire many names in future, but army parents might give special consideration to Harold, 'army power', Herman, 'army man', Herbert, 'shining army', and Hereward, 'army defence'.

Turn over a new leaf

It was watching a film of Woody Allen's that reminded me of tree names for children. Woody, by the way, is seen in a more classical form as Silvester or Sylvester. Silvia is also from the Latin, *silva*, 'wood'.

Willow has been used as a girl's name, and carries a pleasant suggestion of suppleness. Vernon means 'alder tree'; Tamar occurs in the Bible and is 'palm tree'.

An American president with a tree name was Lyndon Baines Johnson. Lyndon refers to a 'hill where lime trees grow'. Olive and Olivia are both related to the 'olive', a tree associated not only with peace, but large families. Greek brides once carried or wore an olive garland as a symbol of fertility.

Put to sea

When long sea journeys were undertaken by young families, emigrating to seek a better life, children were often born at sea. Their names were likely to reflect that fact. Oceanus Hopkins, for instance, was born aboard the *Mayflower* in 1620. The son of John Cotton, a Puritan divine, is mentioned in a letter written by Governor Winthorpe. 'Mrs Cotton was delivered of a son at sea, who was baptized on shore and named Seaborne.' Frequently the name of the ship itself was given to the child. Tremendous McKenzie was born on 1 June 1794, on board HMS *Tremendous*. More recently there was a discussion in a British newspaper about a lady named Lusitania. Two other women who were called Omra and Zealandia wrote in. The editors said that they were sorry to have to say that HMS *Zealandia* was rather an old battleship.

One of the titles of the Virgin Mary is *stella maris*, 'star of the sea'. Maris has been used as a name, and may have led to Marise. The male name Delmar means 'of the sea' as well. Other possibilities include Greek, Thalassa, 'sea', Gaelic, Murdoch, 'sea warrior' and Muriel, 'sea bright' and Old English, Seward, 'sea guardian'.

Isaac Disraeli, in his *Curiosities of Literature*, says that orphan boys who were destined for sea-service were given names like 'Drake, Norris or Blake, after our famous admirals'. To these examples could be added Nelson, Rodney, Hardy and Vernon, and even Admiral itself has been used as a first name. Shakespeare's contribution to this group is his character Marina in *Pericles*. She herself explains that the name was given to her 'for I was born at sea'.

Confer nobility

The British journalist Fiona McCarthy once suggested that when naming a baby, a good test for parents was to put Sir or Lady in front of the proposed name to see how it would sound. Some parents go further. They use Sir or Lady *as* the first name, then follow it with a more normal middle name. Similar title-names are Duke (in some cases a pet form of Marmaduke), Baron and Earl. Mrs Lou Barron, of New York, tells me that one of her husband's relations was Earl Barron. Squire was a fairly common name in the nineteenth century, but seems to have faded away. Also once common as a male name was Noble, but it has been rarely used since the 1920s. All the names which begin with Ethel-, whether for men (Ethelbert, Ethelwyn, etc.) or women (Etheldreda, Ethelinda, etc.), contain the idea of nobility. All are based on the Old English, *aethel*, 'noble'. A similar German name was Adalheidis, 'noble-hood' which has given us both Alice and Heidi.

Freya is the Old Norse way of indicating a 'noble lady', while Nerys is a feminine adaptation of the Welsh, *ner*, 'lord'. Then there is Mona, from the Irish, *muadhnait*, *muadh*, 'noble'. Leonardo da Vinci's Mona Lisa does not, needless to say, bear an Irish name. In her case she is really Madonna, 'my lady', Lisa.

Toughen him up

Parents commonly say that they want a 'strong' name for their son. A similar remark was made to Roy Fitzgerald, who was told that he needed a stronger name if he was to succeed in the tough world of professional acting. He became Rock Hudson.

Rock and Rocky are occasionally used as first names. Craig also occurs, and has a similar meaning. Infinitely more popular has been Peter, based on the Greek word for 'rock'. Other tough names include Farrell, 'man of valour', Griffith, 'strong chief or fighter', and Hardy, 'courageous'. Andrew means 'manly', and Manly itself has been used as a first name. One slightly curious name in this group is Valentine, which carries a suggestion of a little cupid bearing a message of love. In fact, the name, like Valerie, derives from a Latin word which means 'to be strong'.

Have a babe in arms

In early times the weapon by which a man defended himself was of great importance. Perhaps, too, a son was looked upon as the potential defender of his parents. Whatever the reasoning, there are a number of names which refer to a weapon, especially the spear. It is there in Barry, Edgar, Egbert, Oscar, Roger, Gerald and Gerard.

In Australia another weapon name has been very popular for girls in recent years. Parents have taken over an Aboriginal word for the 'boomerang' and named their daughters Kylie. Maybe the parents hope that wherever their daughters roam, they will always come back home.

Make your child happy

There has long been a tradition of bestowing 'happy' names on children, in the hope that they will grow to be like their names. Felicity, for instance, with its variant forms Felicia and Felice, derives from the Latin, *felicitas*, 'happiness'. In a similar way the Latin, *hilaris*, 'cheerful' gave rise at an early date to Hilary, used for both sexes, and the male name Ellery. Latin, *beatus*, 'happy, prosperous' led to Beatrice, which could be translated as 'she who makes others happy'.

A 'happy' name which is now something of a problem is Gay. It is often spelt Gaye to emphasize that it is a name. Parents gave the name to their daughters (and on rare occasions to their sons) before 1960, but it has been little used since the word took on its 'homosexual' meaning.

The outstandingly happy name in the Bible is probably Asher, which means 'what happiness!' He is mentioned in Genesis, the son of Jacob and Zilpah. The name has been little used, probably because it sounds like a sneeze!

Joy, once a pet form of Joyce, became a name in its own right. It could be said to be the English form of Charmian, which is from the Greek, *charma*, 'joy'. Merry has also been in use as an independent name since the nineteenth century, though it began as a pet form of Mercy.

More recent names associated with this group, are Blythe and Jolly. By contrast, modern parents no longer seem to make use of Happy itself as a name. Nineteenth-century records make it clear that it was formerly in regular use as a name for both girls and boys.

Wait and see

In many American Indian tribes, the first thing a father sees after his child is born suggests its name – Sitting Bull or something similar. This wait-and-see policy is sometimes used by other parents. 'Right after she was born,' an American correspondent writes, 'her father glanced out of the window and saw the ivy plant growing on the house, and a mule in the backyard. So he named the baby Ivy Maude. Maude was a popular name for mules at that time – named for the mule that appeared in the Happy Hooligan comic strip.'

Names given in this way are called 'incident names' and can relate to things heard as well as seen. *Concorde* happens to fly overhead as the baby is born, so Concorde becomes the name. A more unusual incident suggested a name for Ruby Lenthall of Bristol, when she was born in 1896. 'I was born at the time two little girls were thrown over the Bristol Suspension Bridge by their father and were saved by the police. One was named Ruby, and that's the reason for my name.'

A bridge figures also in the story of an 'incident name' given to the daughter of Mr and Mrs Tennent. The baby was born in an ambulance which was on its way to the hospital. It was crossing the US 12 Bridge at the time, hence the girl's name – Bridget.

Name him Sue

Johnny Cash's famous song 'A Boy Named Sue' was inspired by Judge Sue Kerr Hicks of Tennessee. The judge died in 1980, aged eighty-four, having encountered lifelong difficulties with his name. His mother, who died a few minutes after his birth, was a Susan and the name was given in her memory. The judge also married a Susan.

Johnny Cash was probably right to say that giving a boy a girl's name will turn him into a fighter. The actor John Wayne, born Marion Michael Morrison, often commented on the battles he was forced to fight as a boy to prove that he was as tough as anyone else.

Sometimes a male name is capable of being turned into a female name. Once again, resorting to fisticuffs seems to be the only solution for the namebearer. 'My first name is Theodore,' says the Laurence boy in *Little Women* by Louisa M. Alcott. 'I don't like it,' he goes on, 'for the fellows called me Dora.' 'How did you make them stop?' asks Josephine. 'I thrashed 'em,' comes the reply.

A long, plaintive article in a British newspaper some years ago told of the difficulties experienced by journalist Vivian White. He wondered whether the explorer Sir Vivian Fuchs had adopted that mode of life in order to get away from 'loonies who thought he was a woman'.

There's an old joke about a man who introduces himself to a stranger. 'I'm Tex.' 'From Texas?' 'No, from Louisiana, but who the hell wants to be Louise?'

Name her George

A boy named Sue may run into problems, but it does not seem to harm a girl to have a male name. The actress Michael Learned copes well, and John Stewart, a lady who died in Boston in 1857, was untroubled throughout her eighty-two years.

Many names which are now thought of as girls' names were originally used for boys: Shirley, Tracy, Florence and Beverley are obvious examples. Other names hover between the sexes: Leslie, Robin, Jay, Terry, Pat and so on. In such cases the name always ends up by becoming feminine. I can find very few examples of names once used for girls that are now exclusively used for boys. William Camden, writing in 1605, listed Douglas very firmly as a girl's name, and to Scottish parents in former times Giles was a feminine name. But the first-name situation in general terms can be summed up as: it is all right for a girl to wear trousers but it is still considered very odd for a boy to wear a skirt.

Make no mistake

Some first names proclaim to the world that the child was deliberately conceived, or 'desired'. Erasmus says this in Greek; Desirée says the same thing in French (with Didier as the male form of the name). Saul in Hebrew means 'asked for'.

Mistakes do occur, of course, and parents occasionally choose to announce the fact in their child's name. A family in Oregon, for instance, named their first son Chance, because they themselves had 'taken a chance' before they married. Their second son became Law, because they were now wed. The British parents who named their daughter Surprise a few years ago claimed that the surprise as far as they were concerned was that a daughter and not a son had been born. The name is fairly certain to be misinterpreted in the future. In 1923 another British family let it be known that they had 'slipped up' when, with a touch of humour, they called their daughter Bloomah.

Try the family Bible

People often say that Old Testament names have become fashionable again in recent years. Some of them have, and there are plenty of young men who are Adam or Benjamin, David, Jonathan, Nathaniel, Daniel or Joshua. You may have to cast your net slightly wider to find an Aaron, Adlai, Amos, Caleb, Darius, Elias, Ezra, Gideon, Jacob, Jethro, Joel, Jonah, Lemuel, Moses, Noah, Phineas, Reuben, Saul, Seth or Solomon, though all were once common.

In times past men also received some of the rarer biblical names such as Cush and Gad, Ham, Kish, Lot, Job, Nebuchadnezzar and Jehoshaphat. The last- named became the subject of a mild oath. When a man was surprised in the nineteenth century he was likely to exclaim, 'Jumping Jehoshaphat!'

The choice of girls' names from the Old Testament is much more limited, since fewer women are named there. The favourite names have been, and remain, Abigail, Deborah, Hannah, Leah, Naomi, Rachel, Rebecca, Ruth and Sarah. Eve has been curiously neglected in English-speaking countries, though it is common throughout Europe. Other interesting possibilities, once far more usual than they are today, include Dinah, Esther, Adah, Bathsheba, Tamar, Beulah, Hephzibah, Keziah, Vashti, Zipporah, Martha and Miriam. Perhaps it is even time to restore Jezebel and Delilah.

Another 'restoration' could be Salome, best known as the name of the girl who danced before King Herod and demanded the head of John the Baptist as a reward. Salome has a beautiful meaning, 'peace', and a beautiful sound. So I thought at least, but when I said as much to an American friend her comment was, 'You couldn't possibly call a girl Salami.'

Scale new heights

Lovers of serious music have a habit of reflecting their interest in the name they choose for their child. It's not for nothing that there are boys to be found bearing names like Haydn, Rossini and Handel.

Musicians might occasionally find inspiration in the instruments they play. Viola is an obvious example, though its common use was certainly caused by its flower meaning rather than its instrumental associations. A trumpeter could perhaps name a son Jubal, from a Hebrew word which means 'horn, trumpet'. Kit could be used by a fiddler. It was formerly the name of a small fiddle much used by dancing masters.

A different approach is hinted at by the name of the writer Harper Lee. The actress who was born Rosetta Jacobs certainly liked the idea of being a player. She changed her name to Piper Laurie. It was a family in Honolulu, though, who really managed to scale the heights of inventiveness. The parents reflected their love of music by naming their children Dodo, Rere, Mimi, Fafa, Soso, Lala, Sisi and Octavia.

Humour them

A lady telephoned me one day when I was doing a radio phone-in and said that her last name was Ireland. Her own first name was Treasure and she had a sister, Coral. She sounded quite happy about it, and indeed the evidence suggests that those landed with names of this kind do not seem to bear a grudge against their parents. Presumably they have grown up in a general atmosphere of good humour.

I have a photograph of a smiling Miss Merry Christmas in my files, though she complained to the reporter of silly telephone calls each Christmas. She has a partial namesake in Merry Christmas Trees of Ohio, a lady whose brothers are named Jack Pine Trees and Douglas Fir Trees.

Some last names are rather funny in themselves. They will look a little odd no matter which first name precedes them. I have met those who would put my own name, Dunkling, into that category. Odd or not, I tell them, it has been an English name for at least a thousand years and in an early form is mentioned in the Domesday Book.

I don't think my own name was in the collection of the late George F. Hubbard of New York, who often sent me his finds. I quote a few of them below to demonstrate that in some cases there is little parents can do when they bestow a first name to correct the influence of the last name.

Lucille Kisses
Burroughs Lovingood
Sophie Mewing
Annie Nails
Yale Pecker
Irmgard Quapp

Douglas Cantelope
Minnie Goodcuff
David Feeblecorn
Nell Upole
Adelina Sloog
Albert Quish
Belle Nuddle
Richard Puff
Malcolm Moos
Margaret Middleditch
Louis Leaky
Arabella Hong
Alice Everyday
Wentworth Fling
Charles Gummey

Spell it out

The problem with many names is that they can be spelt in different ways. Should you use Ann or Anne, Steven or Stephen, Catherine or Katharine? Some parents will decide by the look of the name in its different forms, others will be influenced by other criteria. Steven would be unacceptable to me, for instance, as a modern innovation, yet it is now slightly more common than Stephen.

It would normally be foolish to spell a name in a different way just to give it a fresh look (Dickens laughed at a pretentious young man who changed Simon to Cymon), though one can sympathize with parents who like the sound of names like Siobhán and Aisling, but suspect that the spellings will cause difficulty. They sometimes use phonetic spellings – such as Shavon and Ashling – in an attempt to cope with the problem. One of my own favourite names is Agnes, though it sounds awful when mispronounced in the modern way. Indicating its correct pronunciation, by spelling it Annis or Anyes, would in this case be a good idea.

Be mythological

Like the Bible and the works of Shakespeare, the world of classical mythology offers a collection of possible names. I mention some of them below, but would caution any parents who think of using one to check its pronunciation carefully.

Men: Achilles, Actor, Adonis, Aeneas, Aeson, Ajax, Alastor, Alexander, Apollo, Atlas, Cadmus, Cupid, Eros, Eryx, Hector, Hercules, Hesperus, Hyperion, Icarus, Ion, Janus, Jason, Jupiter, Leander, Linus, Lycus, Marathon, Mars, Mentor, Mercury, Mestor, Midas, Momus, Myles, Narcissus, Nereus, Nestor, Oedipus, Olus, Orion, Orpheus, Pallas, Pan, Pandarus, Paris, Perseus, Phineus, Phoenix, Pluto, Priam, Pyramus, Remus, Theseus, Troilus, Ulysses, Vulcan, Zetus, Zeus.

Women: Alcestis, Althaea, Andromeda, Antigone, Aphrodite, Arachne, Arethusa, Ariadne, Artemis, Atalanta, Athena, Aurora, Bellona, Calliope, Calypso, Camilla, Cassandra, Chloë, Cilla, Clio, Cyrene, Daphne, Dia, Diana, Dione, Doris, Echo, Electra, Ersa, Europa, Evadne, Fauna, Flora, Harmonia, Helen, Helice, Hermione, Hippolyta, Ianthe, Irene, Iris, Ismene, Lara, Laverna, Lavinia, Leda, Libya, Luna, Maia, Meda, Medea, Melia, Metis, Minerva, Niobe, Nyx, Pandora, Penelope, Persephone, Phaedra, Philomela, Phoebe, Phyllis, Rhea, Selene, Sibylla, Thea, Thetis, Venus, Vesta.

Have a love affair

Love was regularly used as a first name in Britain for some three hundred years. Sometimes it became Lovie or Lovey. Loveday was also used, especially for a child born on a loveday, a day appointed for the settlement of disputes.

The Cornish name Kerensa or Kerenza is based on 'love', as are the Welsh names Ceri, Ceredig and Caradog. The French, *aimée*, 'loved' has given us Amy, while Amabel is from the Latin, *amabilis*, 'lovable'. A 'beloved' child could also be called Cara, Carita or Carissa. David is from a Hebrew word of that meaning.

Parents who use these names would no doubt say that the baby is there to be named because of an act of love, so why not make the choosing of its name a love affair.

Put them in their place

Florence Nightingale, the great heroine of the Crimean War, was born in Florence. Her sister was born in Naples, which less obviously suggested a name, but the city had earlier been named Parthenope by the Greeks after a legendary siren. The name means 'face of a maiden', and was duly given to Florence's sister.

Toban looks as if it might be an obscure biblical name, but it was given to a boy born in Manitoba. My own daughter was born in Stockholm, which was hardly suitable as a first name in itself, but at least the place of birth suggested that she be given a Swedish name.

My American colleague Cleveland Kent Evans of Omaha, who has made himself the most informed person on first-name usage in the US, thinks that this kind of naming is a good idea, and he is well placed to voice an opinion.

Protect the family name

A woman normally gives up her family name when she marries. It can be kept in the family by bestowing it as a first or middle name for a child.

Many last names have become common as first names, and for different reasons. At one time there was a tendency to 'borrow' aristocratic family names and use them as first names in order to imply that there was a family connection. Percy, Sidney, Russell, Neville, Mortimer and the like were used in this way. In the US the trend was for the last names of admired public figures – military, political or religious leaders – to be used as first names. This was the original reason for using names like Grant, Lee, Washington, Lincoln, Wesley and Calvin. The modern use of Kelly as a first name probably stems from admiration of Grace Kelly, as she appeared in films like *High Society*. Grace was thought to be a little old-fashioned, but Kelly struck just the right note.

Famous bearers of last names as first names include Stevie Wonder – Steveland, not Steven – and Hoagy Carmichael, who was born Hoagland Howard Carmichael.

Pronounce judgement

Charmian is a charming name, but how do you pronounce it? Some speakers make it sound like 'charm' followed by -ian. Others say *Sharmian*. Those who have studied Greek are likely to pronounce it *Karmian*. It can easily happen that you like the name when it is pronounced in one way, but not so much when it is pronounced in another. Perhaps the only thing to do is to ask as many people as possible how they pronounce it. That will give you some idea of what will happen in future.

British and American speakers often disagree about how a name should be pronounced. My own name is pronounced *Lezlie* in Britain, *Lesslie* in the US. The comedian Bob Hope has explained that he was forced to change his name when he went to America. Until that time he had been Leslie Hope, but when he heard himself being addressed as Less Hope, with jokes about being hopeless, he had to do something about it.

Give a name that wears well

The name that wears best of all is probably Spencer. A 'spencer' has been applied to various items of clothing. In the eighteenth century it was a short double-breasted overcoat, as worn by the second Earl Spencer. Then it became the name of a close-fitting jacket worn by women and children. Now it applies to a short coat or jacket.

Miss Hilary Pimm, who has been collecting unusual personal names for many years, tells me that she has seen Mink and Ermine used as girls' names. Strictly speaking these are animal names, but Miss Pimm is no doubt right to think that their use was inspired by the thought of luxurious fur coats.

Sing her praises

It is said that a pretty girl is like a melody, and she can certainly bear a melodious name. Melody itself was the name of one of my eighteenth-century ancestors, and the name is still in regular use, sometimes spelt Melodie. On its use in the US the novelist Calder Willingham, in *Providence Island* remarks, 'The name Melody's not unusual in the South. I knew a girl in school from Kentucky whose name was Melody. After a while we got used to the name, it was kind of cute.'

Carol looks like a musical name, but strictly speaking it has more to do with the name Charles, through its Latinized form *Carolus*, than with the Christmas carol. Carmen is another slightly deceptive name. It looks as though it must derive from the Latin, *carmen*, 'song', but it is taken from one of the titles of the Virgin Mary, Santa Maria del Carmen. 'Carmen' in that case is the Spanish form of a Hebrew word which occurs in the Bible as Carmel. It means 'garden, orchard'.

But there are thousands of girls who bear names that were suggested by a particular song. Sometimes the parents are not even aware that a song has influenced them when they name their daughters Michelle, Claire, Laura, Louise and so on. All they know is that a name is there in their minds, and that it has pleasant associations. A musical name, it seems, like the melody itself, lingers on.

Make it plain

There's a general feeling that boys should be given down-to-earth, no-nonsense names, while girls should be given something more fancy. Plain Jane may feel that there is something to be said for the fancy theory, but fancy names create their own problems. Take a name like – well, like Fancy, for instance. The name's occasional use may have been inspired by Miss Fancy Day, a character in Thomas Hardy's *Under the Greenwood Tree*. Another literary character who bears it is the heroine of the novel *Fancy* by Robert Krepps. One of this young lady's admirers is made to exclaim, 'What a wonderful name you have, my Fancy. It's a name for love.'

But just think for a moment of what a real-life Fancy would have to endure. She would constantly be told by her fancy-man that 'a little of what he fancies does him good'. She would hear never-ending comments about her fancy dress, for which she no doubt paid a fancy price. In spring her young man's thoughts of love would lightly turn to Fancy. Few girls would fancy having to put up with that kind of thing for very long. My guess is that they would soon be changing their name to Jane.

Be consistent

For some parents 'family planning' means having a

theme which runs through the children's names. At the turn of the century, when flower names were especially popular, it was not unusual for a family to consist of a whole bouquet of flowers, with daughters named Rose, Iris, Daisy and the like.

An even simpler theme is to make all the family names begin with the same letter. Thus, the Mayards of Abbeville, Louisiana, used sixteen names beginning with O for their children: Odile, Odelia, Odalia, Olive, Oliver, Olivia, Ophelia, Odelin, Octave, Octavia, Ovide, Onesia, Olite, Otto, Ormes and Opta. The Hickok family of Bellingham, Washington, made use of Zarnell, Zane, Zorin, Zellum, Zale, Zolund, Zerrill, Zatha, Zorina, Zelpha and Zella – less names than the Mayards but perhaps rather zanier and zippier.

Another American family named seven daughters Marybeth, Marykay, Marysue, Maryjan, Marypat, Marylynn and Maryrose. It is interesting to speculate what they would have named a son.

Finally, it is not difficult to guess the first name of the father who named his daughters Bobbyjoe, Bettyjoe and Billyjoe.

Keep count

Most parents would be enraged if they were told that their child was to be numbered rather than named, but some parents *choose* to number their children. They usually do it in Latin, borrowing names that were used by the Romans. For them it was more important than it is for us to indicate a child's position in the family. As it happens, in some parts of Africa a child still receives a special name which clearly indicates how many brothers or sisters have already been born.

We tend to favour some of the Roman number names more than others. Octavia has been well used, for instance, and sometimes has little or no connection with 'eighth'. I have known it used for a girl born in October (originally the eighth month), and occasionally it refers to a birth on the eighth of the month. In the nineteenth century, when families were larger, it was often legitimately given to an eighth child, becoming Octavius for a boy.

The first child in a Roman family could be a Primus or Prima, Primitivus or Primitiva. Primus is now associated with a trade name, and calling a child 'primitive' would not help his or her passage through life. Prima has been used in modern times: it carries the happy suggestion that the girl concerned may become a prima donna or prima ballerina. Primula provides an alternative, still with the meaning 'first'. A Roman family could have continued with names based on Secundus, Secunda; Tertius, Tertia; Quartinus, Quartina; Quintus, Quinta; Sextus, Sexta; Septimus, Septima; Octavius, Octavia; Nonus, Nona; Decimus, Decima.

It is not necessary to use a Latin name, as is shown by Ten Pilling of Alberta. He says that he was born at the tenth hour of the tenth day of the tenth month, weighed ten pounds at birth and was the tenth child in the family.

Professor Weekley in *Jack and Jill* mentions an English lady whose first name was Undecima, 'eleventh'. He also suggests that Vicesimus, 'twentieth', Knox was probably the record-holder in this area. He adds that for one set of parents enough was enough: they named a son Ultimus, 'last'.

Order things differently

The order in which children arrive can be indicated in other ways than by number names. The American writer Elsdon C. Smith mentions a Mormon family who named their children as follows: Abigail Bertha,

Caroline Daisy, Edward Frank, George Harold, Ida Jane and Katharine Libby.

Needless to say, the idea of alphabetical naming has occurred to others. Mr and Mrs A. W. Bowlin of Bonifay, Florida, managed to get through all twenty-six letters, though with signs of increasing difficulty towards the end. Eventually their family comprised Audie Bryant, Curtis Drue, Era Fay, Grady Hampton, Ida Jennette, Knola Leantha, Millard Nathan, Olevia Penelope, Quincy Ruth, Sarah Thelma, Ulysses Venson, Wilson Xana and Yon Zirckle.

Add a touch of seasoning

Children who are born at Christmas tend to lose out on birthday presents and celebrations, but they do at least get special names. The French Noel and Noelle are popular, as is Natalie, a name which commemorates the Nativity. It has a Russian form, Natasha. Carol, Holly and even Christmas itself can also be used to name children born at this time.

Easter is another season which can attract special names. An Easter child may become Pascal or Pascale, from the Latin, *Pascha*, 'Easter'. In nineteenth-century records the name Easter itself is often found, but I suspect that it is frequently meant to be Esther. An English correspondent tells me that she was named Palm because of her birth on Palm Sunday, the week before Easter.

One of the best-known literary names derives from the Easter season. The Sunday following Easter Day is known as Low Sunday. It has an alternative name, derived from the opening words of the Introit of the Latin mass said that day: *Quasi modo geniti infantes* (As newborn babes . . .). In Victor Hugo's novel *The Hunchback of Notre Dame*, Quasimodo receives his name because he is found abandoned on Quasimodo Sunday.

Other seasonal possibilities include Verna or Vernal, both derived from the Latin, *verna*, 'spring' and used to name children born at this time. More recently, American parents have begun to use Autumn as a first name. One can see why: thanks to the poet John Keats it conjures up rich visions of 'mellow fruitfulness'.

Go to church

A correspondent tells me that Ebba became one of her daughter's names because she was baptized in St Ebba's Church in Northumberland. Another correspondent chose James for her son because she and her husband were married in St James's Church six years previously.

A church could suggest a name in other ways. Dickens jokes with the idea in *Our Mutual Friend*, where Miss Abbey Potterson is the landlady of a pub. She is, of course, an Abigail, but Dickens tells us that some of her customers were firmly convinced that 'she was named after, or was in some way related to, the Abbey of Westminster'. Since Dickens wrote those words a real 'church' name has appeared on the scene, borne notably by the actor Kirk Douglas.

Be a purist

The seventeenth-century Protestants who were known as Puritans do not seem to have liked the name. Although they were very fond of 'virtuous' names, they carefully avoided using Purity itself. I can find no evidence that this name has ever been used in that form, though it exists in other forms. Catherine, or Katharine, is usually associated with the Greek word which means 'pure'. Agnes, and the biblical name Zaccheus, have the same meaning.

Virginia probably belongs here. 'My name's Virginia – Virgin for short but not for long,' says a character in Joseph Heller's *Something Happened*. The name seems to attract jokes. The last lady I met who bore it said she had been known as Creeper throughout her schooldays. The Greek name Parthenia also means 'virgin'.

Innocent has frequently been a papal name. For a girl Imogen could be used, the name of the heroine of Shakespeare's *Cymbeline*. It has come down to us in that form, but in the source Shakespeare used the name was Innogen, derived from the Latin, *innocens*, 'innocent'.

Keep it under your hat

You will think that I'm talking through my hat if I mention that a hat could suggest a suitable first name, but Busby Berkeley wouldn't have agreed. Berkeley was the Hollywood dance director who was responsible for many huge production numbers, especially well known for the kaleidoscopic effects he obtained. A 'busby' is the very tall fur cap worn by certain British guardsmen. No one seems to know where the word came from, or why it was Busby Berkeley's first name.

Trilby O'Ferrall was the heroine of a novel by George du Maurier, published in 1894. She is the artist's model who comes under the influence of Svengali. The stage version of *Trilby* introduced the soft felt hat which became known as a trilby. It would be quite legitimate to name a girl Trilby – the girl's name actually came first.

That is true also of Fedora, originally the name of a character in a play by Sardou. Add Tammy to the list, named for Burns' Tam O'Shanter, and you'll see that the idea is not as crazy as it seems.

Praise her to the skies

The actress Celeste Holm bears a name which derives from the Latin, *caelestis*, 'heavenly'. Her parents no doubt thought that she was heaven-sent.

The young lady who was on board the first People Express flight from Gatwick to Newark a few years ago bore the name Skye for a slightly different reason. Her American parents were great travellers, and had previously made good use of Sir Freddie Laker's Skytrain. Skye was three years old at the time of the People Express flight and had already crossed the Atlantic seventeen times, so her name appeared to have some justification.

Look on the bright side

No one wants to be a Bert these days. I have two friends called Albert and Gilbert who insist on being known as Al and Gil, yet the 'bert' in their names proclaims them to be 'bright' in every sense. Names containing this indication of splendour were once immensely popular. There were Cuthberts, Huberts, Herberts, Lamberts, Wilberts, Ruperts, Ethelberts, Egberts, Humberts, Engelberts and the like on all sides, not to mention the Bertrams and Bertrands. One such name remains one of the most consistently popular in the English-speaking world – Robert, but try calling a man who bears this name Bert instead of Bob or Rob and see where it gets you.

The American actor Burt Lancaster has managed to live with the sound of Bert, but everyone knows he's a Burt, not a Bert, and that somehow makes his name acceptable. Our Germanic ancestors would have found that remark extraordinary. For them it was the mark of highest distinction to be a Bert of one kind or another.

Send her victorious

Victoria, from the Latin word for 'victory', was made world-famous as a name by Queen Victoria but was not actually much used during her reign. Ordinary parents seemed to think that it was all right to name a son Albert, but it would have been considered presumptious to name a daughter after the queen. As it happens, Elizabeth was one of the most popular names for girls during Victoria's reign. Victoria itself has been most widely used during Elizabeth's reign. Other victorious names for girls include Berenice, or Bernice as it often appears, Nicole and Nicola. Nicola is used as a girl's name only in Britain. It is an Italian form of Nicholas, but was thought to be feminine because of the -a ending. Eunice also belongs here. It is derived from the Greek word for 'victorious'.

Boys can be made into winners by naming them Victor, Vincent, Nicholas, Nicodemus or Sigmund. The first two of these are Latin, the second two Greek, while Sigmund is based on the German, *Sieg*, 'victory'. In spite of its meaning, however, Nicodemus is just about the worst possible name anyone could give to a boy, according to a famous passage about the influence of names in the eighteenth-century novel *Tristram Shandy*, by Laurence Sterne.

Get the message

Probably the most extraordinary names ever given to children were those used by a group of extremists – religious fanatics who introduced the idea of 'slogan' names. Unfortunately they helped to bring ridicule upon their Puritan colleagues who expressed their religious faith in a more reasonable fashion, especially with the virtue names such as Faith, Hope and Charity.

Canon Bardsley made a special study of the slogan names in his *Curiosities of Puritan Nomenclature*. His investigation of English parish registers of the sixteenth and seventeenth centuries revealed that children had been called Fear-the-Lord, Fight-the-good-fight-of-faith, Good-work, Hate-evil, Help-on-high, Jesus-Christ-came-into-the-world-to-save, Job-raked-out-of-the-ashes, Learn-wisdom, Love-well, Search-the-Scriptures, Sorry-for-sin, Stand-fast-on-high, What-God-will. Zeal-of-the-land Busy, a character in Ben Jonson's *Bartholomew Fair*, was typical of the playwright's reaction to such extremes.

The public found their own way to put the bearers of such names in their place. The gentleman who was officially If-Christ-had-not-died-for-thee-thou-hadst-been-damned Barebone was known to one and all as Damned Barebone.

Give a classy name

The writer Jane Duncan, who was brought up in Scotland, refers in one of her books to her family's 'code of rules about names'. There were certain names which it was all right for her family to use – names like Janet, Elizabeth, Catherine, Isobel, Duncan, George and John. There was another group of names used by the local gentry – Victoria, Alexandra, Lydia, Deborah, Edward, Torquil, Anthony and Michael. It would have been considered presumptuous for those who were not gentry to make use of those names. There was even a third group of names which were looked down upon by both upper and middle class. No respectable family in Jane Duncan's neighbourhood would name a daughter Gladys, Wendy, Muriel or Doris. No sons in those households became Victor, Barry, Robin or Albert.

Jane Duncan's family evidently accepted its place in the social hierarchy. The more usual situation is for parents to imitate the habits of those they consider to be above them. If those on high choose to reintroduce Daisy for their daughters, and favour Thomas for their sons, then the use of those names will inevitably spread downwards.

While there are very few first names which remain 'upper class' because of this imitation process, there are some names which can be labelled 'working class' because they have been consistently rejected at higher level. That description, in Britain at least, would apply in recent years to Tracy, Sharon, Joanne, Lisa, Julie, Karen, Angela, Kelly and Kerry; Jason, Gary, Lee, Craig, Carl, Wayne, Scott, Shane and Dean. Those parents who gave such names have been, as it were, out-classed.

Name the day

In some parts of Africa a child is always given a name which indicates on which day of the week it was born. In our own society children can also receive day names of different kinds.

Sunday, Monday, Tuesday and the rest are used from time to time as first names. The actress Tuesday Weld, though, who gained a great deal of publicity because of her name, has explained that Tuesday was a childish corruption of her real name, Susan. Miss Weld was actually born on a Friday. The French form of Tuesday, Mardi, is also used as a first name, while Sunday also occurs as Spanish/ Portuguese Domingo.

The day of the month on which a child is born can

also suggest its name. The British newspaper, the *Daily Mail*, reported in November 1978 that a girl had been named Friday February Eleven Biddle because of her birth on that day. An American girl who was born on Friday the thirteenth was named Lucky. The British actress Una Stubbs received her name because she was born on the first of the month, though having a name which means 'one' caused amused comment when she visited Italy. There is an old joke about a boy who arrived on the last day of the month and was therefore named Bill.

Some days already have special names which can be transferred to a child. Michaelmas (29 September) has been used as a first name, and Tiffany was formerly the name given to a girl born on the Epiphany (6 January). The late George F. Hubbard's collection of unusual personal names included Labor Day Johnson and Thanksgiving Carraker.

Bide your time

A girl can be named for the time of day when she is born. An early morning birth can lead to Dawn, for instance, though other possibilities include Aurora, for the Roman goddess of the dawn, Oriana, which is based on the idea of the sun's rising, and Roxana, which derives from the Persian word for 'dawn'.

Eve, a pleasant name at any time, would be particularly suitable for a girl born in the evening. Sunset has also been used for a girl born at that time.

Names for children born at night usually refer to the fact that stars were shining at the time. The Latin, *stella*, 'star' leads to the names Stella and Estelle. Another Latin word, *astralis*, 'of the stars', has given us Astra. The Persian word for 'star' lies behind the name Esther. Star itself has occasionally been used in modern times.

The Latin word *nocturnus* means of the night, by

night, and I have seen Nocturna used as a girl's name. In modern Britain the name might run into a few problems because of certain slang words.

Take it out of store

Some parents have little difficulty in choosing a name for their child; they've had one in store for many years. Girls, especially, seem to make early decisions. They name a doll in childhood and ultimately transfer that name to their baby.

Researchers have also noted a kind of delay factor in name popularity. Some years ago in America a television series featured three young men who were named Jason, Joshua and Jeremy. Teenage girls at the time tended to hero-worship one or other of them. Several years later all three names began to appear in the name-popularity charts, the girls concerned having married and become mothers. It is curious to think that there must be some people who were virtually 'named' many years before they were born.

Study the subject

Catherine Cameron, author of *The Name Givers*, discovered an American family who showed a degree of originality in the naming of their children. Their first son was called Stanford; they then graduated to twins called Duke and Tulane. Further university children followed, named Harvard, Princeton, Auburn and Cornell. The mother really ought to have been known as Alma Mater.

Be a bit of a lad

Long before Boy George appeared on the pop scene, Boy had been used as a first name. It is strange that Boy seems more acceptable as a name than Girl would be. Perhaps it is linked to the fact that when you are pleased about something you exclaim 'Oh, boy!' and not 'Oh, girl!' Two other names of a similar type, not in general use, are Laddie and Chappie. The latter was chosen by a London family a year after their son's birth. Agreement on a more usual name had proved to be impossible.

A slightly older name, in every sense, is Charles (or Carl, Karl). The name derives from the same word which gave us 'churl', but the original meaning was not 'churlish' but 'man'. Man itself was adopted by the artist Man Ray. He would never reveal his real Russian Jewish first name.

Take the middle road

If there is a name that one of the parents likes very much, but the other does not, or there is a name which would honour a respected person but which is now rather old-fashioned, it can always become a middle name. Most people in English-speaking countries have one middle name, but several can be used if the parents wish. In 1986 a British family attracted a lot of media attention when they bestowed over a hundred middle names on their child, saying that they simply couldn't decide which one to use.

In the nineteenth century another British family decided to give their daughter a choice of names by covering the alphabet. Their daughter emerged as Anna Bertha Cecilia Diana Emily Fanny Gertrude Hypatia Inez Jane Kate Louise Maud Nora Ophelia Quince Rebecca Starkey Teresa Ulysis Venus Winifred Xenophone Yetty Zeno Pepper.

Lead her up the garden path

Flower people were with us long before the 1960s.

Parents turned to the garden for name ideas at least a hundred years earlier. Flower names blossomed on all sides in the latter half of the nineteenth century, and they're still with us today.

The Bible had shown the way with names like Susannah, Hebrew, 'lily' and Hadassah, 'myrtle'. There were also Greek names such as Daphne, 'laurel', Chloë, 'young green shoot' and Rhoda, 'rose'. Rose itself was one of the earliest English flower names to be used.

Especially well used have been Lily, Myrtle, Daisy, Iris, Laurel, Pansy, Primrose, Rosemary, Bryony and Veronica. Heather was first used before the end of the century, though it became really popular fifty years later. This name also occurs in its Latin form as Erica.

Other flower names I have noted are Amaryllis, Angelica, Camellia, Coronella, Fern, Hortensia, Jasmine, Jonquil, Marigold, Poppy, Saffron, Crocus, Eglantine, Lavender, Lilac, Magnolia, Mimosa, Nigella, Primula, Snowdrop (also in its Welsh form Eirlys), Sorrel, Syringa, Tansy, Yasmine and Zinnia.

If the language of flowers is taken into account, these names become 'meaningful' in a new way. Sorrel is 'affection', for instance. Tansy is 'I declare war against you'. Flower itself was once used as a first name. It is still used, translated into the Greek Anthea, Latin Flora, French Fleur, Welsh Blodyn. You can also name a girl Carmel, 'garden'.

Join the in-sect

The most popular insect name by far is 'honey-bee', which appears in either its Hebrew form, as Deborah, or as the Greek Melissa. Other insect names are very rare, though one thinks of Lady Bird Johnson, wife of President Lyndon Baines Johnson. A 'ladybird' is usually a 'ladybug' to Americans, so perhaps the name didn't so obviously suggest the little beetle dedicated to Our Lady.

I once commiserated in print with a lady who was Ima June Bugg before she married. The lady concerned wrote to say that she had enjoyed bearing that name, created by a father who had 'a great sense of humour'.

Put it in black and white

It has probably come about accidentally, but there are now distinct groups of names which are used almost exclusively by either black or white families. If we imagine a group of American teenagers, for instance, and are told that their names are Amy, Megan, Julie, Kristine, Susan, Bonnie, Colleen, Kelly, Kathleen, Heidi, Laura, Rebecca and Jennifer; Matthew, Joshua, Scott, Bradley, Adam, Peter, Jeffrey, Daniel, Jeremy, Todd and Alan, then we could be sure that nearly everyone of them was white. Any young blacks in the group would have come from decidedly middle-class families.

In a similar way, had the names been Kenya, Ayanna, Keisha, Ebony, Toya, Tameka, LaTonya, Yolanda, Felicia, Tasha, Katina, Wanda, Ericka, Patrice and Monique; Tommie, Roosevelt, Lamont, Kelvin, Jermaine, Deshawn, Demetrius, Darnell, Cornell, Cedric, Antoine, Reginald, Willie, Tyrone, Deon and Marlon, then the group would have been overwhelmingly black.

Not all names can be distinguished ethnically at a given time. Just as in Britain some names are acceptable at all social levels, so in the US some names ignore racial barriers. Teenagers who are Kimberly, Sherry, Danielle, Terri, Tracy, Andrea, Stacie, Stephanie or Sharon; Donald, Kevin, William, Randall, Kenneth, Benjamin, Raymond, Aaron,

Keith or Eric are amongst those whose names give no indication of their racial background.

It is interesting to note that one of the names that appealed almost equally to black and white parents, just before President Reagan entered the White House, was Ronald.

Use a Christian name

For me Christian names are a particular kind of first name, chosen because of the Christian beliefs of the parents. The American writer Mary McCarthy has pointed out that in Catholic families they 'are chosen for the spiritual qualities of the saints they are taken from. The saint a child is named for is supposed to serve, literally, as a model or pattern to imitate; your name is your fortune and it tells you what you are or must be.'

In many Christian countries boys are named Jesus. That name is almost never used in English-speaking countries, though both Jason and Joshua, which are variant forms of it, are quite common. Christ is an element in names like Christopher and Christine. It is also there in the most Christian of all names, Christian itself, which has enjoyed something of a revival in recent years.

Consult the calendar

Each day of the year is the feast-day of one or more saints. A glance at the calendar of saints may therefore suggest a name for a child born on a particular day. A well-known bearer of such a name was the late Valentine Orde, a distinguished musician, born on 14 February 1889.

The problem with this system is that a child has to choose the right day to be born. 1 March would make a boy David, 24 June would make him John, and so on. No problem there. If he came a few days later, however, he might find himself going through life as Winwaloe, Gerasimus or Phocas.

Turn it around

It's very difficult to be original when naming a child. If you decide to depart from the usual run of things and do something different, you're likely to discover later that you have walked down a well-trodden path. Plenty of people, for instance, have had the idea of taking a familiar name, shuffling its letters around, and thus producing a new name. Many others have simply spelt a name backwards. There's even a technical term – ananym – for a name produced by reversed spelling.

The name of this type that has been most generally used is Senga. It occurs nearly always in Scotland, where Agnes was immensely popular over a long period, but then acquired an old-fashioned image. Some parents wanted to keep in touch with the name, but gave it a new look. The use of Senga in Scotland has been widespread, and suggests that the name was used in literature, or was borne by a public figure at one time. No other name of this type has gained such general acceptance.

I was once introduced to a young lady called Kirry, as I thought. In fact her name turned out to be Cire, and her father was Eric. I remember remarking to her that she was not as backward as her name seemed to suggest. I have heard also of an Adnil whose mother was a Linda. It was the father who chose the name, explaining that he wanted his daughter to be as unlike her mother as possible. Perhaps there was a similar reason for the Azile I saw mentioned in a parish register. Her mother's name was certainly Eliza.

The former football correspondent of *The Times* newspaper once told me that he had named his son Ti, 'it' backwards, because he and his wife had been referring to 'it' for so long. I see also that Professor Weekley, in his book *Jack and Jill*, mentions someone whose name was Emorb Brome. He also came across a girl named Ronaele by her mother, Eleanor. Nor is the back-spelling phenomenon confined to English-speaking countries. Russian parents in the 1920s and 1930s, for instance, sometimes used the name Ninel, 'Lenin' in reverse, to name their children.

Names have varying fortunes when treated in this way. A Tessa becomes an asset when she's facing the other way. When a Dennis turns round, his name seems to hint at a murky past.

Listen to the weather forecast

'Our priest,' an American correspondent once told me, 'noticed how nervous I was during a storm. He took time out to explain to me about rain being one of God's greatest gifts. What he said that evening stuck with me, and when my daughter was born she was truly a gift from God, so I called her Raine.' And why not? The name is only a minor variant of Raina, which has been in use for many years. George Bernard Shaw may be responsible for that, having introduced a character of the name in *Arms and the Man*. Shaw was not inventing a weather name, simply making use of a well-established Russian variant of Regina.

A true weather name is Storm, made well known by the British novelist Storm Jameson. I have also come across an American girl called Stormy. Tempest was used to some extent in the nineteenth century, but did not become popular. It had probably been suggested by the last name.

Gisele does not look like a name of this type, but another of my correspondents tells me that in her case its use was inspired by a tropical hurricane of that name which was raging in Wellington Harbour at the time of the baby's birth.

Misty is occasionally found, having been launched by a popular song. Cloud is very rare, even in France where they have a Saint Cloud. There is a Greek name Iola which has the poetical meaning 'dawn cloud'.

I have no record of Snow being used as a first name, though it does occur in its Welsh form Eira. In the US there are girls called Nevada, usually because they were born in that state, but the Spanish word *nevada* actually means 'snowy'. Most of the names I've mentioned so far are used for girls, but one weather-type name for boys is Sunny. This doesn't mean that girl babies are wet and windy while boy babies always smile sweetly. It has more to do with Sunny and Sonny sounding the same. Sunny would cause considerable confusion if applied to a girl. The problem does not occur in Welsh, and Heulwen, 'sunshine', is used for girls. The idea of comparing a boy to the sun, by the way, is of great antiquity. The Hebrew name Samson means 'like the sun'.

One more 'weather' name, though it is one that is unlikely to be mentioned in the weather forecast, is Rainbow. Barbara Rainbow Fletcher is the author of *Don't Blame the Stork*, an amusing 'cyclopoedia of unusual names' published in 1981. The name is also found in its Welsh form, Enfys. An ideal name, one would have thought, for the daughter of a Sunny and Raine.

Brook no arguments

Mrs de Winton-Jewers once wrote to me from South Africa to explain why she and her husband named their daughter Tamar. 'The River Tamar is the natural boundary between Cornwall and Devonshire. My husband is a Cornishman; we met and married in Devon.' At the time of naming, the parents were unaware that Tamar occurs as a first name in the Bible. It has the meaning 'palm tree'.

Jordan, Douglas, Shannon and Sabrina are all river names that have been used as first names. A glance at a list of English river names suggests that many more could easily be a source of inspiration. I am thinking of names like Allen, Avon, Blythe, Boyd, Brent, Connor, Cory, Dane, Dee, Devon, Eden, Glen, Greta, Kennet, Kent, Kenwyn, Lark, Lea, Orwell, Perry and Warren. There are also rivers called Don, Len, Ray and Sid. The River Medina, which divides the Isle of Wight, has lent its name to many young ladies.

Thames does not seem to have been used as a first name, though its earlier form Tamesa would serve very well. And for those with only a stream nearby instead of a fully fledged river, there are the possibilities Brook, Brooke or Brooks.

Take a bird's eye view

In the short story by Rudyard Kipling, *Without Benefit of Clergy*, a son is born to an Indian girl as a result of her liaison with an Englishman. The couple decide to call him Tota, 'parrot'. Kipling explains that the parrot is 'regarded as a sort of guardian spirit in most native households', so the name would not be thought strange. Parrot would hardly be a suitable name in our own society. It seems likely that Polly has almost disappeared from use as a girl's name because of its connection with the bird.

Bird names in general, however, have been used quite successfully. Male names of this kind include Gawain or Gavin, 'hawk, eagle', Ingram, 'raven' and

Jonah, 'dove', but most of the bird names are for girls. Young girls, after all, have been referred to as 'birds' for centuries, and that expression is still used informally, in Britain at least. It was a fairly natural development for Birdie, 'little bird', to be used as a first name. Avis, from the Latin word for 'bird', also occurs, though there is no evidence that the Romans themselves ever used it as a name. On the other hand, the Bible sanctions the use of 'bird' as a name for either sex. The male form is Zippor, the female Zipporah – as borne by Noah's wife. In modern Wales one can also meet an Aderyn, whose name is Welsh for 'bird'.

Robin is now thought of as a girl's name connected with the bird, though it began as a pet form of Robert and was at first used for boys. Some parents think it necessary to give it a feminine form, and make it Robyn, Robina, Robena or Robinetta, but Robin itself will probably be feminine enough in the future.

The novelist Marie Corelli, who was fond of inventing new names for her characters, was ultimately responsible for the success of Mavis in the 1930s. She was the first to use this poetical word for a song thrush as a girl's name, in her book *The Sorrows of Satan*. Jay has also been fairly widely used, but parents don't necessarily have a bird in mind when they bestow it. It is often used to link with another name beginning with J.

Other bird names that occur in the records include Linnet (which becomes Llinos in its Welsh form), Merle, Starling, Pheasant, Lark (also found as the French Alouette, perhaps suggested by a well-known French song), Heron, Swan, Merlin and Finch. Not everyone realizes that these are girls' names. Merlin Johnson, writing to a newspaper on one occasion, lamented the fact that, when she attended birthday parties as a young child, hostesses always assumed she was a boy and prepared an appropriate present.

The kind of thinking that can lie behind the choice of a name of this type was indicated by the American writer Sinclair Lewis in *Cass Timberlane*: 'I did think . . . that I'd like to have a daughter named Lark. I know it was a kind of fancy name, but I want her to be what I always wanted to be and never could – swift and clean and belonging to the upper air, not touched with earth.'

Be virtuous

It was the Puritans of the sixteenth century who introduced the so-called 'virtue' names, such as Faith, Hope and Charity. Such names seem also to have appealed to the Russians. Lenin's wife, for instance, was Nadia, 'hope'. That name is found also as Nada, along with Vera, 'faith'.

Amongst the more popular virtue names have been Patience, Felicity, Grace, Constance, Honour, Clemency, Mercy, Prudence, Unity and Verity. Amity and Comfort have become rare, and many such names have disappeared. Modern parents would be unlikely to use Abstinence, Donation, Fear, Humility, Lamentation, Obedience, Perseverance, Repentance, Temperance or Tribulation, but all these occur in early parish registers. As a reminder to themselves and their children of their mortal nature, some Puritans used names like Dust, Earth and Ashes. At first glance these names seem incredible, yet Dusty Springfield was the winner of the European Song Contest some years ago, Eartha Kitt is a famous singer, and Ash is probably the nickname of many an Ashley or Ashleigh.

I was once 'arrested' by a police dog whose name turned out to be Justice. That was another Puritan first name, along with Assurance, Belief, Diffidence, Diligence, Discretion, Faithful, Gracious, Honesty,

Piety and Providence. Virtue itself was also used. It does seem as if the Puritans were trying to tell their children something.

Be economical

When the family name is already a first name it is tempting to 'economize', as B. S. Johnson suggested in his novel *Travelling People*. He was explaining why his central character was called Henry Henry.

Echo-names of that type do occur fairly regularly – not just near-misses, such as Robert Roberts or Evan Evans, but true echoes, such as Thomas Thomas, Alexander Alexander, Smith Smith. The last of these, Smith Smith, has been used more often than you might think. The Index of Births, compiled for the Registrar General, shows plenty of examples for England and Wales, though most of them occur in the nineteenth century. The last Smith Smith seems to have been named in 1929. In 1858 a boy was named Smith Follows Smith.

The American writer N. I. Bowditch, in his *Suffolk Surnames*, mentions people named Livingston Livingston, Tubervill Tubervill and Sir Cresswell Cresswell, an English judge. The late George F. Hubbard of New York, an avid collector of unusual names, discovered a Boyle O'Boyle and a man called Dominick Dominick Dominick. Another name in Mr Hubbard's collection was Rose Rose, recalling a once-popular song which began 'Rose, Rose, I love you'.

Alexander Alexander will be known to the readers of Jane Duncan's novels. The writer's husband of that name features in them, though he is usually referred to by his nickname, Twice. Charles Dickens also refers to an echo-name in *The Perils of Certain English Prisoners*: 'The beautiful unmarried young

English lady was Miss Maryon. The novelty was that her Christian name was Marion too. Marion Maryon. Many a time I have run off those names in my thoughts, like a bit of verse.'

Be poetical

If Marion Maryon was like a 'bit of verse' to Charles Dickens, what would he have made of Della Stella Serritella of Chicago, or Miss Trudy Moody of New York? Both were able to claim membership of the 'My Name Is A Poem Club', founded by someone called Hugh Blue. The club was being promoted in the 1950s by the American journalist E. V. Durling. One of the club's rules was that a married woman was ineligible for membership if it was her husband's name which completed the rhyme. The feeling was that too many women might otherwise be tempted to enter into the holy state of matrimony for the wrong reason – because they were desperate to join the club. One would have thought that they were more likely to get married because they were already in the club. By that, of course, I mean that they would want a change of last name in order to *stop* being Heather Feather, Nancy Clancy, or whatever. The club's membership at one time included a Jane Cane, Newton Hooton, Max Wax, Hollie Jolley and Dale Vale. Some people deliberately used pet forms of their first names in order to achieve the necessary effect. Thus Kenneth and Penelope Tenny of San Francisco, insisted on being known as Kenny and Penny Tenny. In various records I have come across a Larry Harry Barry, a Hester Pester, a Phoebe McKeeby, a May Day, a Vinch Finch and a Mollie Wollie, all of whom may have been unaware that membership of this select band was theirs for the asking.

Needless to say, I'm not seriously suggesting that parents should inflict this kind of name on their child, though some people choose to adopt them for themselves. There is the American stunt performer Evel Knievel, for instance, who was born Robert Craig Knievel. It is said that his behaviour as a youth suggested the nickname Evil. He amended this to Evel to match the last four letters of his family name – which perhaps suggests yet another way of naming a baby?

To stay with poetical parents for a moment, I am thinking of forming a 'Rhyming Relations Club'. Eligible for membership will be families consisting of parents and children with rhyming names such as Karen, Darren, Sharon; Johnny, Connie, Bonnie, Lonnie, Ronnie. Think of Jolly and Holly Forsyte in John Galsworthy's *Forsyte Saga*. There's also the family in *Trouble on Lost Mountain* by Joel Chandler Harris. The father in the latter story is touchingly proud of his daughter's name: 'This is my gal, Babe. I'm name' Abe an' she's name' Babe, sort er rimin' like.'

Try a new angle

Salmon occurs as a man's name in the Bible, but fishy names are few and far between. Those that look fishy aren't necessarily what they seem. Salmon, for instance, is thought to derive from a word meaning 'garment'. An Australian correspondent once told me of her ancestor, who was named Dolphin. The woman concerned was born on the ship of that name while her parents were on their way to their new homeland.

Ronan Coghlan, author of *Irish Christian Names*, says that his own first name means 'little seal'. Another writer on names, Bowditch, mentions a lady called Sardina, Italian for 'sardine'. Such names remain rare, though parents often refer to their children affectionately as Shrimp or Winkle. In the nineteenth century, when boys were sometimes given family names as first names, Fisher was fairly commonly used. When they became eligible bachelors later in their lives, such men were no doubt considered to be a good catch.

Be a vegetarian

The vegetable garden may not seem very inspiring if you are stuck for a name, though you could always call your son Spud. Then there's Fabian, which probably derives from the Latin, *faba*, 'bean'. An elderly gentleman of that name could therefore legitimately be addressed as 'old bean'.

While we're on the subject of terms of address, it's commonly said that the French call their loved ones 'my little cabbage' (*mon petit chou*). It's true that *chou* means 'cabbage', but it also refers to a small cake, the delicacy the French have in mind when they use the expression. Just as *chou* does not necessarily mean 'cabbage', so Lettuce, used as a girl's name, does not necessarily mean the salad vegetable. It is really a form of Lettice, which in turn is from the Latin, *laetitia*, 'joy, delight'. Girls who bore this name, which was once fairly popular, were usually known as Letty or Tish. The novelist Josephine Tey hints that it was nevertheless not a name to inspire its bearer with 'gladness'. In *Miss Pym Disposes* there is a character who 'remembered the day on which the fourth form had discovered her christened name to be Laetitia: a shame she had spent her life concealing.'

Try your luck

The Romans had a saying, *nomen est omen* (a name is an omen). They really believed that the name given to a child would help decide its destiny. They therefore frequently gave their children 'lucky' names, such as Fortunatus, Fortuna or Boniface. The last of these meant 'of good fate'.

Faustus, the Latin word for 'lucky', also formed the basis of many names. The Romans turned it into Faustillus, Faustinianus and Faustinus for men, Fausta, Faustina, Faustinia for women. Modern parents with similar beliefs in omens sometimes use Lucky or Luckie as first names. I don't know whether such names really do bring good fortune, but I see that a gentleman whose name was Luck Nash was listed as a bankrupt in 1857. A less obvious 'lucky' name was borne by the actress Yootha Joyce. She once told me that her first name, which her father borrowed from a New Zealand dancer, meant 'goddess of luck'.

Use a remarkable name

A passing remark by a friend or relative, seeing the new baby for the first time, can suggest a suitable name. A correspondent tells me that her daughter became Serena because a visitor happened to say that she looked so serene.

There are two well-known instances in literature where a baby is named in a similar way. In John Galsworthy's *Forsyte Saga* Soames goes to see his daughter for the first time. His wife Annette happens to refer to her baby as '*ma petite fleur*' (my little flower). The father seizes on the word. '*Fleur*,' repeated Soames. '*Fleur*! we'll call her that.'

An even more famous incident occurs in *Gone With The Wind* by Margaret Mitchell. 'The name agreed upon for the child was Eugenie Victoria, but that afternoon Melanie unwittingly bestowed a name that clung. . . . Rhett leaning over the child had said: "Her eyes are going to be pea green." "Indeed they are not," cried Melanie indignantly, "they are going to be blue ... as blue as the bonnie blue flag." "Bonnie Blue Butler," laughed Rhett, and Bonnie she became until even Scarlett and Rhett did not recall she had been named for two queens.'

Be alphabetical

The letters of the Greek alphabet have inspired many parents in the past, and Alpha has been especially well used for a first child. The letter, after all, is used symbolically in the Bible. 'I am the Alpha and the Omega,' God says, according to the Revelation of St John, meaning, 'I am the Beginning and the End.' The name has been used for both sexes, and when given to a boy makes him sound, in normal use, as if he's just another Alf.

Omega has also been reasonably well used, presumably to signal that he or she will be the last child in the family. In modern times people might think that the parents had named the child in honour of a Swiss watch.

Gamma is rarely used, but I have records of three girls named Delta. A river delta is named because it resembles the triangular shape of the Greek letter. It is to be hoped that the girls who bore the name did not resemble it.

Theta is very rare, but Zetas are not difficult to find. Pi was also used a few years ago by a Canadian family. They explained that in geometry pi could never be finally calculated, and that the name therefore represented infinity. I imagine that most people will think she was named because she was a 'sweety-pie'.

Put a smile in their eyes

Families which have an Irish ancestry often like to

show the connection in the names of their children. Irish parents themselves sometimes make use of a book such as *Irish Names For Children* by Patrick Woulfe, or *Irish First Names* by Ronan Coghlan.

Such names seem to have a special flavour for some people. In an article in *The Times* in 1983, Penny Perrick was discussing the impact of Irishmen who travelled abroad for their holidays. She remarked, 'When an Irishman dedicates himself to a line, he is unstoppable. His very name reeks of passion. Most are named after legendary local heroes – the sort of names that shorthand typists will murmur softly to themselves as they write love letters which will not be answered.'

Be that as it may, the most typical Irish names for boys, in my view, are Aidan, Bernard, Brendan, Brian, Cathal, Ciarán, Colin, Colm, Connor, Cormac, Cornelius, Daire, Declan, Denis, Dermot, Diarmuid, Donal, Eamonn, Eimar, Enda, Eoghan, Eoin, Eugene, Fergal, Flannan, Garrett, Gerard, Joseph, Kevin, Kieran, Liam, Niall, Padraig, Patrick, Ronan, Seamus, Sean, Shane. (In some instances I have given both Irish and English forms of the same name – Ciaran, Kieran; Diarmuid, Dermot.)

Corresponding names for girls would be Aileen, Áine, Aisling, Aoife, Bernadette, Bridget, Ciara, Deirdre, Eileen, Elaine, Erin, Ethna, Fidelma, Geraldine, Gráinne, Ita, Kathleen, Mairead, Majella, Maura, Muirne, Niamh, Nuala, Orla, Róisín, Shelia, Sinéad, Siobhán, Sorcha, Teresa, Una.

Take the low road

Scotland has not only the most famous monster in the world, but also the most aptly named. 'Nessie' not only links the creature, if she exists, to Loch Ness; it uses the diminutive form of Agnes, which was once a very popular Scottish name.

Certain names which are thought to be Scottish are used far more by families living outside Scotland than within – Kirk and Bonnie are obvious examples. I have nevertheless included them in the selection of typically Scottish first names. I have taken them from a book I published in 1978, *Scottish Christian Names*.

Boys: Adair, Alasdair, Alpin, Andrew, Angus, Arran, Athol, Aulay, Blair, Broderick, Bruce, Calum, Cameron, Campbell, Clyde, Cosmo, Crawford, Denholm, Diarmid, Donald, Douglas, Drummond, Dugald, Erskine, Ewan, Farquhar, Fergus, Finlay, Forbes, Fraser, Gilchrist, Graeme, Gregor, Hamish, Iain, Keir, Kirk, Lachlan, Ludovic, Magnus, Malcolm, Maxwell, Mungo, Murdoch, Murray, Ramsay, Roderick, Rory, Ross, Rowan, Stuart, Torquil, Wallace.

Girls: Ailsa, Alana, Alexina, Alexis, Alison, Antonia, Beathag, Bonnie, Brenda, Catriona, Christy, Edwina, Eilidh, Elsa, Elspeth, Esmé, Fenella, Fiona, Heather, Ina, Innes, Iona, Isla, Ismay, Janet, Jeanette, Jessie, Katrine, Kirsten, Kirstie, Mairi, Malvina, Morag, Morna, Morven, Osla, Rhona, Senga, Sheena, Shona, Sinnie, Thora, Tina.

Make them welcome in the hillsides

American writers on names now seem to be convinced that Megan is an Irish name, probably because of the character in Colleen McCullough's *The Thorn Birds*. Megan remains as Welsh as it has always been, used in Wales itself and by families living in other countries who like to indicate their Welsh connections.

Those with a special interest in Welsh first names should consult *A Book of Welsh Names* by Trefor Rendall Davies, *Welsh Names For Children* by Ruth

Stephen or *Welsh Personal Names* by Heini Gruffudd. My own selection of typically Welsh names would include the following:

Boys: Aled, Alun, Arwel, Arwyn, Awen, Bleddyn, Bryn, Brynmor, Carwyn, Cemlyn, Ceri, Cledwyn, Dafydd, Deinol, Dewi, Dyfan, Dylan, Edryd, Eifion, Eilir, Elfed, Elgan, Elis, Elwyn, Emrys, Emyr, Eryl, Eurig, Euros, Eurwyn, Gareth, Geraint, Gerlad, Gerwyn, Gethin, Glyndwr, Gruffydd, Gwilym, Gwyn, Gwynfor, Hefin, Huw, Iestyn, Ieuan, Ifan, Iolo, Iwan, Llyr, Melfyn, Morgan, Owain, Rhodri, Rhydian, Rhys, Tudur, Wyn.

Girls: Angharad, Anwen, Arwenna, Bethan, Bronwen, Carys, Catrin, Ceinwen, Ceri, Cerian, Cerys, Delyth, Einir, Eirian, Eirlys, Elen, Eleri, Elin, Eluned, Enfys, Ffion, Gwerfyl, Heulwen, Llinos, Lona, Lora, Lowri, Mai, Mair, Medi, Megan, Meironwen, Menna, Meriel, Mererid, Myfanwy, Nerys, Nesta, Nia, Olwen, Rhiain, Rhiannon, Sian, Sioned.

Pair them off

If you have twins you will get plenty of daft suggestions for pairs of names. Someone is bound to suggest Pete and Repeat or Kate and Duplicate. Then will come Jack and Jill, Adam and Eve, Romeo and Juliet. I'm not sure who got at the Evans family of Dubuque, Iowa, in 1962 but they named their twins Bing and Bang.

Thomas actually means 'twin' in Aramaic, as does the Greek Didymus and the Latin Geminus. All of these have feminine forms – Tamsin, Didyma, Gemina. I wouldn't mind betting, though, that the twin brother or sister of a Thomas would end up being called Jerry by classmates.

Other possibilities include using two names which have the same letters in different order, such as Amy and May, Noel and Leon, or using the same name in different languages. This might lead to Joy and Felicity, Melissa and Deborah, John and Ian. They could also be named for a common theme: two flower names, for instance, such as Daisy and (Sweet) William.

Get them interested

When the new baby already has a brother or sister, parents often feel that the older child should be encouraged to take an interest by helping to choose its name. One way of achieving this result, avoiding suggestions that are unsuitable, is to write potential names on slips of paper and put them into a hat. 'Impossible' names are quietly extracted. The child then draws the name from the hat, 'choosing' it in a way that most children find acceptable.

Fashion a name

Elsewhere in this book (pages 256–265) I have given lists of the most popular names at different times. The lists showing which names are currently being most used are especially important. Unless parents consult such a list they are likely to get a shock about five years after naming baby, when their child goes to school for the first time. Suddenly the name which they thought was, if anything, slightly unusual and distinctive turns out to be the name which dozens of other parents in the area chose in the same year.

Ideally a first name should distinguish its bearer from everyone around – when there are several Emmas or Pauls in the same class it can become rather confusing. There is also another disadvantage to names which reach the very top of the popularity charts. Eventually everyone realizes just how popular those names are and stops using them. The effect of that is to date the names concerned. Think of what happened to the Joans, Joyces and Bettys of the 1930s. At some time in the future Sarah, Emma and Claire will be as firmly attached to the 1980s, making the age of the women who bear those names all too apparent. Names to avoid at all costs, for girls especially, are those which are clearly becoming less popular after a spell in the limelight. The safest names of all are those which hover in the middle of the charts for a generation or two.

If you're determined to be fashionable, spot the names which are rising through the charts. If you want to be individualistic about naming your baby, avoid those names which appear in the top fifties altogether.

Compromise

It is not unusual for a husband and wife to find that they have completely different ideas about what to name their baby. Mary Lassiter, in her book *Our Names, Our Selves*, suggested a way of reaching a compromise solution. I have modified her ideas slightly, but the system works like this:

1. the husband and wife each choose about ten names which could be used for the child;
2. two lists of all twenty names are written out;
3. each partner awards a number of points, say from one to ten, to each of the names;
4. both partners agree to accept the name which emerges with the highest number of points when their respective 'scores' are added together.

Mrs Lassiter says that she and her husband had reached stalemate because she wanted to name her daughter Rachel, while he wanted Julia. When it came to awarding points, Mrs Lassiter gave Rachel ten and Julia only one. Her husband gave Julia ten points and Rachel only one. They then discovered that they had both given Rebecca, a name reasonably acceptable to both, enough points to make it the winner. Five years after naming their daughter Rebecca, Mrs Lassiter was able to report that both parents and Rebecca herself felt satisfied with the compromise name.

Do your own thing

If none of the ideas I've put forward appeals to you, use your own imagination. Parents are always surprising me with their sources of inspiration. From computer read-outs of first names given in recent years to American children I extract the following slightly unusual names: boys: Artery, Change, Chip, Demon, Marvel, Monsieur, Qupid, Shiny, Sultan, Tory: girls: Common, Destiny, London, Passion, Sparkle, Tomorrow.

British records also contain a few surprises. Children with the surname Smith, for instance, have at various times been given the first names Tram, Same, Raper, Mystic, Energetic, Dozer, Barman and Ark. Streaker Smith was named in 1845, the son of Ann Smith, *née* Streaker.

What would you say to a first name which appears to mean 'clotted blood'? The American writer Gore Vidal has made it well known and it attracts no undue attention. As it happens, Gore as a family name has another meaning altogether, to do with a 'triangular piece of land'.

I could continue with examples indefinitely, but one more will do. A boy born in England in 1880, for reasons which are unknown to me, was given the first name Farewell.

4,000 FIRST NAMES

Dictionary and Index to names mentioned in the 101 Interesting Ideas section

A

A (m.) the letter used as a name (p. 12)

Aaron (m.) Hebrew, meaning doubtful, perhaps 'high mountain' (pp. 33, 55)

Abbey (f.) also *Abbie*, *Abby*. Pet forms of Abigail (p. 45)

Abda (m.) Hebrew, 'servant'

Abdiel (m.) Hebrew, 'servant of God'

Abdon (m.) Hebrew, 'little servant'

Abdul (m.) also *Abdullah*. Arabic, 'servant of God'

Abednego (m.) Aramaic, 'servant of Nabu' (p. 16)

Abel (m.) Hebrew, 'breath, vapour' or Assyrian, 'son'

Abia(h) (m.) a form of Abijah

Abiathar (m.) Hebrew, 'Father of abundance'

Abida (m.) Hebrew, 'the Father knows'

Abidan (m.) Hebrew, 'my Father is judge'

Abiel (m.) Hebrew, 'my Father is God'

Abiezer (m.) Hebrew, 'my Father is help'

Abigail (f.) Hebrew, 'my Father rejoices' (pp. 20, 34, 43, 45)

Abihail (m.), 'my Father is mighty'

Abijah (m.) Hebrew, 'my Father is Jehovah'

Abimelech (m.) Hebrew, 'my Father is king'

Abinadab (m.) Hebrew, 'my Father is generous'

Abinoam (m.) Hebrew, 'my Father is gracious'

Abiram (m.) Hebrew, 'my Father is on high'

Abishag (f.) Hebrew, meaning uncertain

Abishua (m.) Hebrew, 'my Father is noble'

Abner (m.) Hebrew, 'my Father is the lamp or light'

Abraham (m.) Hebrew, 'father of a multitude'

Abram (m.) Hebrew, 'my Father is on high'

Absalom (m.) Hebrew, 'my Father is peace'

Abstinence (m., f.) the word used as a name (by the Puritans) (p. 62)

Achbor (m.) Hebrew, 'the mouse' (p. 5)

Achilles (m.) Greek, 'lipless' (p. 37)

Actor (m.) Greek, 'chief, leader'. The word 'actor' is Latin, 'doer' (p. 37)

Ada (f.) pet form of Adelaide (p. 24)

Adah (f.) Hebrew, 'ornament' (p. 34)

Adaiah (m.) Hebrew, 'Jehovah has adorned himself'

Adair (m.) Scottish form of Edgar (p. 70)

Adalheidis (f.) Germanic, 'nobility' (p. 28)

Adaline (f.) a form of Adeline

Adam (m.) Hebrew, 'of red earth' (pp. 13, 14, 33, 55, 71)

Adamina (f.) also *Adamine*, *Adamette*. Feminine forms of Adam (p. 13)

Addie (f.) pet form of Adeline, Adelaide

Adela (f.) short form of Adelaide

Adelaide (f.) Germanic, 'nobility'

Adèle (f.) French, pet form of Adelaide

Adelia (f.) fanciful form of Adela

Adelina (f.) Latinized form of Adelaide (p. 36)

Adeline (f.) variant of Adelina

Adeliza (f.) blend of Adèle and Liza

Aden (m.) place name or variant of Aidan

Aderyn (f.) Welsh, 'bird' (p. 61)

Adina (m, f.) Hebrew, 'delight'

Adlai (m.) Hebrew, 'my ornament' (p. 33)

Admiral (m.) the word used as a name (p. 27)

Adnil (f.) Linda spelt backwards (p. 57)

Adolf (m.) Germanic, 'noble wolf' (p. 5)

Adolphus (m.) Latinized form of Adolf

Adonis (m.) Greek, 'lord' (p. 37)

Adria (f.) feminine form of Adrian

Adrian (m.) Latin, 'from the city of Adria in Italy'

Adriana (f.) Italian feminine form of Adrian

Adrienne (f.) French feminine form of Adrian

Aeneas (m.) Greek, 'praiseworthy' (p. 37)

Aeson (m.) Greek, 'ruler' (p. 37)

Afra (f.) also *Affery*. Forms of Aphra

Agatha (f.) Greek, 'good'

Agnes (f.) Greek, 'pure, chaste' (pp. 36, 46, 57, 69)

Agneta (f.) Latin, derivative of Agnes

Ahab (m.) Hebrew, 'brother of the Father'

Ahaz (m.) also *Ahaziah*. Hebrew, 'Jehovah grasps [in order to guide]'

Ahmad (m.) also *Ahmed*. Arabic, 'the most praised'

Aiah (m.) Hebrew, 'vulture'

Aibhlin (f.) Irish form of Eileen

Aidan (m.) Gaelic, 'fire' (p. 69)

Aileen (f.) a variant of Eileen (p. 69)

Ailie (f.) pet form of Ailis (Gaelic, Alice) or Ailsa

Ailsa (f.) from the island rock called Ailsa Craig at the mouth of the Clyde (p. 70)

Aimée (f.) French, 'loved'

Aine (f.) Irish, an ancient name now linked with Anna (p. 69)

Ainslie (m., f.) family name and place name of uncertain origin

Aisha (f.) Arabic, 'woman'

Aisling (f.) Irish, 'dream, vision' (pp. 36, 69)

Aithne (f.) a form of Ethne

Ajax (m.) Greek, 'eagle' (p. 37)

Alain (m.) French form of Alan

Alaine (f.) feminine form of Alain (but not used in France)

Alaister (m.) a form of Alasdair

Alan (m.) Gaelic, of uncertain meaning, possibly 'rock' or 'noble' (pp. xi, 55)

Alana (f.) feminine form of Alan (p. 70)

Alaric (m.) Germanic, 'noble ruler'

Alasdair (m.) Gaelic, form of Alexander (p. 70)

Alastair (m.) also *Alaster*. Variant of Alasdair

Alastor (m.) Greek, 'avenger' (p. 37)

Alban (m.) Latin, 'citizen of Alba' (p. 14)

Albany (m.) Gaelic, 'rock, mountain', alluding to Scotland or Great Britain

Albert (m.) Germanic, 'noble bright' (pp. 36, 47, 48, 50)

Alberta (f.) feminine form of Albert or from the Canadian province of this name

Albertina (f.) Latinized feminine form of Albert

Albertine (f.) French feminine form of Albert

Albin (m.) Latin, 'white'

Albion (m.) a variant of Albany (p. 11)

Albreda (f.) Germanic, 'elf-counsel'

Alby (m.) pet form of Albert

Alcestis (f.) Greek, 'power of the home' (p. 37)

Alda (f.) Germanic, 'old'

Alden (m.) Old English, 'old friend'

Aldo (m.) Italian form of Germanic name, 'old'

Aldous (m.) variant of Aldo

Aldred (m.) Old English, 'old counsel'

Aldwyn (m.) Old English, 'old friend'

Alec (m.) also *Aleck*. Pet forms of Alexander

Aled (m.) Welsh river name (p. 71)

Alester (m.) variant of Alasdair

Alethea (f.) Greek, 'truth'

Alette (f.) French diminutive of Latin, 'wing'

Alex (m.) pet form of Alexander

Alexa (f.) feminine form of Alexis or Alexander

Alexander (m.) Greek 'defender of men' (pp. 37, 63)

Alexandra (f.) feminine form of Alexander (p. 49)

Alexandria (f.) variant of Alexandra or from the Egyptian place name

Alexandrina (f.) also *Alexandrine*. Feminine forms of Alexander

Alexia (f.) variant of Alexa

Alexina (f.) also *Alexine*. Scottish feminine forms of Alexander (p. 70)

Alexis (m., f.) Greek, 'helper' (p. 70)

Alf (m.) pet form of Alfred (p. 68)

Alfie (m.) diminutive of Alf

Alfred (m.) Old English, 'elf-counsel'

Alfreda (f.) feminine form of Alfred

Alfredo (m.) Spanish/Italian form of Alfred

Algar (m.) Old English, 'elf-spear'

Algerine (f.) the family name Alger adapted to first name use (p. 17)

Algernon (m.) Norman French, 'with whiskers or moustaches'

Algie (m.) pet form of Algernon

Ali (m.) Arabic, 'the highest'

Alic (m.) also *Alick*. Variants of Alec(k)

Alice (f.) Germanic, 'of noble kind' (pp. 28, 36)

Alicia (f.) Latinized form of Alice

Alida (f.) variant of Alda

Alina (f.) pet form of Adelina

Aline (f.) pet form of Adeline

Alisa (f.) Russian form of Alice

Alisdair (m.) variant of Alasdair

Alisha (f.) phonetic spelling of Alicia

Alison (f.) French diminutive of Alice (p. 70)

Alissa (f.) modern variant of Alicia

Alistair (m.) variant of Alasdair

Alix (f.) variant of Alice or feminine form of Alexander

Allan (m.) variant of Alan

Allana (f.) variant of Alana

Allaster (m.) variant of Alasdair

Allegra (f.) Italian, 'lively, joyful'

Allen (m.) variant of Alan (p. 60)

Allena (f.) also *Allene.* Feminine forms of Allen

Allie (f.) pet form of Alice, Alison

Allison (m., f.) male usage is from the family name, otherwise a variant of Alison

Ally (m.) pet form of Alasdair, Alexander

Allyson (f.) variant of Alison

Alma (f.) Latin, 'nurturing, kind', or from the river Alma in the Crimea (p. 26)

Almina (f.) also *Almina.* Variants of Elmina

Almira (f.) Arabic, 'princess'

Almond (f.) from the tree

Aloisa (f.) also *Aloisia.* Feminine forms of Aloysius

Alonso (m.) also *Alonzo.* Pet forms of Alphonso

Alouette (f.) French, 'lark' (p. 61)

Aloysius (m.) Latin form of Louis

Alpha (m., f.) the first letter of the Greek alphabet, used to symbolize 'the beginning, first' (p. 68)

Alphonso (m.) of uncertain meaning, probably 'battle ready'

Alpin (m.) Gaelic, 'white' (p. 70)

Althaea (f.) Greek form of Althea (p. 37)

Althea (f.) Greek, 'shrub which heals, i.e. the marsh mallow'

Alun (m.) Welsh form of Alan (p. 71)

Alured (m.) short form of Latin Aluredus (Alfred)

Alva (m., f.) also *Alvah (m.)*. Hebrew, 'height'

Alvar (m.) Old English, 'elf-army'

Alverdine (f.) Latinized feminine form of Alfred

Alvie (m., f.) pet form of Alvin or Alvina

Alvin (m.) Old English, 'elf-friend' or 'noble-friend'

Alvina (f.) also *Alvine*. Feminine forms of Alvin

Alvis (m.) possibly a variant of Elvis

Alvyn (m.) variant of Alvin

Alwin (m.) also *Alwyn*. Variants of Alvin

Alwyna (f.) also *Alwyne*, *Alwynne*. Feminine forms of Alwin

Alycia (f.) variant of Alicia

Alys (f.) Welsh form of Alice

Alysia (f.) variant of Alicia

Alyson (f.) variant of Alison

Alyssa (f.) variant of Alissa

Amabel (f.) Latin, 'lovable' (p. 37)

Amal (m.) Hebrew, 'difficulty'

Amalia (f.) Latin, 'industrious'

Amanda (f.) Latin, 'fit to be loved'

Amariah (m.) Hebrew, 'Jehovah speaks'

Amaris (f.) feminine form of Amariah

Amaryllis (f.) the flower name (p. 54)

Amasa (m.) Hebrew, 'Jehovah carries'

Amasiah (m.) Hebrew, 'Jehovah carries'

Amata (f.) Latin, 'loved'

Amaziah (m.) Hebrew, 'Jehovah is strong'

Amber (f.) a reference to 'yellowish brown' or ambergris, used for necklaces, etc. (pp. 14, 15)

Amberetta (f.) diminutive of Amber

Ambrose (m.) Greek, 'immortal'

Ambrosina (f.) also *Ambrosine*, *Ambrozine*. Feminine forms of Ambrose

Amelia (f.) Latin, 'industrious'

America (f.) The name of the country, a Latin feminine form of Amerigo, ultimately from Alberic, 'elf-ruler' (pp. 10, 11)

Amethyst (f.) the precious stone (p. 15)

Amia (f.) Latinized form of Amy

Amias (m.) variant of Amyas

Amica (f.) Latin, 'beloved friend'

Amice (f.) French form of Amica

Amie (f.) French, 'friend' or variant of Amy

Amina (f.) pet form of Williamina

Aminta (f.) Italian feminine of Amintore, 'protector'

Amity (m., f.) the word used as a name (by the Puritans) (p. 62)

Ammiel (m.) Hebrew, 'my uncle is God'

Amminadab (m.) Hebrew, 'my uncle is generous'

Ammizabad (m.) Hebrew, 'my uncle has made a gift'

Amnon (m.) Hebrew, 'faithful'

Amok (m.) Assyrian, 'capable'

Amon (m.) Hebrew, 'faithful'

Amos (m.) Hebrew, 'carrier' (p. 33)

Amplias (f.) Greek, 'vine'

Amy (f.) French, 'loved' (pp. 37, 55, 71)

Amyas (m.) Latin, 'loved of God'

Anaiah (m.) Hebrew, 'Jehovah answers'

Anabella (f.) variant of Annabella

Anan (m.) Hebrew, 'storm-cloud'

Ananiah (m.) Hebrew, 'Jehovah has shown himself'

Anastasia (f.) Greek, 'resurrection' (p. 19)

Anders (m.) Scandinavian (occasionally Scottish) form of Andrew

Andra (m., f.) Gaelic form of Andrew or a feminine form of Andrew
André (m.) French form of Andrew
Andrea (f.) feminine form of Andreas (p. 55)
Andreas (m.) Latin form of Andrew
Andrée (f.) French feminine form of André
Andrette (f.) modern feminine form of André
Andrew (m.) Greek, 'manly, virile' (pp. 28, 70)
Andrewina (f.) also *Andria*, *Andrietta*, *Andrianna*, *Andrienne*, *Andrina*, *Andrine*. Feminine forms of Andrew
Andromeda (f.) Greek, 'ruler of men' (p. 37)
Andronicus (m.) Greek, 'conqueror of men'
Andy (m.) diminutive of Andrew
Aneirin (m.) variant of Aneurin
Anetta (f.) also *Anette*. Variants of Annetta, Annette
Aneurin (m.) based on Welsh, 'gold', or Welsh form of Latin word for 'honour'
Angel (m, f.) Greek, 'messenger, angel'
Angela (f.) feminine of Angel (p. 50)
Angèle (f.) French form of Angela
Angelene (f.) variant of Angeline
Angelia (f.) variant of Angela
Angelica (f.) the flower name (p. 54)
Angelika (f.) German form of Angelica
Angelina (f.) Italian diminutive of Angela
Angeline (f.) French form of Angelina

Angelique (f.) French form of Angelica
Angelita (f.) Spanish diminutive of Angela
Angelo (m.) Italian/Spanish form of Angel
Angharad (f.) Welsh, 'much loved' (p. 71)
Angie (f.) pet form of Angela, Angelina, etc.
Angus (m.) Gaelic, 'unique choice' (p. 70)
Angusina (f.) feminine form of Angus
Anice (f.) variant of Annice
Anika (f.) variant of Annika
Anis (f.) variant of Annis
Anise (f.) variant of Annice
Anita (f.) Spanish diminutive of Ann
Ann (f.) English form of Hannah (p. 36)
Anna (f.) Greek and Latin form of Hannah (p. 24, 25, 53)
Annabel (f.) variant of Amabel
Annabella (f.) Latin form of Annabel
Annabelle (f.) Frenchified form of Annabel
Annalie (f.) pet form of Anneliese
Annalisa (f.) English form of Anneliese
Annamarie (f.) blend of Anna and Marie
Annaple (f.) Scottish form of Annabel
Anne (f.) French form of Ann (p. 36)
Anneliese (f.) German blend of Anna and Liese (Elisabeth)
Annemarie (f.) blend of Anne and Marie
Annetta (f.) Latinized form of Annette
Annette (f.) French diminutive of Anne (p. 67)

Annice (f.) probably English form of Greek, Anysia, 'fulfilment, completion'

Annie (f.) diminutive of Ann (p. 35)

Annika (f.) Swedish diminutive of Ann

Annis (f.) a phonetic spelling of Agnes as formerly pronounced or a variant of Annice (p. 36)

Annita (f.) variant of Anita

Annmaria (f.) also *Annmarie.* Blends of Ann and Marie

Annora (f.) early variant of Honoria

Annthea (f.) modern variant of Anthea

Anny (f.) variant of Annie

Anona (f.) Latin, 'pineapple' (p. 7)

Anouska (f.) Russian pet form of Ann

Anselm (m.) Germanic, 'divine-helmet'

Anselma (f.) feminine form of Anselm

Anthea (f.) Greek, 'flower' (p. 54)

Anthony (m.) from Latin Antonius, a Roman clan name of uncertain meaning. Incorrectly linked with Greek, *anthos*, 'flower', which caused the 'h' to be added unnecessarily (p. 49)

Antigone (f.) Greek, 'contrary birth, incestuous conception' (p. 37)

Antione (m.) modern US form of Antoine

Antoine (m.) French form of Antony (p. 55)

Antoinette (f.) French feminine form of Antoine

Anton (m.) German form of Antony

Antonette (f.) variant of Antoinette

Antonia (f.) Latin feminine of Antony (p. 70)

Antonina (f.) Italian feminine of Antonio

Antonino (m.) Italian form of Antony

Antonio (m.) Italian/Spanish form of Antony

Antony (m.) from the Roman clan name Antonius, of uncertain meaning

Anwen (f.) also *Anwyn*. Welsh, 'very beautiful' (p. 71)

Anya (f.) phonetic spelling of Anna as pronounced in Spanish

Anyes (f.) a spelling of Agnes to indicate its French pronunciation (p. 36)

Aoife (f.) Irish form of Eva, Eve (p. 69)

Aphra (f.) Hebrew, 'dust'

Aphrodite (f.) Greek, 'foam-born' (p. 37)

Apollo (m.) Greek, 'destroyer' (p. 37)

April (f.) from the month. Apryl is also found (p. 8)

Aquila (m.) Latin, 'eagle'

Arabella (f.) Latin, 'yielding to prayer' (p. 36)

Arachne (f.) Greek, 'spider' (p. 37)

Araminta (f.) invented by Sir John Vanbrugh for his play *The Confederacy* (1705). She is the wife of Moneytrap, which no doubt links with 'mint'

Archelaus (m.) Greek, 'leader or ruler of the people'

Archer (m.) a use of the family name, meaning 'bowman'

Archibald (m.) Germanic, 'excellent, noble-bold'

Archie (m.) pet form of Archibald

Areta (f.) Greek, 'virtue'

Aretas (m.) Arabic, 'metal worker'

Arethusa (f.) Greek, 'excellence' (p. 37)

Arfon (m.) Welsh place name

Ariadne (f.) Greek, 'very holy one' (p. 37)

Ariane (f.) French form of Ariadne

Ariel (m.) Hebrew, 'lion of God' or 'hearth of God'

Arjay (m.) formed by the letters R and J (p. 8)

Ark (m.) the word used as a name (p. 74)

Arleena (f.) also *Arlena, Arlene.* Variants of Arline (p. 21)

Arletta (f.) diminutive of Caroletta or Carletta

Arline (f.) a pet form of Caroline

Armand (m.) French form of Herman

Armando (m.) Spanish form of Herman

Arnaud (m.) French form of Arnold

Arno (m.) probably a pet form of Arnold

Arnold (m.) Germanic, 'eagle-power'

Aron (m.) variant of Aaron

Arran (m.) Scottish place name (p. 70)

Arthene (f.) feminine form of Arthur

Artemas (m.) Greek, 'gift of the goddess Artemis'

Artemis (f.) Greek, 'safe and sound' (pp. 17, 37)

Artery (m.) the word used as a name (p. 74)

Arthur (m.) Celtic, 'bear' (p. 5)

Arthuretta (f.) feminine form of Arthur

Arthurina (f.) also *Arthurine*. Feminine forms of Arthur

Arwel (m.) a Welsh name of uncertain meaning (p. 71)

Arwen (f.) also *Arwenna*, *Arwyn (m.)* Welsh, 'muse' (p. 71)

Asa (m.) Hebrew, 'healer'

Asaiah (m.) Hebrew, 'Jehovah has made'

Asaph (m.) Hebrew, 'God adds' or 'God gathers'

Ashby (m.) place name/family name, 'farm near ash trees'

Asher (m.) Hebrew, 'what happiness!' (p. 30)

Ashes (m., f.) the word used as a name (by the Puritans) (p. 62)

Ashlea (m., f.) also *Ashlee*, *Ashleigh*. Variants of Ashley (p. 62)

Ashley (m., f.) place name/family name, 'ash wood' (pp. 9, 62)

Ashlie (f.) variant of Ashley

Ashling (f.) phonetic spelling of Aisling (p. 36)

Ashton (m.) place name/family name, 'ash tree farm'

Asia (f.) from the continent (p. 117)

Aspasia (f.) Greek, 'welcome'

Assurance (m., f.) the word used as a name (by the Puritans) (p. 62)

Asta (f.) pet form of Astrid, Augusta or Anastasia

Aston (m.) place name/family name, 'eastern settlement'

Astra (f.) Latin, 'of the stars' (p. 51)

Astrid (f.) Old Norse, 'divinely beautiful' (p. 10)

Atalanta (f.) Greek, 'unswaying' (p. 37)

Atarah (f.) Hebrew, 'crown'

Athalaiah (f.) Hebrew, 'Jehovah is exalted'

Athelstan (m.) Old English, 'noble-stone'

Athene (f.) also *Athena*. Greek goddess of wisdom. Probably 'of Athens' (p. 37)

Athol (m.) Scottish place name/family name (p. 70)

Atlas (m.) Greek, 'he who endures' (p. 37)

Auberon (m.) Germanic, 'noble-bearlike'

Aubert (m.) French form of Albert

Aubrey (m.) Germanic, 'elf-counsel'

Auburn (m.) a use of the word for 'reddish-brown', or of the US place name (pp. 14, 52)

Audie (m.) pet form of Edward (p. 44)

Audley (m.) English place name/family name

Audra (f.) modern variant of Audrey

Audrey (f.) simplified form of Etheldreda

August (m.) German form of Augustus

Augusta (f.) feminine form of Augustus or Augustin(e) (p. 8)

Augustina (f.) feminine form of Augustine

Augustine (m.) Latin diminutive of *augustus*, 'venerable'

Augustus (m.) Latin, 'venerable' (p. 8)

Aulay (m.) Gaelic form of Olave (p. 70)

Aurelia (f.) Latin feminine of Aurelius 'gold' (p. 14)

Auriel (f.) Latin, 'gold'

Aurora (f.) Latin, Roman goddess of the dawn. (pp. 37, 51)

Aurore (f.) French form of Aurora

Austen (m.) variant of Austin

Austin (m.) spoken form of Augustine (p. 3)

Austyn (m.) modern variant of Austin

Autumn (f.) the word used as a name (p. 45)

Ava (f.) phonetic spelling of Eva as pronounced in several countries

Aveen (f.) modern diminutive of Ava

Averil (f.) Old English, 'boar-battle' (p. 5)

Avery (m.) variant of Alfred

Avice (f.) Latin feminine of Avitius, of unknown meaning

Avis (f.) also *Avisa*, *Avise*. Latin, 'bird', or variants of Avice (p. 61)

Avner (m.) Hebrew form of Abner

Avon (f.) river name (p. 60)

Avril (f.) French form of April (p. 8)

Awen (m.) Welsh, 'muse' (p. 71)

Axel (m.) Scandinavian pet form of Absalon

Ayanna (f.) perhaps a development from Juliana or a similar name (p. 55)

Ayesha (f.) variant of Aisha

Ayleen (f.) variant of Aileen

Aylmer (m.) Old English, 'noble-famous'

Azaniah (m) Hebrew, 'Jehovah has heard'

Azarel (m.) Hebrew, 'God has helped'

Azariah (m.) Hebrew, 'Jehovah has helped'

Azaziah (m.) Hebrew, 'Jehovah shows himself to be strong'

Azel (m.) Hebrew, 'noble'

Azile (f.) Eliza spelt backwards (p. 57)

Aziza (m.) Hebrew, 'Jehovah shows himself to be strong' (p. 24)

Azriel (m.) Hebrew, 'my help is God'

Azubah (f.) Hebrew, 'abandoned, forsaken'

Azure (f.) the word used as a name (p. 14)

B

Babe (f.) the word used as a name (p. 65)

Babette (f.) French diminutive of Barbara or Elizabeth

Baden (m.) from the family name of Lord Baden-Powell

Bailey (m.) family name meaning 'bailiff'

Baker (m.) occupational family name

Baldwin (m.) Germanic, 'bold friend'

Bang (m.) the word used as a name, twin brother of Bing (p. 71)

Bani (m.) short form of Benaiah

Barak (m.) Hebrew, 'lightning flash'

Barbara (f.) Greek, 'strange, foreign' (p. 14)

Barbary (f.) early form of Barbara

Barbie (f.) pet form of Barbara

Barbra (f.) modern spelling of Barbara

Barclay (m.) Scottish form of Berkeley

Barker (m.) from the family name, which means 'tanner' or 'shepherd'

Barman (m.) family name (p. 74)

Barnabas (m.) Hebrew, 'son of encouragement'

Barnaby (m.) English form of Barnabas

Barnard (m.) variant of Bernard

Barnes (m.) place name/family name, connected with 'barns'

Barnet(t) (m.) place name/family name, connected with 'burnt land'

Barney (m.) pet form of Barnabas

Baron (m.) family name or use of social title (p. 28)

Barrett (m.) family name

Barrie (f., m.) place name/family name, or a pet form of Bernice, Berenice, or a variant of Barry

Barrington (m.) place name/family name

Barron (m.) variant of Baron

Barry (m.) Irish, 'spear, javelin' (pp. 29, 50)

Barrymore (m.) family name

Bartholomew (m.) Aramaic, 'son of Tolmai or Talmai'

Bartle (m.) pet form of Bartholomew

Bartlett (m.) family name linked with Bartholomew

Barton (m.) place name/family name

Baruch (m.) Hebrew, 'blessed'

Barzillai (m.) Hebrew, 'of iron'

Basemath (f.) Hebrew, 'perfumed'

Basil (m.) Greek, 'kingly' (p. 6)

Basilia (f.) also *Basilie.* Feminine forms of Basil

Bassett (m.) family name linked with 'smallness'

Bathia (f.) variant of Bethia

Bathsheba (f.) Hebrew, 'daughter of opulence' (p. 34)

Battle (f.) family name (p. 26)

Baubie (f.) Scottish pet form of Barbara

Bea (f.) pet form of Beatrice (p. 12)

Beata (f.) Latin, 'blessed'

Beathag (f.) Gaelic, 'life' (p. 70)

Beatrice (f.) Latin, 'she who makes happy' (pp. 12, 18, 29)

Beatrix (f.) early variant of Beatrice

Beattie (f.) pet form of Beatrice or family name

Beau (m.) French, 'handsome'

Beaumont (m.) French place name/English family name meaning 'beautiful hill'

Bebai (m.) Assyrian, 'infant'

Becher (m.) Hebrew, 'young camel'

Becky (f.) pet form of Rebecca

Bede (m.) Old English, 'prayer'

Bedelia (f.) fanciful Irish variant of Bridget

Beeri (m.) Hebrew, 'of the well'

Bela (m.) Hebrew, 'swallowed up'

Belief (m., f.) the word used as a name (by the Puritans) (p. 62)

Belinda (f.) Germanic, 'serpent', i.e. 'cunning' (p. 17)

Bell (m., f.) family name

Bella (f.) Latin, 'pretty', or pet form of Isabella, Annabella, etc. (p. 10)

Belle (f.) French, 'beautiful' (pp. 10, 36)

Bellona (f.) Latin, 'war' (p. 37)

Ben (m.) pet form of Benjamin, Benedict, etc. and of Reuben

Benaiah (m.) Hebrew, 'Jehovah builds'

Benedetta (f.) Italian feminine form of Benedict

Benedict (m.) Latin, 'blessed' (p. 22)

Benedicta (f.) feminine of Benedict

Benedine (f.) feminine form of Benedict (p. 22)

Bengt (m.) Swedish form of Benedict

Benita (f.) Spanish feminine of Benito

Benito (m.) Spanish pet form of Benedicto, or Benedict

Benjamin (m.) Hebrew, 'son of the right hand' (pp. 9, 33, 55)

Benmichael (m.) Hebrew, 'son of Michael'

Benn (m.) family name linked with Benedict

Bennet(t) (m.) English forms of Benedict

Benny (m.) also *Bennie*. Pet forms of Benjamin, Benedict, etc.

Benny Mae (f.) feminine form of Benedict Mady (p. 22)

Benoni (m.) Hebrew, 'son of my sorrow'

Benson (m.) family name linked with Benedict

Bent (m.) Danish form of Benedict

Bente (f.) Danish feminine of Bent

Bentley (m.) place name/family name linked with 'coarse grass' (p. 3)

Beraiah (m.) Hebrew, 'Jehovah has created'

Berechaiah (m.) Hebrew, 'Jehovah blesses'

Berenice (f.) Greek, 'bringer of victory' (p. 48)

Beresford (m.) place name/family name

Berkeley (m.) place name/family name linked with 'birch wood'

Bernadette (f.) feminine of Bernard (p. 69)

Bernadina (f.) also *Bernadine*, *Bernadene*. Feminine forms of Bernard

Bernal (m.) also *Bernel*. Germanic, 'bear-power'

Bernard (m.) Germanic, 'bear-brave' (pp. 5, 69)

Bernardette (f.) variant of Bernadette

Bernardina (f.) also *Bernardine, Bernardene.* Variants of Bernadina, etc.

Bernice (f.) variant of Berenice (p. 48)

Berry (m., f.) pet name of Bernard, Bernice, Beryl, etc. or a use of the word 'berry' (p. 7)

Bert (m.) pet form of Bertram, Albert, Hubert, Egbert, Gilbert, etc. (pp. 47, 48)

Berta (f.) German form of Bertha

Bertha (f.) Germanic, 'bright, splendid' (p. 43, 53)

Berthold (m.) Germanic, 'bright-power'

Bertie (m.) pet form of Bertram, Albert, etc.

Bertina (f.) also *Bertine.* Pet forms of Albertina, Albertine

Bertram (m.) Germanic, 'bright-raven' (p. 47)

Bertrand (m.) Germanic, 'bright-shield' (p. 47)

Berwyn (m.) Old English, 'bear-friend'

Beryl (f.) the name of a jewel (pp. 14, 15)

Bessie (f.) also *Bessey.* Pet forms of Elizabeth

Beta (f.) pet form of Elizabeth in some countries, but probably from the Greek letter B

Beth (f.) pet form of Elizabeth

Bethan (f.) also *Beth-Ann, Beth-Anne, Bethanne.* Shortened forms of Elizabeth-Ann(e), used especially in Wales (p. 71)

Bethany (f.) Hebrew (biblical place name), 'house of the poor man' or 'house of Ananiah'

Bethel (m., f.) Welsh family name, 'son of Ithel', or biblical place name 'house of God' or pet form of Elizabeth

Bethia (f.) variant of Bithiah, or a variant of Gaelic Beathag, 'life'

Betsy (f.) also *Betsey*. Variants of Betty

Bette (f.) French form of Betty

Bettina (f.) Spanish/Italian form of Betty

Bettine (f.) French diminutive form of Bette

Betty (f.) pet form of Elizabeth (p. 73)

Bettyjoe (f.) blend of Betty and Joe (p. 42)

Beulah (f.) Hebrew, 'married' (p. 34)

Bevan (m.) Welsh family name, 'son of Evan'

Beverley (m., f.) also *Beverly*. Place name/family name linked with 'beaver stream' (pp. 5, 32)

Bevis (m.) place name/family name

Bianca (f.) Italian 'white' (p. 14)

Biddie (f.) Irish pet form of Bridget

Biggy (f.) pet form of Abigail (p. 20)

Bill (m.) pet form of William (pp. 20, 51)

Billie (m., f.) pet form of William or Wilhelmina

Billie-Jean (f.) blend of Billie and Jean

Billy (m.) pet form of William

Billyjoe (f.) blend of Billy and Joe (p. 42)

Bina (f.) pet form of Sabina, Robina, Albina, etc.

Bing (m.) in Bing Crosby's case, from a cartoon character named Bingo (p. 71)

Birch (m.) place name/family name linked with 'birch trees'

Birdie (f.) 'Little bird' (p. 61)

Birgitta (f.) Swedish form of Bridget

Bithia (f.) Egyptian, 'queen'

Bittan (f.) pet form of Birgitta

Björn (m.) Scandinavian 'bear' (p. 5)

Blaine (m.) family name 'devotee of St Blane'

Blair (m.) Scottish family name linked with 'flat land' (p. 70)

Blaise (m.) Latin, 'stutterer, cripple'

Blake (m.) family name linked with 'black' or 'pale' (pp. 14, 27)

Blanche (f.) French, 'white' (p. 14)

Bleddyn (m.) Welsh, 'wolf' (p. 71)

Blodwen (f.) also *Blodwyn*. Welsh, 'fair, white flower'. Perhaps a translation of Blanchefleur, one of Boccaccio's heroines

Blodyn (f.) Welsh, 'flower, blossom' (p. 54)

Bloomah (f.) adapted form of 'bloomer' (mistake) (p. 33)

Blossom (f.) a use of the word as a name

Bluebell (f.) from the flower

Blythe (f.) adaptation of 'blithe' (pp. 30, 60)

Boadicea (f.) name of the early British queen, of unknown meaning

Boaz (m.) Hebrew, 'in him is strength'

Bob (m.) pet form of Robert (pp. 14, 20, 47)

Bobbie (m., f.) pet form of Robert or Roberta
Bobbyjoe (f.) blend of Bobby and Joe (p. 42)
Bolton (m.) place name/family name
Bonar (m.) French, 'gentle, courteous'
Bonheur (f.) French, 'happiness' (p. 13)
Boniface (m.) Latin, 'of good fate' (p. 67)
Bonita (f.) Spanish, 'pretty' (p. 10)
Bonnie (f.) a use of the Scottish word meaning 'pretty, healthy-looking' (pp. 10, 55, 65, 68, 70)
Booth (m.) family name
Boris (m.) Slavonic, 'battle, fight' (p. 26)
Boy (m.) the word used as a name (p. 52)
Boyce (m.) family name linked with 'wood'
Boyd (m.) Gaelic, 'yellow (hair)' (pp. 14, 60)
Boyle (m.) Irish family name (p. 63)
Brad (m.) pet form of Bradley or Bradford
Bradford (m.) place name/family name, 'broad ford'
Bradley (m.) place name/family name, 'broad clearing' (p. 55)
Brady (m.) family name
Bram (m.) Dutch pet form of Abraham
Bramwell (m.) place name/family name, 'broom well' or 'bramble well'
Brandee (f.) variant of Brandy (p. 4)
Branden (m.) variant of Brandon

Brandi (f.) also *Brandie*. Variants of Brandy. (p. 4)

Brandon (m.) place name/family name, 'hill covered with broom', or (in Ireland) 'descendant of Brendan'

Brandy (f.) a use of the word as a name (p. 4)

Branwell (m.) variant of Bramwell

Brenda (f.) Old Norse, 'sword', but used as feminine of Brendan (p. 70)

Brendan (m.) Irish, 'stinking hair' (p. 69)

Brendon (m.) variant of Brendan

Brent (m.) place name/family name, 'high place' or 'descendant of one who was burnt [i.e. branded as a criminal]' (p. 60)

Brett (m.) Latin, 'Briton' or Breton'

Brewster (m.) occupational family name, 'female brewer'

Brian (m.) an Irish name of unknown meaning (p. 69)

Briana (f.) also *Briane*, *Briann*, *Brianna*, *Brianne*. Feminine forms of Brian

Brice (m.) variant of Bryce

Bride (f.) English form of Bridget

Bridget (f.) Irish, 'the high one' (pp. 31, 69)

Bridgett(e) (f.) modern variants of Bridget

Bridie (f.) Irish pet form of Bridget

Brigham (m.) place name/family name, 'hamlet near a bridge'

Brigid (f.) also *Brighid*. Irish forms of Bridget

Brigitta (f.) Latinized form of Bridget influenced by Birgitta

Brigitte (f.) French form of Bridget

Brinley (m.) place name/family name, 'burnt clearing'

Briony (f.) variant of Bryony

Brita (f.) pet form of Birgitta

Britannia (f.) Latin, 'Britain' (p. 11)

Brittany (f.) name of French province

Briton (m.) the word used as a name (p. 11)

Britt (f.) also *Britta*. Pet forms of Birgitta

Broderick (m.) family name, 'brother' (p. 70)

Bronwen (f). also *Bronwyn*. Welsh, 'white breast' (p. 71)

Brook (m., f.) also *Brooke*, *Brooks*, *Brookes*. Family name linked with 'brook' (p. 60)

Bruce (m.) Norman place name/Scottish family name (p. 70)

Brucine (f.) feminine of Bruce

Brunetta (f.) feminine of Bruno

Bruno (m.) Germanic, 'of dark complexion' or 'bear-like'

Bryan (m.) variant of Brian

Bryant (m.) family name linked with Brian (p. 44)

Bryce (m.) Scottish family name

Bryden (m.) place name/family name

Bryn (m.) Welsh, 'hill, mound', or pet form of Brynley, Brynmor (p. 70)

Brynley (m.) variant of Brinley

Brynmor (m.) Welsh place name, 'great hill' (p. 71)

Bryon (m.) variant of Brian

Bryony (f.) the plant name (p. 54)

Buck (m.) family name, 'male deer' (p. 20)

Bud (m.) also *Buddy*. Ultimately from 'brother'

Bunni (m.) Hebrew, 'Jehovah builds'

Bunny (f.) pet form of Bernice or Berenice

Burnet(t) (m.) family name

Burroughs (m.) family name, 'worker at the manor house' (p. 35)

Burt (m.) pet form of Burton, or variant of Bert (p. 47)

Burton (m.) place name/family name, 'farm near a fort'

Busby (m.) place name/family name, 'shrub farm' (p. 46)

Buster (m.) nickname for a jovial, active boy

Byron (m.) place name/family name, 'cow shed'

C

Cadel(l) (m.) Welsh, 'battle' (p. 26)

Caesar (m.) Latin, 'hairy child'

Cadmus (m.) pre-Greek, 'east' (p. 37)

Cain (m.) Hebrew, 'blacksmith' (p. 10)

Cain (f.) Welsh, 'beautiful' (p. 10)

Caitlin (f.) Irish form of Kathleen

Caitriona (f.) Irish form of Catriona

Caleb (m.) Hebrew, 'dog' (pp. 5, 33)

Calliope (f.) Greek, 'beautiful voice' (p. 37)

Calum (m.) Gaelic form of Columba or pet form (in Scotland) of Malcolm (p. 70)

Calvert (m.) occupational family name, 'calf-herder'

Calvin (m.) Latin, 'bald' (p. 39)

Calypso (f.) Greek, 'concealer' (p. 37)

Camelia (f.) also *Camellia.* From the flower (p. 54)

Cameron (m.) Scottish clan and family name, 'crooked nose' (p. 70)

Camilla (f.) Latin, name of a queen but meaning unknown (p. 37)

Camille (f.) French form of Camilla

Campbell (m.) Scottish clan and family name, 'crooked mouth' (p. 70)

Canada (f.) The name of the country used as a first name (p. 11)

Candace (f.) title of Ethiopian queens, of unknown meaning (p. 24)

Candi (f.) pet form of Candace, Candice (p. 24)

Candice (f.) variant of Candace (p. 24)

Candida (f.) Latin, 'dressed in white [like a candidate for office]' (p. 14)

Candis (f.) variant of Candice

Candy (f.) pet form of Candace, Candice, or a use of the word (p. 24)

Cara (f.) Latin, 'dear' (p. 38)

Caradoc (m.) variant of Caradog

Caradog (m.) Welsh, 'love' (p. 37)

Caren (f.) variant of Karen

Carey (m.) Irish family name

Carina (f.) Italian diminutive of Cara, 'my dear one'

Carine (f.) French form of Carina

Carissa (f.) variant of Charissa (p. 38)

Carita (f.) Latin diminutive of Cara (p. 38)

Carl (m.) Germanic, 'man, countryman' (pp. 50, 53)

Carla (f.) feminine of Carl

Carleen (f.) also *Carlene*. Feminine forms of Carl

Carletta (f.) shortened form of Caroletta

Carley (f.) also *Carlie*. Pet forms of Carleen, etc.

Carlina (f.) shortened form of Carolina or feminine of Carl

Carline (f.) shortened form of Caroline

Carling (f.) family name linked with Charles (p. 4)

Carlo (m.) Italian form of Charles

Carlos (m.) Spanish form of Charles

Carlotta (f.) Italian feminine form of Carlo

Carlton (m.) place name/family name, 'churls' settlement'

Carly (f.) variant of Carley

Carlyn(n) (f.) shortened forms of Carolyn(n)

Carmel (f.) Hebrew, 'orchard, garden'. A biblical place name (pp. 40, 54)

Carmela (f.) Italian form of Carmel

Carmelina (f.) Italian diminutive of Carmela

Carmelita (f.) Spanish diminutive of Carmel

Carmella (f.) Latinized form of Carmel

Carmen (f.) from a title of the Virgin Mary in Spanish, Santa Maria del Carmen (Carmel) or Latin, *carmen*, 'song' (p. 40)

Carol (f.) pet form of Carolina, Caroline but popularly associated with Christmas carol (pp. 9, 40, 44)

Carola (f.) Latinized form of Carol

Carol-Ann(e) (f.) popular modern blend of Carol and Ann(e)

Carole (f.) French form of Carol

Caroleen (f.) modern variant of Caroline

Carolin (f.) occasional variant of Carolyn

Carolina (f.) Latin form of Caroline

Caroline (f.) Italian feminine form of Carlo (Charles) (p. 44)

Carolyn (f.) also *Carolynn*, *Carolynne*, *Carolyne*. Modern variants of Caroline

Caron (m.) name of a Welsh saint

Carpus (m.) Greek, 'fruit'

Carrie (f.) pet form of Carolina, Caroline, Carolyn

Carrol (m.) English form of Irish Cearbhall or Dutch Karel, Polish Karol, Rumanian Carol, etc. all forms of Charles

Carry (f.) early variant of Carrie

Carson (m.) family name. The American writer Carson McCullers 1917–67 was a feminine bearer of the name (p. 22)

Carter (m.) occupational family name

Carthach (m.) Celtic name based on 'love'

Cartwright (m.) occupational family name

Carwyn (m.) Welsh, 'blessed love' (p. 71)

Cary (m.) place name/family name, 'pleasant stream'

Caryl (f.) also *Caryle*, *Caryll*, *Carylle*. Variants of Carol, or Welsh, 'love'

Caryn (f.) probably variant of Karen

Carys (f.) Welsh, 'love' (p. 71)

Casey (m, f.) pet form of Casimir or Irish family name, 'watchman', also a variant of Cassie

Casimir (m.) Polish, 'proclamation of peace'

Caspar (m.) variant of Jaspar

Cassandra (f.) Greek, possibly 'entangler of men' or feminine form of Alexander (p. 37)

Cassie (f.) pet form of Cassandra

Casson (m.) family name

Castle (m.) family name, 'one who worked in a castle'

Catalina (f.) Spanish form of Catherine/ Katharine

Cater (m.) occupational family name, 'caterer, furnisher of household provisions'

Caterina (f.) Italian form of Catherine/ Katharine or variant of Catriona

Cathal (m.) Irish, 'battle-mighty' (p. 69)

Catharine (f.) variant of Catherine

Catherine (f.) French form of Katharine, normally explained as Greek, 'pure' (pp. 36, 45, 49)

Cathleen (f.) variant of Kathleen

Cathrine (f.) modern variant of Catherine

Cathy (f.) pet form of Catherine

Catrin (f.) Welsh form of Catherine (p. 71)

Catrina (f.) variant of Catriona, or Caterina

Catriona (f.) Gaelic form of Catherine (pp. 18, 70)

Cearbhall (m.) Irish name of unknown meaning, usually anglicized as Carrol(l) or Charles

Cecil (m.) Latin clan name, 'blind'

Cecile (f.) French feminine form of Cecil

Cecilia (f.) Latin feminine of Cecil (p. 53)

Cecily (f.) English form of Cecilia

Cedric (m.) also modern variant *Cedrick*.

Variants of Cedrych or (originally) of Cerdic (p. 55)

Cedrych (m.) Welsh name of unknown meaning, possibly variant of Caradog

Ceinlys (f.) Welsh, 'beautiful and fair'

Ceinwen (f.) Welsh, 'beautiful and blessed' (p. 71)

Celena (f.) variant of Selina

Celeste (f.) Latin, 'heavenly' (p. 47)

Celestine (f.) also *Celestina.* French and Latin diminutives of Celeste

Celia (f.) Latin feminine of Caelius, a Roman clan name of unknown meaning, but regarded as a pet form of Cecilia (p. 18)

Celina (f.) variant of Selina

Céline (f.) French pet form of Marceline

Cemlyn (m.) Welsh place name, 'bent lake' (p. 71)

Cephas (m.) Aramaic, 'rock'

Cerdic (m.) English form of Ceredig

Ceredig (m.) Welsh, 'kind, beloved' (p. 37)

Ceri (m.) Welsh river name (p. 71)

Ceri (f.) Welsh, 'love' (pp. 37, 71)

Cerian (f.) Welsh diminutive of Ceri (p. 71)

Ceridwen (f.) Welsh, 'blessed poetry'

Cerise (f.) French, 'cherry' (p. 7)

Cerri(e) (f.) variants of Ceri

Cerys (f.) Welsh, 'love' (p. 71)

Chad (m.) Old English saint's name of unknown meaning

Chaim (m.) variant of Hyman

Chance (m.) the word or last name used as a first name (p. 33)

Chanel (f.) also *Channel*. French family name and trade name of a famous perfume (p. 13)

Change (m.) the word used as a name (p. 74)

Chantal (f.) French place name, 'stony place' used in honour of Saint Jeanne de Chantal

Chantel (f.) also *Chantell*, *Chantelle*, *Chantele*. Modern (English) versions of Chantal

Chappie (m.) 'Chap' adapted to first name use (p. 53)

Charis (f.) Greek, 'grăce'

Charissa (f.) diminutive of Charis

Charity (f.) the word used as a name (pp. 15, 49, 62)

Charleen (f.) also *Charlena*, *Charlene*. Modern feminine forms of Charles

Charles (m.) Old English, 'man, husbandman' (pp. 36, 40, 53)

Charlesena (f.) also *Charlesina*. Modern feminine forms of Charles

Charlotta (f.) Latinized form of Charlotte

Charlotte (f.) French form of Carlotta, feminine of Charles

Charlton (m.) place name/family name, 'settlement of free peasants' (p. 11)

Charmaine (f.) also *Charmain*. Latin feminine form of a Roman clan name of unknown meaning, but suggested by a 1920s song

Charmian (f.) Greek, 'joy' (pp. 18, 30, 39)

Chatty (f.) pet form of Charlotte

Chavon (f.) also *Chavonne*. Variants of Siobhan

Chay (m.) pet form of Charles

Chaz (m.) abbreviated (written) form of Charles now used as a name

Chelsea (f.) place name, 'landing place for chalk or limestone' (p. 11)

Chelsie (f.) variant of Chelsea influenced by Elsie, Kelsie

Chère (f.) also *Cher*. French, 'dear one'

Cheralyn (f.) variant of Cherilyn

Chereen (f.) variant of Shereen

Chèrie (f.) French, 'dear one, darling'

Cherilyn (f.) also *Cherilynn*, *Cherilynne*. Diminutives of Cheryl

Cherrie (f.) variant of Chèrie or Cherry

Cherril(l) (f.) variants of Cheryl

Cherrilyn (f.) also *Cherrilynn*, *Cherrilynne*. Variants of Cherilyn

Cherry (f.) pet form of Charity and in modern times of Cheryl, also a modern variant of

Chèrie. Perhaps occasionally a use of the word as name (pp. 7, 14)

Cheryl (f.) also *Cheryle, Cheryll, Cherylle.* Probably diminutive of Cherry influenced by Beryl

Chester (m.) place name/family name, 'Roman camp'

Chet (m.) pet form of Chester

Chevon (f.) also *Chevonne.* Variants of Siobhan

Chip (m.) the word used as a name, perhaps with reference to 'chip off the old block' (p. 74)

Chloë (f.) Greek, 'young green shoot' (pp. 37, 54)

Chlorine (f.) the word used as a name (p. 25)

Chris (m., f.) pet form of Christopher, Christine, etc.

Chrisanda (f.) blend of Christine and Amanda/Miranda

Chrissie (f.) also *Chrissy.* Pet forms of Christine

Christ (m.) Greek, 'anointed' (p. 56)

Christa (f.) German pet form of Christiane

Christabel (f.) also *Christabella, Christabelle.* An invented name intended to mean 'fair follower of Christ'

Christal (f.) variant of Crystal

Christen (f.) modern variant of Kristen

Christian (m.) Latin, 'follower of Christ' (p. 56)

Christiana (f.) early feminine form of Christian

Christiann (f.) also *Christianna*. Variants of Christiana

Christie (m.) Scottish diminutive of Christopher

Christina (f.) feminine form of Christian (p. 14)

Christine (f.) French form of Christina (p. 56)

Christmas (m., f.) occasional use of the word as a name (pp. 35, 44)

Christobel (f.) variant of Christabel

Christopher (m.) Greek, 'one who carries Christ (in his heart)' (p. 56)

Christy (f.) Scottish pet form of Christina, Christine (p. 70)

Chuck (m.) pet form of Charles

Ciara (f.) probably Irish feminine of Ciarán, 'black' (p. 69)

Cicely (f.) Latin feminine of Cecil

Cilla (f.) pet form of Priscilla. In Greek mythology the name is from Greek, *cillos*, 'ass' (p. 37)

Cinderella (f.) English form of Cendrillon, 'little cinder girl'

Cindy (f.) also *Cindi*. Pet form of Cynthia, Lucinda, Cinderella, etc.

Cire (f.) Eric spelt backwards (p. 57)

Cissie (f.) also *Cissy*. Pet forms of Cicely, Cecily

Clair (m.) Latin, 'bright, shining, clear'

Claire (f.) French form of Clara (pp. 41, 73)

Clancy (m.) Irish family name, 'descendant of red-haired warrior' (p. 14)

Clara (f.) Latin, 'bright, shining, clear'

Clare (f.) English form of Clara

Clarence (m.) Latin, 'of Clare', the name of a dukedom

Claribel (f.) originally a male name but used occasionally as a diminutive of Clare

Clarice (f.) Italian diminutive of Clara

Clarinda (f.) former diminutive of Clara

Claris (f.) variant of Clarice

Clarissa (f.) Latinized form of Clarice

Clarisse (f.) French form of Clarissa

Clarita (f.) Spanish diminutive of Clara

Clark (m.) also *Clarke*. Occupational family name, 'cleric, scholar, secretary' (p. 9)

Clarrie (f.) pet form of Clara, Clarissa, etc.

Claud (m.) English form of Claudius

Claude (m., f.) French form of Claudius or Claudia

Claudelle (f.) diminutive of French Claude

Claudette (f.) French diminutive of Claude

Claudia (f.) Latin feminine of Claudius

Claudine (f.) French diminutive of Claude

Claudius (f.) Latin, 'lame', a famous Roman clan name

Clay (m.) occupational family name, 'worker in clay pit'

Clayton (m.) place name/family name, 'settlement near a clay-pit'

Cledwyn (m.) Welsh river name (p. 71)

Clement (m.) Latin, 'mild, merciful'

Clementia (f.) Latin, 'mildness'. Clemency was the spoken form of this name (p. 62)

Clementina (f.) feminine form of Clement

Clementine (f.) French form of Clementina

Cleo (f.) pet form of Cleopatra, though the jazz singer Cleo Laine is a Clementina

Cleopatra (f.) Greek, 'fame of her father'

Cleveland (m.) place name/family name, 'hilly district' (p. 38)

Cliff (m.) pet form of Clifford, Clifton

Clifford (m.) place name/family name, 'ford near a slope'

Clifton (m.) place name/family name, 'settlement near a cliff'

Clint (m.) pet form of Clinton (p. 16)

Clinton (m.) place name/family name, 'settlement near a hill' (p. 16)

Clio (f.) Greek, 'fame, renown' (p. 37)

Clive (m.) place name/family name, 'cliff'

Clodagh (f.) Irish river name

Clotilda (f.) Germanic, 'famous-battle'

Cloud (m., f.) a use of the word, though the name of the French saint is ultimately a form of Louis (p. 59)

Clyde (m.) Scottish river name (p. 70)
Coco (f.) normally a childish nickname derived from names beginning with Co- (p. 13)
Cody (m.) Irish/American family name, 'helper'. Also an American place name
Coleen (f.) variant of Colleen
Coletta (f.) pet form of Nicoletta
Colette (f.) pet form of Nicolette
Colin (m.) pet form of Nicholas (p. 69)
Colina (f.) feminine form of Colin
Colleen (f.) Irish, 'girl' (pp. 10, 55)
Collette (f.) variant of Colette
Colley (m.) family name, 'black-haired'
Collin (m.) variant of Colin
Collins (m.) family name linked with Colin
Collis (m.) family name, 'black-haired'
Colm (m.) Irish, 'dove' (p. 69)
Colman (m.) family name linked with Colm
Colston (m.) place name/family name
Colville (m.) Norman place name/family name
Colvin (m.) family name
Colwyn (m.) Welsh place and river name
Comfort (f.) family name or the word used as a name (p. 62)
Common (m.) probably a family name (p. 74)
Conan (m.) Gaelic, 'high'
Concetta (f.) Italian, '(Immaculate) conception'
Concorde (f.) French, 'friendly agreement' (p. 31)

Connie (f.) pet form of Constance (p. 65)

Connor (m.) also *Conor*. Irish, 'high desire' (pp. 60, 69)

Conrad (m.) Germanic, 'brave counsel'

Conroy (m.) Irish family name

Constance (f.) Latin, 'constancy, firmness' (p. 62)

Constant (m.) the word used as a name, or a pet form of Constantine

Constantia (f.) Latin, 'constancy'

Constantine (m.) Latin, 'firm, constant'

Conway (m.) also *Conwy*. Welsh river name

Cook (m.) occupational family name

Cooper (m.) occupational family name

Cora (f.) Greek, 'maiden' (p. 10)

Coral (f.) the word used as a name (pp. 15, 35)

Coralie (f.) French diminutive of Cora

Coralina (f.) also *Coraline*, *Coralyn*. Diminutives of Coral influenced by Carolina, etc.

Corbet(t) (m.) also *Corbit(t)*. Family name, 'black hair'

Cordelia (f.) Latin, 'heart' (p. 18)

Cordell (m.) occupational family name, 'maker, seller of cord'

Corey (m.) Irish family name linked with Godfrey

Corey (f.) pet form of Corinne, Cornelia. Occurs as Corey Ann, Corey Lee, etc.

Corinne (f.) also *Corin, Corina, Corine, Corinn, Corinna*. Diminutive forms of Cora

Cormac (m.) Irish, 'charioteer' (p. 69)

Cornelia (f.) Latin feminine form of Cornelius

Cornelius (m.) Latin, 'horn', a famous Roman clan name (p. 69)

Cornell (m.) place name/family name (pp. 52, 55)

Cornwallis (m.) family name linked with Cornwall

Corona (f.) used in coronation years

Coronella (f.) the flower name (p. 54)

Correen (f.) also *Correne*. Variants of Corinne

Correy (m.) also *Corrie*. *see* Corey

Corrin (f.) also *Corrina, Corrine, Corrinna, Corrinne*. Variants of Corinne

Cortez (m.) Spanish place name/family name

Cory (m.) variant of Corey (p. 60)

Cosmo (m.) Greek, 'order' (p. 70)

Coulson (m.) family name linked with Nicholas

Courtney (m., f.) French place name/family name linked with Courtenay in France

Cozbi (f.) Hebrew, 'luxuriant'

Craig (m.) Gaelic, 'rock' (pp. 28, 50, 65)

Craven (m.) place name/family name

Crawford (m.) Scottish place name/family name, 'ford where crows gather' (p. 70)

Creature (m., f.) a name formerly given before birth (p. 5)

Cressida (f.) Shakespearian name of unknown meaning. *The Oxford Dictionary of English Christian Names* considers that its use is 'an aberration of taste for which there is no accounting'. (p. 18)

Cresswell (m.) also *Creswell.* Place name/family name, 'stream where cress grows' (p. 63)

Crispin (m.) Latin, 'curly'. Crispian is the Shakespearian variant

Crista (f.) variant of Christa

Cristal (f.) variant of Crystal

Cristina (f.) also *Cristine.* Modern variants of Christina, Christine

Crocus (f.) the flower name (p. 54)

Crofton (m.) place name/family name

Crosby (m.) place name/family name, 'village with a public cross'

Crowther (m.) occupational family name, 'fiddle-player'

Crystal (m., f.) originally a pet form of Christopher. Later a use of the word as a name (p. 15)

Cupid (m.) Latin, 'desire' (p. 37)

Curt (m.) variant of Kurt, or pet form of Curtis

Curtis (m.) family name, 'courteous' (p. 44)

Cush (m.) Hebrew, 'Ethiopian' (p. 33)

Cuthbert (m.) Old English, 'famous-bright' (p. 47)

Cymon (m.) fanciful variant of Simon (p. 36)

Cynthia (f.) Greek title of the moon goddess (p. 17)

Cyprian (m.) Latin, 'man from Cyprus'

Cyrene (f.) Greek, 'mistress of the bridle' (p. 37)

Cyril (m.) Greek, 'lord, ruler'

Cyrus (m.) Persian, 'shepherd'

D

Dacian (m.) Latin, 'inhabitant of Dacia' (now in Rumania)

Dafydd (m.) Welsh form of David (p. 71)

Dagmar (f.) Nordic, 'day famous' or 'glory of the day'

Dahlia (f.) for the flower

Daimen (m.) variant of Damon

Daire (m.) an ancient Irish name of unknown meaning. *Daireen (f.)* is also found (p. 69)

Daisy (f.) for the flower (pp. 42, 44, 50, 54, 72)

Dajuan (m.) variant of Dejuan

Dale (m.) family name, 'dweller in a valley' (pp. 25, 64)

Daley (m.) variant of Daly

Dalila (f.) variant of Delilah

Dallas (m., f.) Scottish place name/family name

Dalphon (m.) Assyrian, 'sleepless'

Daly (m.) Irish family name, 'assembly'

Damaris (f.) Greek, 'calf'

Damian (m.) Greek, 'to tame'

Damien (m.) French form of Damian

Damon (m.) modern variant of Damian

Dan (m.) Hebrew, 'to judge'. Also a pet form of Daniel

Dana (f., m.) pet form of Daniela. The actor Dana Andrews was a Daniel

Dane (m.) family name indicating Danish ancestors or English river name (p. 60)

Daneen (f.) also *Danella, Danetta, Danette, Danice*. Modern feminine forms of Dan or Daniel

Daniel (m.) Hebrew, 'God is judge' (pp. 12, 33, 55)

Daniela (f.) also *Daniele, Daniella*. Variants of Danielle

Danielle (f.) French feminine form of Daniel (p. 55)

Danise (f.) also *Danita*. Modern feminine forms of Dan or Daniel

Danna (f.) variant of Dana

Danny (m.) pet form of Daniel

Dante (m.) Latin, 'enduring, obstinate'

Daphne (f.) Greek, 'laurel' (pp. 37, 54)

Darby (m.) variant of Derby

Darcy (m., f.) Norman place name/family name or an Irish family name, 'dark man'. Found also as D'Arcy and D'Arcie, with modern variants Darcey, Darcee, Darci

Darell (m.) variant of Darryl

Daren (m.) variant of Darren

Darin (m.) variant of Darren linked with the singer Bobby Darin

Darius (m.) Persian, 'one who upholds good' (p. 33)

Darlene (f.) also *Darleen, Darla.* Adaptations of 'darling'

Darnell (m.) place name/family name, 'hidden nook' (p. 55)

Daron (m.) variant of Darren

Darrell (m.) variant of Darryl

Darrellyn (f.) feminine form of Darryl

Darren (m.) Irish family name (p. 65)

Darryl (m.) family name

Daryllyn (f.) feminine form of Daryl

Daryn (m.) variant of Darren

Dave (m.) pet form of David

Daveen (f.) also *Davena, Davene, Davenia, Davenne.* Variants of Davina

David (m.) Hebrew, 'beloved' (pp. 33, 36, 38, 57)

Davida (f.) feminine form of David

Davina (f.) Scottish feminine form of David

Davis (m.) also *Davison, Davy.* Family names linked with David

Dawn (f.) the word used as a name (p. 51)

Dawna (f.) also *Dawne, Dawnetta, Dawnielle, Dawnysia.* Modern variants of Dawn

Dawson (m.) family name linked with David

Dax (m.) French place name

Dayle (m.) variant of Dale

Dayna (f.) variant of Dana

Dean (m.) family name, 'valley' or 'leader of ten churchmen' (p. 50)

Deana (f.) feminine form of Dean or variant of Diana

Deandre (m.) André with fashionable prefix De- much used by black American families in the 1980s

Deane (f.) variant of Diane

Deanna (f.) modern variant of Diana (p. 12)

Deanne (f.) variant of Diane

Debbie (f.) also *Debby*. Pet forms of Deborah

Deborah (f.) Hebrew, 'bee' (pp. 34, 49, 54, 72)

Debra (f.) modern variant of Deborah

Decima (f.) Latin, 'tenth', name of Roman goddess of childbirth (p. 43)

Decimus (m.) Latin, 'tenth' (p. 43)

Declan (m.) name of an Irish saint but of unknown meaning (p. 69)

Dee (f., m.) family name or pet form of names beginning with D- (pp. 12, 60)

Dee Ann (f.) variant of Diane

Deena (f.) variant of Dina

Deinol (m.) also *Deiniol*. Welsh, 'attractive, charming' (p. 71)

Deirdre (f.) also *Deidre*. Irish, 'fear' or 'one who rages' (p. 69)

Dejuan (m.) Juan with De- prefix. *See* Deandre

Del (m., f.) also *Dell*. Pet form of names beginning with Del- or of Derek

Delia (f.) Greek place name, or pet form of Bedelia, Cordelia

Delicia (f.) Latin, 'delight'

Delilah (f.) Hebrew, 'amorous, coquette' (p. 34)

Delise (f.) also *Delisa*, *Delisha*. Variants of Delicia

Dell (m.) variant of Del (p. 25)

Della (f.) pet form of Adella (p. 64)

Delma (f.) pet form of Fidelma

Delmar (m.) place name, 'the sea' (p. 27)

Delores (f.) variant of Dolores

Delpha (f.) also *Delphe*, *Delphia*. Pet forms of Philadelphia

Delphine (f.) Greek place name linked with 'dolphin'

Delroy (m.) modern variant of Elroy

Delta (f.) Greek letter D used as a name (p. 68)

Delwen (f.) Welsh, 'pretty-white'

Delyse (f.) French form of Delicia

Delysia (f.) variant of Delicia

Delyth (f.) Welsh, 'pretty' (p. 71)

Demarco (m.) also *Demario*. Marco and Mario with De- prefix. *See* Deandre

Demelza (f.) Cornish place name, 'hill fort'

Demetrius (m.) Greek, 'of Demeter [goddess of cultivated soil]' (p. 55)

Demon (m.) the word used as a name (p. 74)

Dene (m.) variant of Dean

Dene (f.) variant of Deana

Denese (f.) also *Deneice*. Variants of Denise

Denham (m.) place name/family name, 'hamlet in a valley'

Denholm (m.) Scottish place name/family name (p. 70)

Denice (f.) variant of Denise

Denis (m.) French form of Dennis (p. 69)

Denise (f.) French feminine form of Denis

Dennis (m.) English form of Greek Dionusios, god of wine (p. 58)

Dennison (m.) family name linked with Dennis

Denny (m.) pet form of Dennis

Denton (m.) place name/family name, 'settlement in a valley'

Denver (m.) place name/family name, 'Danes' crossing place'

Denyce (f.) also *Denyse*. Variants of Denise

Denys (m.) early French form of Dennis

Denzel (m.) also *Denziel*, *Denzil*, *Denzill*, *Denzyl*. Cornish place name/family name

Deon (m.) ultimately a variant of Denis (p. 55)

Derby (m.) place name/family name, 'village with deer park'

Derek (m.) also *Dereck*. English forms of Theodoric

Derenda (f.) also *Derinda*. Feminine forms of Derek

Deric (m.) also *Derick*, *Derik*. Variants of Derek

Dermot (m.) Irish, 'envy free' (p. 69)

Derreck (m.) also *Derrek*, *Derrick*, *Derrik*. Variants of Derek

Derrie (m., f.) also *Derry*. Irish place name/family name (Derry) with Derrie mainly being used as feminine form

Deryck (m.) also *Deryk*, *Deryke*. Fanciful variants of Derek

Deryn (f.) from Welsh Aderyn, 'bird'

Desdemona (f.) Greek, 'misery'

Deshawn (m.) Shawn with De- prefix. *See* Deandre (p. 55)

Desirée (f.) French, 'desired' (p. 33)

Desmond (m.) Irish family name, 'man from south Munster'

Destiny (f.) the word used as a name (p. 74)

Detta (f.) pet form of Benedetta

Devin (m.) variant of Devon

Devon (m.) place name, or river name (p. 60)

Devona (f.) feminine form of Devon

Devorah (f.) Hebrew form of Deborah

Devra (f.) shortened form of Devorah

Dewayne (m.) Wayne with De- prefix. *See* Deandre

Dewey (m.) family name linked with Dewi

Dewi (m.) Welsh form of David (p. 71)

Dexter (m.) family name indicating a 'female dyer'

Dia (f.) Greek, 'godlike one' (p. 37)

Diamond (f.) the word used as a name

Dian (f.) variant of Diana, Diane

Diana (f.) Latin, 'divine', goddess of the moon (pp. 17, 37, 53)

Diane (f.) French form of Diana

Dianna (f.) variant of Diana

Dianne (f.) variant of Diane

Diarmid (m.) Scottish form of Dermot (p. 70)

Diarmuid (m.) Irish form of Dermot (p. 69)

Dick (m.) pet form of Richard

Dickon (m.) also *Dicken*. Early pet forms of Richard

Didier (m.) French masculine form of Desirée (p. 33)

Didyma (f.) feminine of Greek Didymus, 'twin' (p. 71)

Diedre (f.) also *Dierdre*. Variants of Deirdre

Diego (m.) Spanish form of James

Dieter (m.) Germanic, 'people-army'

Diffidence (f.) the word used as a name (by the Puritans) (p. 62)

Digby (m.) place name/family name, 'settlement by a ditch'

Diligence (m., f.) the word used as a name (by the Puritans) (p. 62)

Dillan (m.) also *Dillon*. Irish family names or variants of Dylan

Dilwyn (m.) place name, 'secret or shady place'

Dilys (f.) Welsh, 'genuine, sincere'

Dina (f.) pet form of Bernadina or variant of Dinah

Dinah (f.) Hebrew, 'judged'. Could be considered a feminine form of Dan or Daniel (p. 34)

Dinero (m.) Spanish, 'money' (p. 20)

Dion (m.) short form of Dionysus

Dione (f.) Greek, 'divine' (p. 37)

Dionna (f.) also *Dionne*. Feminine forms of Dion or family name

Dionysia (f.) feminine of Dionysus

Dionysus (m.) also *Dionysius*, *Dionusios*. Latin and Greek forms of the name of the Greek god of wine, anglicized as Dennis

Dirk (m.) pet form of Diederick, itself the Dutch form of Derek

Discretion (m., f.) the word used as a name (by the Puritans) (p. 62)

Dives (m.) also *Divers*. Traditionally Dives is the name of the 'rich man' in the parable related in Luke 16

Divina (f.) Latin, 'divine'

Dixie (m.) also *Dixee*. Family name linked to a chorister (who regularly said 'I have spoken' in Latin). In America associated with the southern states

Dixon (m.) family name, 'Dick's son'

Doctor (m.) the word used as a name (p. 22)

Dodo (m.) Hebrew, 'His beloved'. Linked with David

Dodo (f.) pet form of Dorothy (p. 35)

Dolly (f.) also *Dollie*. Pet forms of Dorothy

Dolores (f.) Spanish Maria de los Dolores, 'Mary of Sorrows'

Dolphin (f.) name of a ship used as a first name (p. 65)

Dolphus (m.) pet form of Adolphus

Domingo (m.) Spanish, 'Sunday' (p. 50)

Dominic (m.) Latin, 'the lord'

Dominica (f.) feminine form of Dominic

Dominick (m.) variant of Dominic (p. 63)

Dominique (f.) French feminine form of Dominic

Don (m.) also *Donn*. Pet forms of Donald, Donovan, etc. (p. 60)

Donal (m.) Irish form of Donald (p. 69)

Donald (m.) Gaelic, 'world mighty' (pp. 55, 70)

Donalda (f.) also *Donaldina, Donaleen, Dona.* Feminine forms of Donald

Donation (m., f.) the word used as a name (by the Puritans) (p. 62)

Donavon (m.) variant of Donovan

Donella (f.) also *Donita.* Feminine forms of Donald

Donna (f.) Italian, 'lady', probably from Madonna, 'my lady'

Donna-Maria (f.) also *Donna-Marie.* Italian, 'Lady Mary'

Donnell (m.) Irish family name

Donnella (f.) variant of Donella or feminine of Donnell

Donovan (m.) Irish family name, 'dark brown'

Donte (m.) form of Donato, 'gift'

Dora (f.) pet form of Dorothy, Dorothea, Theodora, Isadora (p. 31)

Dorcas (f.) Greek, 'roe, gazelle' (p. 5)

Doreen (f.) diminutive of Dora, influenced by Kathleen, Maureen, etc.

Dorette (f.) modern variant of Dora

Doria (f.) variant of Doris

Dorian (m.) Greek, 'man from Doris [in central Greece]'

Dorice (f.) variant of Doris

Dorinda (f.) diminutive of Dora

Doris (f.) Greek, 'woman from Doris (in central Greece)' (pp. 37, 50)

Dorita (f.) diminutive of Dora

Dorothea (f.) Greek, 'gift of God'

Dorothy (f.) English form of Dorothea

Dorrit (f.) family name linked with Dorothy

Dory (m.) pet form of Isidore

Dot (f.) also *Dottie*. Pet forms of Dorothy

Dougal (m.) Irish, 'black stranger' (p. 14)

Douglas (m.) Gaelic river and place name/family name, 'black water' (pp. 32, 35, 36, 60, 70)

Douglasina (f.) feminine form of Douglas

Dowsabel (f.) early spoken form of Dulcibella (p. 24)

Dozer (m.) family name, 'dweller near willow grove' (p. 74)

Drake (m.) family name referring especially to Sir Francis Drake (p. 27)

Dreena (f.) also *Drena*. Pet forms of Andrena

Drew (m.) pet form of Andrew

Drina (f.) pet form of Alexandrina

Drue (m.) family name, 'lover' (p. 44)

Drummond (m.) Scottish family name (p. 70)

Drusilla (f.) Roman name of unknown meaning

Duane (m.) Irish family name, 'black'

Dudley (m.) place name/family name

Dugald (m.) variant of Dougal (p. 70)

Duke (m.) pet form of Marmaduke or family name or a use of the title as name (pp. 28, 52)

Dulcibella (f.) also *Dulcibel.* Latin, 'sweetly beautiful' (p. 24)

Dulcie (f.) Latin, 'sweet' (p. 24)

Dulcinea (f.) Spanish, 'sweet, mild'

Duncan (m.) Gaelic, 'brown warrior' (pp. 14, 49)

Dunstan (m.) place name/family name, 'stony hill'

Duplicate (f.) the word used as a name (for a twin sister of Kate) (p. 71)

Durand (m.) Latin, 'enduring'

Dust (m., f.) the word used as a name (by the Puritans) (p. 62)

Dustin (m.) place name/family name or variant of Thurstan, 'Thor's stone' (p. 9)

Dustine (f.) feminine form of Dustin

Dusty (f.) the word used as a name (p. 62)

Dwayne (m.) popular variant of Duane

Dwight (m.) family name

Dyer (m.) occupational family name

Dyfan (m.) Welsh, 'ruler of a tribe' (p. 71)

Dylan (m.) name of a Welsh sea-god, perhaps 'son of the waves' (p. 71)

Dylis (f.) variant of Dilys

Dympna (f.) also *Dymphna.* Name of an early Irish saint

Dyson (m.) family name linked with Dennis

E

Eamon(n) (m.) Irish form of Edmond (p. 69)

Eardley (m.) place name/family name

Earl (m.) family name or the title used as a name (p. 28)

Earlene (f.) also *Earlean, Earleen, Earlena, Earlina, Earlinda.* Feminine forms of Earl

Earnest (m.) variant of Ernest

Earth (m., f.) the word used as a name (by the Puritans) (p. 62)

Eartha (f.) the word 'earth' plus feminine ending (p. 62)

Easter (f.) the word used as a name or a variant of Esther (p. 44)

Ebba (f.) a short form of Ermenburga, Germanic, 'universal territory' (p. 45)

Ebed (m.) Hebrew, 'servant'

Eben (m.) Hebrew, 'stone'

Ebenezer (m.) Hebrew, 'stone of help'

Ebony (f.) the word used as a name (pp. 14, 55)

Echo (f.) Greek, 'sound, noise' (p. 37)

Ecky (f.) pet form of Rebecca (p. 20)

Eda (f.) pet form of Edith or Old English, 'rich, happy'

Eddie (m.) pet form of Edward, Edgar, etc.

Eddie (f.) pet form of Edwina, etc. Popular with a second name, such as Eddie Mae.

Eden (m., f.) Hebrew, 'delight', pleasantness' or English river name (p. 60)

Edgar (m.) Old English, 'prosperity-spear' (p. 29)

Edie (f.) pet form of Edith

Edith (f.) Old English, 'rich-war'

Editha (f.) former variant of Edith

Edmee (f.) French feminine form of Edmond

Edmond (m.) French form of Edmund

Edmund (m.) Old English, 'rich-protector'

Edna (f.) Hebrew, 'pleasure, delight' or pet form of Edwina

Edric (m.) Old English, 'property-powerful'

Edryd (m.) Welsh, 'restoration' (p. 71)

Edward (m.) Old English, 'property-guardian' (pp. 44, 49)

Edwin (m.) Old English, 'prosperity-friend'

Edwina (f.) also *Edweena, Edwena, Edwyna.* Feminine forms of Edwin (p. 70)

Edwy (m.) Old English, 'prosperity-war'

Edwyn (m.) variant of Edwin

Edyth (f.) also *Edytha, Edythe.* Variants of Edith

Effie (f.) also *Eff.* Pet forms of Euphemia (p. 12)

Egan (m.) Irish, 'little fire'

Egbert (m.) Old English, 'bright sword' (pp. 29, 47)

Egerton (m.) place name/family name

Egidia (f.) Latinized feminine form of Giles

Eglantine (f.) the flower name (p. 54)

Eibhlin (f.) Irish form of Eileen or Evelyn, originally Helen

Eifion (m.) Welsh place name (p. 71)

Eifiona (f.) feminine form of Eifion

Eileen (f.) English form of Irish Eibhlin, linked with Evelyn, Helen (p. 69)

Eilidh (f.) Gaelic form of Helen (p. 70)

Eilir (m., f.) Welsh, 'butterfly' (p. 71)

Eilwen (f.) Welsh, 'fair brow'

Eimar (m.) Irish, 'swift' (p. 69)

Einir (f.) Welsh form of Honora (p. 71)

Eira (f.) Welsh, 'snow' (p. 59)

Eirian (f.) Welsh, 'silver' (p. 71)

Eirlys (f.) Welsh, 'snowdrop' (pp. 54, 71)

Eirwen (f.) Welsh, 'white snow'

Elaine (f.) French form of Helen (p. 69)

Elah (m.) Hebrew, 'oak'

Elbert (m.) Old English, 'noble-bright'

Eldon (m.) also *Elden*. Place name/family name, 'Ella's mound'

Eldred (m.) Old English, 'old-counsel'

Eleanor (f.) traditionally linked with Helen: possibly Greek, 'pity, mercy' (p. 58)

Electra (f.) Greek, 'amber' (pp. 14, 37)

Elen (f.) Welsh, 'nymph, angel' (p. 71)

Eleonore (f.) French form of Eleanor

Eleri (f.) Welsh river name (p. 71)

Elfed (m.) Welsh, 'Autumn' (p. 71)

Elfrida (f.) also *Elfreda*. Old English, 'elf-strength'

Elgan (m.) Welsh, 'bright circle' (p. 71)

Eli (m.) Hebrew, '(Jehovah is) raised up'

Elias (m.) Greek form of Elijah (p. 33)

Eliezer (m.) Hebrew, 'my God is help'

Elihu (m.) Hebrew, 'He is my God'

Elijah (m.) Hebrew, 'my God is Jehovah'

Elin (f.) Welsh variant of Elen, or short form of Elinor, or form of Helen (p. 71)

Eliot (m.) also *Aliott*, *Elliot*, *Elliott*. Family names linked with Eli

Elis (m.) Welsh form of Elias (p. 71)

Elisa (f.) pet form of Elisabeth or Elizabeth

Elisabeth (f.) usual European form of Elizabeth

Elise (f.) French diminutive of Elisabeth

Elisha (m.) Hebrew, 'God has helped'

Elissa (f.) name of the Queen of Carthage, perhaps meaning 'wanderer'

Eliza (f.) pet form of Elizabeth (p. 57)

Elizabeth (f.) Hebrew, 'my God is completeness' (pp. 48, 49)

Elkanah (m.) Hebrew, 'God has created'

Elke (f.) Germanic pet form of Alice

Ella (f.) Germanic 'all, entirely'

Ellen (f.) English form of Helen

Ellery (m.) family name, linked with Latin, 'cheerful' (p. 29)

Elli (f.) also *Ellie*. Pet forms of Ellen, Eleanor, etc.

Elliot (m.) also *Elliott*. Variants of Eliot(t)

Ellis (m.) English form of Elias

Elma (f.) pet form of Anselma, Wilhelma, etc.

Elmer (m.) Old English, 'noble-famous'

Eloise (f.) also *Eloisa*. Variant of Aloysia, feminine of Aloysius

Elroy (m.) variant of Leroy, 'the king' (p. 5)

Elsa (f.) German pet form of Elisabeth (p. 70)

Elsie (f.) pet form of Elizabeth (p. 8)

Elspeth (f.) Scottish pet form of Elizabeth (p. 70)

Elton (m.) place name/family name, 'Ella's settlement'

Eluned (f.) Welsh, 'idol, icon' (p. 71)

Elva (f.) English form of Irish Ailbhe. Olive is another form of this name

Elvie (f.) also *Elvy*. Pet forms of Elvina, Elvira

Elvin (m.) variant of Alvin

Elvina (f.) feminine form of Elvin

Elvira (f.) Spanish place name

Elvis (m.) variant of Irish Ailbe or Ailbhe, a name also anglicized as Albert. The district of St Elvis in Pembrokeshire was named for St Ailbe of Munster, who baptised St David

Elwyn (m.) Welsh, 'white brow' (p. 71)

Elysia (f.) based on the word 'elysian'

Emanuel (m.) also *Emmanuel, Immanuel.* Hebrew, 'God is with us'

Emeline (f.) Germanic name of unknown meaning

Emerald (f.) the jewel name (p. 14)

Emerson (m.) family name linked with Emery

Emery (m.) Germanic, 'home-power'

Emil (m.) German form of Emilius

Emile (m.) French form of Emilius

Emilia (f.) variant of Amelia (p. 18)

Emilius (m.) Latin, 'eager, industrious'. Roman Aemilius was a famous clan name

Emily (f.) English form of Emilia or Aemilia, feminine of Emilius (pp. 12, 53)

Emlyn (m.) Welsh place name

Emma (f.) Germanic, 'all embracing' (pp. 12, 18, 72, 73)

Emmanuel (m.) variant of Emanuel

Emmeline (f.) variant of Emeline

Emmerson (m.) variant of Emerson

Emmett (f.) also *Emmet, Emmot.* Family names linked with Emma

Emorb (m.) family name Brome spelt backwards (p. 58)

Emrys (m.) Welsh form of Ambrose (p. 71)

Emyr (m.) Welsh form of Latin Honorius, 'honour' (p. 71)

Ena (f.) pet form of Helena. Variant of Irish Ethne

Enda (m.) Irish, 'bird' (p. 69)

Energetic (m.) the word used as a name (p. 74)

Enfys (f.) Welsh, 'rainbow' (pp. 59, 71)

Engelbert (m.) (p. 47)

Enid (f.) Welsh, 'soul, life'

Ennis (m.) variant of Angus

Enoch (m.) Hebrew, 'inauguration, dedication'

Enos (m.) Hebrew, 'man'

Enrico (m.) Italian form of Henry

Eoghan (m.) Irish form of Eugene (p. 69)

Eoin (m.) Irish form of John (p. 69)

Ephie (f.) pet form of Euphemia

Ephraim (m.) Hebrew, 'fertile'

Ephrathah (f.) Hebrew, 'fruitful'

Eppie (f.) pet form of Euphemia or Hephzibah (p. 23)

Epsie (f.) pet form of Hephzibah (p. 23)

Er (m.) Hebrew, 'watchful'

Era (f.) the word used as a name (p. 44)

Erasmus (m.) Greek, 'beloved, desired' (p. 32)

Erastus (m.) Greek, 'lovable, loving'

Eric (m.) Old Norse, 'ruler of all' (pp. 56, 57)

Erica (f.) also *Ericka*. Feminine forms of Eric or Latin, 'heather' (pp. 54, 55)

Erik (m.) Scandinavian form of Eric

Erin (f.) Gaelic, 'western island' i.e. Ireland (pp. 11, 69)

Erle (m.) variant of Earl

Ermine (f.) the word used as a name (p. 40)

Erna (f.) Irish, 'knowing'

Ernest (m.) Germanic, 'earnestness, vigour'

Ernestina (f.) also *Ernestine*. Feminine forms of Ernest

Ernie (m.) pet form of Ernest

Ernst (m.) German form of Ernest

Eros (m.) Greek, 'sexual love' (p. 37)

Errol (m.) Scottish place name/family name

Errolyn (f.) feminine form of Errol

Ersa (f.) Greek, 'dew' (p. 37)

Erskine (m.) Scottish place name/family name, 'green ascent' (p. 70)

Ervin (m.) also *Ervine*, *Erving*. Variants of Irvin

Eryl (m., f.) Welsh, 'watcher' (p. 71)

Eryx (m.) Greek, 'heather' (p. 37)

Esau (m.) Hebrew, 'shaggy, hairy'

Esma (f.) variant of Esmé

Esmé (m., f.) French, 'esteemed' (p. 70)

Esmée (f.) feminine form of Esmé, which was originally male

Esmeralda (f.) Spanish, 'emerald' (p. 15)

Esmond (m.) Old English, 'grace-protection'

Esperanza (f.) Spanish, 'hope'

Essie (f.) pet form of Esther, Estelle, etc.

Estella (f.) Latin, 'star'

Estelle (f.) French form of Estella (p. 51)

Esther (f.) Assyrian, 'star' (pp. 34, 44, 51)
Ethan (m.) Hebrew, 'constant, permanent'
Ethel (f.) Old English, 'noble' (p. 12)
Ethelbert (m.) Old English, 'noble-bright' (pp. 28, 47)
Etheldreda (f.) Old English, 'noble-strength' (p. 28)
Ethelinda (f.) Germanic, 'noble serpent' (p. 28)
Ethelwyn (m.) Old English, 'noble-friend' (p. 28)
Ethna (f.) variant of Ethne (p. 69)
Ethne (f.) Irish, 'little fire'
Etienne (m.) early French form of Stephen
Etta (f.) pet form of Henrietta, Marietta, Pauletta, etc.
Ettie (f.) pet form of Hetty or a diminutive of Etta
Euan (m.) also *Euen*. Variants of Ewan
Euclid (m.) name of a famous Greek mathematician
Eudora (f.) Greek, 'good gift'
Eugene (m.) Greek, 'well born' (p. 69)
Eugenia (f.) feminine form of Eugene
Eugenie (f.) French form of Eugenia (p. 67)
Eulalie (f.) also *Eulalia*. Greek, 'sweetly speaking'
Eunice (f.) Greek, 'fine victory' (p. 48)
Euphemia (f.) Greek, 'auspicious speech' (p. 12)

Eurig (m.) also *Euros*, *Eurwyn*. Welsh 'gold' (p. 71)

Europa (f.) Greek, 'broad brow' (p. 37)

Eustace (m.) Greek, 'fruitful'

Eutychus (m.) Greek, 'of good fortune, lucky'

Eva (f.) Hebrew, 'living, lively'

Evadne (f.) Greek, of uncertain meaning (p. 37)

Evan (m.) Welsh form of John (p. 63)

Evangeline (f.) also *Evangelina*. Greek, 'good news'

Eve (f.) variant of Eva (pp. 13, 34, 51, 71)

Evel (m.) the word 'evil' adapted to first name use (p. 65)

Evelina (f.) French, 'hazel'

Evelyn (m., f.) Germanic, Avila, a name of uncertain meaning

Everard (m.) Germanic, 'boar-hard' (p. 5)

Everet (m.) also *Everett*, *Everitt*. Family names linked with Everard

Everilda (f.) also *Everhilda*. Variants of Averil

Everton (m.) place name/family name, 'boar farm'

Evette (f.) variant of Yvette

Evita (f.) Spanish pet form of Eva, Eve

Evonne (f.) modern variant of Yvonne

Ewan (m.) variant of Gaelic Eoghan, 'youth' or 'well born' (p. 70)

Ewart (m.) place name/family name, 'homestead near a river' or linked with Edward

Ewen (m.) variant of Ewan

Ezekiel (m.) Hebrew, 'may God make strong'

Ezer (m.) Hebrew, 'help'

Ezra (m.) Hebrew, '[God is] helper' (p. 33)

Ezri (m.) Hebrew, 'my help'

F

Fabian (m.) Latin, 'bean' (p. 66)

Fafa (f.) the note in the musical scale reduplicated (p. 35)

Faith (f.) the word used as a name. Faithful was also used in former times (pp. 49, 62)

Fancy (f.) variant of Fiancée (p. 41)

Fanny (f.) pet form of Frances, occasionally of Stephanie (p. 53)

Farah (f.) Persian, 'joy' (p. 22)

Farewell (m.) the word used as a name or place name/family name, 'beautiful spring' (p. 74)

Farley (m.) place name/family name

Farnham (m.) place name/family name, 'river meadow with ferns'

Faron (m., f.) family name

Farquhar (m.) Gaelic, 'very dear one' (p. 70)

Farrah (f.) variant of Farah (p. 22)

Farrell (m.) Irish family name, 'man of valour' (p. 28)

Fatima (f.) Arabic name of unknown meaning

Fauna (f.) Latin, 'she who favours' (p. 37)

Fausta (f.) also *Faustina, Faustinia, Faustillus (m.) Faustinianus (m.)*. Latin, 'fortunate, lucky' (p. 67)

Faye (f.) also *Fay* . Pet forms of Faith (p. 44)

Fear (m., f.) the word used as a name (by the Puritans) (p. 62)

Fearghas (m.) Gaelic form of Fergus

Fear-the-Lord (m.) a Puritan slogan name (p. 49)

Featherstone (m.) place name/family name, 'four stone'

Fedora (f.) variant of Feodora (p. 46)

Felice (f.) French form of Felicia (p. 29)

Felicia (f.) Latin, 'lucky', feminine form of Felix (pp. 29, 55)

Felicity (f.) English form of Felicia (pp. 29, 62, 72)

Felix (m.) Latin, 'happy, lucky'

Fenella (f.) English form of Fionnghal, a Gaelic name meaning 'white shoulder' (p. 70)

Fenton (m.) place name/family name, 'settlement near a fen'

Fenwick (m.) place name/family name, 'dairy farm in the fen'

Feodora (f.) Russian form of Theodora

Ferdinand (m.) Germanic, 'peace-boldness' (p. 18)

Fergal (m.) Irish, 'man of strength' (p. 69)
Fergus (m.) Gaelic, 'supreme choice' (p. 70)
Ferguson (m.) family name linked with Fergus
Fern (f.) also *Ferne*. The plant name (p. 54)
Fernando (m.) Spanish form of Ferdinand
Fernley (m.) also *Fernleigh*. Place name/family name, 'clearing with ferns'
Ferrari (m.) Italian family name 'Smith' linked with a car firm (p. 3)
Ffion (f.) Welsh, 'foxglove' (p. 71)
Fiancé (m.) the French word for 'betrothed' used as a name
Fidel (m.) Spanish, 'faithful'
Fidelma (f.) blend of Fidel and Mary (p. 69)
Fife (m.) Scottish place name
Fifi (f.) French pet form of Josephine
Fight-the-good-fight-of-faith (m.) Puritan slogan name (p. 49)
Filomena (f.) Italian form of Philomena
Finch (f.) the bird name or family name (p. 61)
Finella (f.) variant of Fenella
Finlay (m.) also *Finley*, *Findlay*. Scottish family name, 'fair hero' (p. 70)
Finola (f.) Irish, 'white shoulder'
Fiona (f.) Gaelic, 'white, fair' (pp. 14, 70)
Firth (m.) place name/family name, 'woodland'
Fisher (m.) occupational family name (p. 66)
Fitz (m.) Norman French, 'son'

Fitzroy (m.) family name, '[illegitimate] son of the king' (p. 5)

Flannan (m.) Irish, 'of ruddy complexion' (p. 69)

Flavia (f.) Latin feminine of Flavius, 'yellow' (p. 14)

Fletcher (m.) occupational family name, 'maker or seller of arrows'

Fleur (f.) French, 'flower' (pp. 54, 67)

Flo (f.) pet form of Florence or Flora

Flora (f.) Latin, 'flower' (pp. 37, 54)

Florann (f.) also *Floranne*. Modern blend of Flora and Ann(e)

Flore (f.) French form of Flora

Florella (f.) also *Florelle*. Modern diminutives of Flora

Florence (f., m.) Latin, 'flourishing', originally a male name. Made famous by Florence Nightingale who was born in Florence (pp. 32, 38)

Floretta (f.) also *Florette*. Variant of French *fleurette*, 'little flower'.

Florian (m.) Latin, 'flowery'

Florida (f.) Spanish, 'flowery', but usually directly from the American state

Florimel (f.) Latin, 'flower and honey'

Florina (f.) also *Florine*, *Florinda*. Diminutives of Flora

Floris (f.) also *Florise*. Latin, 'flower'

Florrie (f.) pet form of Florence or Flora

Flossie (f.) also *Floss*, *Flossy*. Pet forms of Florence

Flower (f.) the word used as a name or the family name (p. 54)

Floyd (m.) family name, 'grey, hoary'

Flurry (m.) pet form of Florence when used for men

Forbes (m.) Scottish place name/family name, 'field, district' (p. 70)

Ford (m.) family name, 'resident near a ford' (p. 3)

Forrest (m.) also *Forest*. Family name, 'dweller in a forest'

Forster (m.) occupational family name, 'forester'

Fortune (f.) the word used as a name, or an English form of Fortuna, Fortunata, feminine of Latin Fortunatus, 'happy, lucky' (p. 67)

Foster (m.) family name

Fran (f., m.) pet form of Frances, Francis

Francene (f.) variant of Francine

Frances (f.) feminine form of Francis

Francesca (f.) Italian feminine of Francesco, or Francis

Francetta (f.) also *Francette*. Diminutive forms of Frances

Francie (f.) diminutive of Frances

Francine (f.) French diminutive of Frances (Françoise)

Francis (m.) Latin, 'a Frenchman' (p. 17)

Francisca (f.) Spanish feminine form of Francisco, Francis

Franco (m.) pet form of Francesco or Francisco

Françoise (f.) French form of Frances

Francyne (f.) variant of Francine

Frank (m.) pet form of Francis (p. 44)

Frankie (m., f.) pet form of Francis, Frances

Franklin (m.) also *Franklyn (m., f.)*. Family name, 'freeholder'

Franz (m.) German form of Francis

Fraser (m.) also *Frazer*. French place name/family name (p. 70)

Fred (m.) pet form of Frederic(k)

Freda (f.) pet form of Winifred

Freddie (m.) also *Freddy*. Pet forms of Frederic(k)

Frederic (m.) French form of Frederick

Frederica (f.) feminine form of Frederic(k)

Frederick (m.) Germanic, 'peaceful ruler' (p. 4)

Frederique (f.) French feminine of Frederic

Freeman (m.) family name, 'free man'

Freya (f.) English form of Swedish Freja, earlier Freyja, 'noble lady' (p. 28)

Friday (f.) the day name (p. 51)

Frieda (f.) pet form of German Friederike, or Frederica

Friend (m., f.) the word used as a name

Fuller (m.) occupational family name

G

Gabi (f.) variant of Gaby

Gabriel (m.) Hebrew, 'man of God'

Gabriella (f.) Italian feminine form of Gabriel

Gabrielle (f.) French form of Gabriella (p. 13)

Gaby (f.) pet form of Gabriella, Gabrielle

Gad (m.) Hebrew, 'fortune, luck' (p. 33)

Gaddiel (m.) Hebrew, 'my fortune is God'

Gael (f.) variant of Gail

Gaenor (f.) Welsh variant of Gaynor

Gail (f.) pet form of Abigail

Gaila (f.) also *Gaile*. Modern variants of Gail

Gaius (m.) Latin, 'to rejoice'

Gale (f.) variant of Gail

Galen (m.) Greek, 'healer' or 'calm'

Gamaliel (m.) Hebrew, 'my reward is God'

Gamma (f.) Greek, third letter of the Greek alphabet used to name a third child (p. 68)

Gareth (m.) Welsh, 'gentle, benign' (p. 71)

Garfield (m.) place name/family name, 'field of spears'

Garner (m.) family name

Garnet (m., f.) also *Garnett*. Family name, 'shelter, protection'

Garnetta (f.) feminine form of Garnet

Garrard (m.) also *Garrat*, *Garrett*. Variants of Gerard (p. 69)

Garrick (m.) family name, 'spear-rule'

Garrie (m.) also *Garry*. Variants of Gary

Garth (m.) family name, 'chief gardener' (p. 25)

Gary (m.) from Gary, Indiana in the case of Gary Cooper. The town was named for Elmer Gary. The family name links with Gerard (p. 50)

Gavin (m.) Scottish form of Gawain (p. 60)

Gawain (m.) Welsh, 'hawk, falcon' (p. 60)

Gay (f.) also *Gaye*. A use of the word 'gay' or of the family name (p. 29)

Gayle (f.) variant of Gail

Gaylord (m.) family name, 'one of high spirits'

Gaynor (f.) variant of Guinevere or Jennifer. Welsh, 'fair and yielding', or 'smooth'

Geber (m.) Hebrew, 'the virile one'

Gedaliah (m.) Hebrew, 'Jehovah has magnified'

Gem (f.) the word used as a name

Gemelle (f.) Latin, 'twin'

Gemina (f.) feminine of Latin Geminus, 'twin' (p. 71)

Gemma (f.) Italian, 'gem' (p. 15)

Gene (m.) pet form of Eugene

Geneva (f.) the Swiss place name or a variant of Genevieve

Genevieve (f.) a Celtic or Germanic name of unknown meaning

Genty (m.) Irish family name linked with 'snow'

Geoffrey (m.) Germanic name, part of which means 'peace'

George (m.) Greek, 'earth-worker, farmer' (pp. 5, 44, 49)

Georgette (f.) French feminine form of George

Georgia (f.) also *Georgiana, Georgianna.* Feminine forms of George

Georgie (m., f.) pet form of George

Georgina (f.) Scottish feminine form of George (p. 13)

Georgine (f.) occasional variant of Georgina

Geraint (m.) Welsh form of a Latin name meaning 'old' (p. 71)

Gerald (m.) Germanic, 'spear-ruler' (p. 29)

Geraldine (f.) feminine form of Gerald (p. 69)

Gerard (m.) Germanic, 'spear-brave' (pp. 29, 69)

Gerasimus (m.) a saint's name of unknown meaning (p. 57)

Gerda (f.) Old Norse, 'protection'

Geri (f.) variant of Gerry

Gerlad (m.) Welsh name of disputed meaning (p. 71)

Germaine (f.) French feminine of Germain, 'German'

Gerrald (m.) variant of Gerald

Gerrard (m.) variant of Gerard

Gerry (m.) pet form of Gerald, Gerard

Gerry (f.) pet form of Geraldine

Gershom (m.) Hebrew, 'exile'

Gertie (f.) pet form of Gertrude

Gertrude (f.) Germanic, 'spear-strength' (p. 53)

Gervaise (f.) French feminine form of Gervase

Gervase (m.) a saint's name of unknown meaning

Gerwyn (m.) Welsh name of disputed meaning (p. 71)

Gethin (m.) Welsh, 'dusky' (pp. 14, 71)

Ghislaine (f.) French feminine form of Ghislain, name of a saint which contains a reference to a 'pledge'

Gianetta (f.) Italian form of Janet

Gibson (m.) family name, 'son of Gilbert'

Gideon (m.) Hebrew, 'hewer, cutter' (p. 33)

Gifford (m.) family name, 'chubby-cheeked, bloated'

Gilbert (m.) Germanic, 'pledge-bright' (p. 47)

Gilchrist (m.) Gaelic, 'servant of Christ' (p. 70)

Gilda (f.) Italian pet form of Ermenegilda, originally a Germanic name possibly meaning 'all-embracing battle'

Gildroy (m.) variant of Gilroy

Giles (m.) French form of Latin Egidius, 'young goat' (pp. 5, 32)

Gill (f.) pet form of Gillian

Gillean (m.) Gaelic, 'servant of St John'

Gillian (f.) English form of Juliana

Gillie (f.) also *Gilly*. Pet forms of Gillian

Gilroy (m.) Celtic family name, 'servant of the red-haired man'

Gina (f.) pet form of Georgina or Regina

Ginette (f.) pet form of Genevieve

Ginger (f.) pet form of Virginia (p. 14)

Giovanna (f.) Italian feminine form of Giovanni (John)

Gipsy (m.) the word used as a name

Gisela (f.) Germanic, 'hostage, pledge'

Gisele (f.) French form of Gisela (p. 59)

Giuseppe (m.) Italian form of Joseph

Gladstone (m.) Scottish place name/family name

Gladys (f.) Welsh form of Claudia (p. 50)

Glanville (m.) Norman place name/family name

Glen (m.) also *Glenn*. Family name, 'dweller in a valley' (pp. 25, 60)

Glenda (f.) Welsh, 'holy and good'

Glendower (m.) English form of Welsh Glyndwr

Glenice (f.) also *Glenis*, *Glenise*. Variants of Glenys

Glenn (m.) variant of Glen

Glenna (f.) feminine form of Glen, Glenn

Glennis (f.) variant of Glenys

Glenton (m.) place name/family name, 'settlement in a valley'

Glenville (m.) also *Glenvil*. Place name/family name

Glenys (f.) Welsh, 'holy, fair'

Glinys (f.) variant of Glynis

Gloria (f.) Latin, 'glory'

Glory (f.) the word used as a name

Glyn (m.) Welsh, 'small valley'

Glyndwr (m.) Welsh family name, probably based on a place name (p. 71)

Glynis (f.) Welsh, 'little valley'

Godfrey (m.) Germanic, 'god-peace'

Godwin (m.) Germanic, 'God-friend'

Golden (f.) the word used as a name

Goldie (f.) modern form of Golden (p. 14)

Golding (m.) family name, 'one with golden hair'

Goliath (m.) Hebrew, 'giant, mighty warrior'

Good-work (m.) a Puritan slogan name (p. 49)

Gordon (m.) Scottish clan and family name of uncertain meaning

Gore (m.) family name, 'triangular piece of land' (p. 74)

Grace (f.) the word used as a name (p. 9, 39, 62)

Gracie (f.) also *Gracey*. Diminutives of Grace

Gracious (m., f.) the word used as a name (by the Puritans) (p. 62)

Grady (m.) Irish family name, 'noble' (p. 44)

Graeme (m.) Scottish form of Graham (p. 70)

Graham (m.) also *Grahame*. Place name/family name, 'Granta's homestead'

Grania (f.) also in the Irish form Gráinne. Irish, 'love' (p. 69)

Grant (m.) family name, 'tall' (p. 39)

Grantley (m.) place name/family name, 'Granta's meadow'

Granville (m.) French place name/family name, 'large town'

Gray (m.) family name, 'one with gray hair'

Greenwood (m.) place name/family name, 'one who lived near or in a green wood'

Greer (f.) family name linked with Gregor

Greg (m.) pet form of Gregor or Gregory

Gregg (m.) variant of Greg

Gregor (m.) German, Norwegian form of Gregory, used in Scotland (p. 70)

Gregory (m.) Greek, 'watchful'

Grenville (m.) also *Grenvil*. Variants of Granvil(le)

Gresham (m.) place name/family name, 'hamlet with grazing land'

Greta (f.) pet form of Margareta (p. 60)

Gretchen (f.) German pet form of Margarete (Margaret)

Gretel (f.) also *Grethel.* German pet forms of Margarete

Greville (m.) Norman place name/family name

Griffith (m.) English form of Welsh Gruffydd, 'powerful chief' (p. 28)

Grigor (m.) Ukrainian form of Gregory

Griselda (f.) probably Germanic, 'grey battlemaid' (p. 17)

Grissel (f.) also *Grizzle.* Pet forms of Griselda (p. 17)

Grover (m.) also *Grove.* Family name, 'one who lived in a grove' (p. 25)

Gruffydd (m.) Welsh form of Griffith (p. 71)

Guinevere (f.) French form of Jennifer

Gus (m.) pet form of Augustus or Augustine (p. 8)

Gussie (f.) pet form of Augusta or Augustina (p. 8)

Gustave (m.) French form of Scandinavian Gustav, Gustaf, 'staff of the gods'

Guy (m.) a Germanic name of unknown origin

Gwen (f.) pet form of Gwendolen

Gwenda (f.) Welsh, 'fair and good'

Gwendolen (f.) Welsh, 'fair, blessed ring'

Gwendoline (f.) English form of Gwendolen

Gwendolyn (f.) North American form of Gwendolen

Gweneth (f.) variant of Gwyneth

Gwerfyl (f.) name of a Welsh female poet, of unknown meaning (p. 71)

Gwilym (m.) Welsh form of William (p. 71)

Gwladys (f.) Welsh form of Gladys

Gwyn (m.) Welsh, 'fair, blessed' (p. 71)

Gwyneth (f.) Welsh, 'happiness'

Gwynfor (m.) Welsh, 'fair lord' (p. 71)

Gwynne (f.) feminine form of Gwyn

Gwynneth (f.) variant of Gwyneth

Gyles (m.) variant of Giles

H

Hadassah (f.) Hebrew, 'myrtle' (p. 54)

Haddon (m.) place name/family name, 'hill with heather'

Hadrian (m.) variant of Adrian

Hadyn (m.) variant of Haydn or Aidan or Haddon

Hagar (f.) Hebrew, 'forsaken'

Haidee (f.) Greek, 'modest'

Hailey (f.) variant of Hayley

Hal (m.) pet form of Henry or Harry

Haley (f.) variant of Hayley

Halina (f.) Polish/Russian form of Helen

Ham (m.) Hebrew, possibly 'to be hot' (p. 33)

Hamilton (m.) place name/family name

Hamish (m.) a form of Seumas, Gaelic James (p. 70)

Hamlet (m.) diminutive of the Norman name Hamo, 'home' (p. 18)

Hammond (m.) family name

Hampton (m.) place name/family name (p. 44)

Handel (m.) German family name linked with Hans (John) (p. 34)

Handley (m.) also *Hanley*. Place name/family name, 'high wood clearing'

Hank (m.) Dutch pet form of Hendrik (Henry)

Hannah (f.) Hebrew, 'favour' (pp. 24, 34)

Hans (m.) form of John in several languages, from Latin Johannes

Happy (m., f.) the word used as a name (p. 30)

Harcourt (m.) Norman place name/family name

Hardy (m.) family name, 'hardy, courageous' (p. 27, 28)

Hargreaves (m.) place name/family name, 'grove with hares'

Harlan (m.) Germanic, 'army-land'

Harley (m.) place name/family name, 'hare wood'

Harmonia (f.) Greek, 'harmony' (p. 37)

Harold (m.) Old English, 'army-power' (pp. 26, 44)

Haroldene (f.) feminine form of Harold

Harper (m., f.) occupational family name, 'harp-maker or player' (p. 34)

Harriet (f.) feminine form of Harry or Henry

Harrington (m.) place name/family name

Harriot (f.) also *Harriott*. Variants of Harriet

Harris (m.) also *Harrison*. Family names linked with Harry

Harry (m.) spoken form of Henry (p. 64)

Hartley (m.) place name/family name, 'stag wood or hill' (p. 5)

Harvard (m.) place name/family name linked with Hereward (p. 52)

Harvey (m.) Celtic, 'battle ardent'

Harwood (m.) place name/family name, 'hare wood'

Hate-evil (m.) Puritan slogan name (p. 49)

Hattie (f.) also *Hatty*. Pet forms of Harriet

Havelock (m.) Old Norse, 'sea-sport'

Hawthorn (m.) also *Hawthorne*. Place name/family name, 'place where hawthorns grew'

Hayden (m.) place name/family name

Haydn (m.) appears to be the family name of the composer Joseph Haydn but used in Wales as a variant of Aidan (p. 34)

Haydon (m.) place name/family name

Hayley (f.) place name/family name, 'hay

meadow' introduced by the actress Hayley Mills (p. 9)

Haywood (m.) occupational family name, 'Bailiff'

Hazel (f.) from the tree (p. 14)

Headley (m.) variant of Hedley

Healey (m.) family name, probably 'ingenious' (p. 3)

Heath (m.) place name/family name

Heather (f.) the plant name (pp. 54, 64, 70)

Heaton (m.) place name/family name, 'high place'

Hebe (m.) Greek, 'youth'

Heber (m.) Hebrew, 'companion'

Hector (m.) Greek, 'holding fast' (p. 37)

Heddus (f.) Welsh, 'peace' (p. 4)

Hedley (m.) place name/family name, 'clearing overgrown with heather'

Hedwig (f.) German, 'struggle, strife'

Hedy (f.) pet form of Hedwig

Hefin (m.) Welsh, 'summery' (p. 71)

Heidi (f.) German pet form of Adelheid or Adalheidis (Adelaide) (pp. 28, 55)

Helen (f.) Greek, 'the shining one' (pp. 15, 37)

Helena (f.) Latinized variant of Helen (p. 18)

Hélène (f.) French form of Helen

Helga (f.) Nordic, 'holy'

Helice (f.) Greek, 'of the same age' (p. 37)

Héloise (f.) French form of Eloise

Help-on-high (m.) Puritan slogan name (p. 49)

Henderson (m.) family name linked with Henry

Henley (m.) place name/family name, 'high clearing'

Henri (m.) French form of Henry

Henrietta (f.) English form of French Henriette, feminine of Henri (Henry)

Henrik (m.) Swedish form of Henry

Henrika (f.) feminine form of Henrik

Henry (m.) Germanic, 'home-ruler' (pp. 3, 63)

Henryk (m.) Polish form of Henry

Hephzibah (f.) Hebrew, 'my delight is in her' (pp. 23, 34)

Hepsey (f.) also *Hepsie*, *Hepsy*. Pet forms of Hephzibah (p. 23)

Herald (m.) family name linked with Harold

Herbert (m.) Germanic, 'army-bright' (pp. 26, 47)

Hercules (m.) Greek, 'glory of Hera' (p. 37)

Hereward (m.) Old English, 'army-defence' (p. 26)

Herman (m.) Germanic, 'army-man' (p. 26)

Hermia (f.) short form of Hermione

Hermione (f.) feminine form of Hermes, the Greek messenger of the gods (p. 37)

Heron (f.) the bird name (p. 61)

Hervey (m.) variant of Harvey influenced by its French form Hervé

Hesperus (m.) Greek, 'evening star' (p. 37)

Hester (f.) variant of Esther (pp. 15, 64)

Hetta (f.) German pet form of Hedwig

Hettie (f.) also *Hetty*. Pet forms of Hester, Henrietta

Heulwen (f.) Welsh, 'sunshine' (pp. 59, 71)

Hew (m.) Welsh variant of Huw (Hugh)

Hewitt (m.) also *Hewlett, Hewson*. Family names linked with Hugh

Hezekiah (m.) Hebrew, 'my strength is Jehovah'

Hezir (m.) Hebrew, 'wild boar, pig'

Hilary (m, f.) Latin, 'cheerful' (p. 29)

Hilda (f.) Germanic, 'battle' (p. 26)

Hildegarde (f.) Germanic, 'battle-stronghold'

Hildred (f.) Old English, 'battle-counsel'

Hillary (m., f.) variant of Hilary

Hilma (f.) Scandinavian pet form of Wilhelmina

Hilton (m.) place name/family name

Hippolyta (f.) Greek feminine of Hippolytus, which possibly means 'stampeding horses' (pp. 5, 37)

Hiram (m.) Hebrew, 'my brother is on high'

Hoagie (m.) pet form of Hoagland, a family name (p. 39)

Hobart (m.) variant of Hubert

Hollie (f.) variant of Holly (p. 64)

Hollis (f.) family name, 'one who lived near holly bushes or a holm oak'

Holly (f.) the plant name. In Galsworthy's *Forsyte Saga* Jolly and Holly are the son and daughter of Jolyon and Hélène Forsyte (pp. 44, 65)

Homer (m.) Greek, 'hostage, pledge'

Honesty (m., f.) the word used as a name (by the Puritans) (p. 62)

Honor (f.) also *Honora*, *Honorah*. Latin, 'woman of honour'

Honoria (f.) Roman form of Honor

Honour (f.) English form of Honor (p. 62)

Hope (f.) the word used as a name (pp. 49, 62)

Horace (m.) English form of a famous Roman clan name Horatius, of unknown meaning

Horatia (f.) feminine form of Horatio

Horatio (m.) variant of Horace influenced by Italian Orazio (p. 5)

Hortensia (f.) Latin feminine of Hortensius, a Roman clan name of unknown meaning. Also a flower name (p. 54)

Howard (m.) family name

Howell (m.) variant of Welsh Hywel

Hubert (m.) Germanic, 'mind-bright' (p. 47)

Huckleberry (m.) the word for 'blueberry' used as a name (p. 7)

Hudson (m.) family name linked with Hugh or Richard

Hugh (m.) Germanic, 'mind, soul' (p. 64)

Hughie (m.) also *Hughey*, *Hughy*, *Huey*. Pet forms of Hugh

Hugo (m.) Latin form of Hugh

Huldah (f.) also *Hulda*. Hebrew, 'weasel, mole' (p. 5)

Humbert (m.) Germanic, 'famous-giant' (p. 47)

Humility (f.) the word used as a name (by the Puritans) (p. 62)

Humphrey (m.) Germanic, 'peace' plus another element of unknown meaning (p. 4)

Hunter (m.) occupational family name

Huw (m.) Welsh form of Hugh (p. 71)

Hyacinth (m., f.) the flower name (p. 17)

Hylda (f.) variant of Hilda

Hylton (m.) variant of Hilton

Hyman (m.) Hebrew, 'life'

Hymie (m.) also *Hy*. Pet forms of Hyman

Hypatia (f.) Greek, 'highest' (p. 53)

Hyperion (m.) Greek, 'going over' (p. 37)

Hywel (m.) Welsh, 'eminent, conspicuous'

I

Iago (m.) Welsh form of James

Iain (m.) Scottish Gaelic form of John (p. 70)

Ian (m.) variant of Iain (p. 72)

Ianthe (f.) Greek, 'violet flower' (pp. 14, 37)

Icarus (m.) Greek, 'dedicated to the moon-goddess Car' (p. 37)

Ichabod (m.) Hebrew, 'where is the glory?'

Ida (f.) Germanic, 'youthful' (p. 44)

Idris (m.) Welsh, 'ardent lord'

Idwal (m.) Welsh, 'rampart of the lord'

Ieasha (f.) also *Ieashia, Ieeshia, Iesha.* Variants of Aisha

Iestin (f.) Welsh form of Justine

Iestyn (m.) Welsh form of Justin (p. 71)

Ieuan (m.) Welsh form of John (p. 71)

Ifan (m.) a Welsh form of John (p. 71)

If-Christ-had-not-died-for-thee-thou-hadst-been-damned (m.) a Puritan slogan name (p. 49)

Ifor (m.) Welsh, 'lord' or variant of Ivor

Ignatious (m.) also *Ignatius, Ignacious, Inigo.* Greek name of unknown meaning

Igor (m.) Russian form of Ingvar

Ike (m.) pet form of Isaac, but associated with Dwight D. Eisenhower, whose nickname it was

Ilona (f.) Hungarian form of Helen

Ilse (f.) also *Ilsa.* German pet forms of Elisabeth

Ima (f.) variant of Emma (p. 55)

Imelda (f.) Italian form of a Germanic name, 'all-embracing battle' (p. 26)

Immanuel (m.) variant of Emanuel

Imogen (f.) also *Imogene*. Latin, 'innocent' (pp. 18, 46)

Ina (f.) pet form of Georgina, Clementina, Martina, Christina, etc. (p. 70)

India (f.) the name of the country used as a name (p. 11)

Ines (f.) Italian pet form of Agnese (Agnes)

Inez (f.) Spanish form of Agnes (p. 53)

Inga (f.) pet form of Ingeborg, an Old Norse name, 'Ing's protection'. Ing was the god of fertility

Inge (f.) German form of Inga

Ingram (m.) Germanic, 'Anglian raven' (p. 60)

Ingrid (f.) Old Norse, 'Ing beautiful'. *See* Inga (p. 9)

Ingvar (m.) Old Norse, 'Ing's warrior'. *See* Inga

Inigo (m.) Basque form of Ignatious

Innes (m.) Gaelic, 'island' (p. 70)

Innocent (m.) the word used as a name (p. 46)

Iola (f.) Greek, 'dawn cloud' (p. 59)

Iolanthe (f.) Greek, 'violet flower'

Iolo (m.) Welsh, 'lord value' (p. 71)

Ion (m.) Greek, 'going' (p. 37)

Iona (f.) name of a Scottish island (p. 70)

Iorwerth (m.) Welsh, 'lord worth'

Ira (m.) Hebrew. Explained variously as 'watchful' or 'ass'

Irene (f.) also *Irena*. Greek, 'peace' (pp. 4, 37)

Iris (f.) the flower name, also the Greek goddess of the rainbow (pp. 37, 42, 54)

Irma (f.) German pet form of Irmgard and similar names, where the first element is 'whole, universal'

Irmgard (f.) Germanic, 'all-embracing fence' (p. 35)

Irvin (m.) also *Irvine*, *Irving*. Scottish place name/ family name

Irwin (m.) Old English, 'boar-friend'

Isa (f.) pet form of Isabella

Isaac (m.) Hebrew, 'may God laugh'

Isabel (f.) Spanish form of Elizabeth

Isabella (f.) Italian form of Elizabeth (pp. 17, 18)

Isabelle (f.) French form of Isabel, Isabella

Isador (m.) variant of Isidore

Isadora (f.) also *Isidora*. Greek feminine form of Isidore

Isaiah (m.) Hebrew, 'Jehovah is salvation'

Isidore (m.) Greek, 'gift of Isis'. Adopted by Spanish Jews and subsequently associated with Jewish families

Isla (f.) Scottish river name (p. 70)

Ismay (f.) family name (p. 70)

Ismene (f.) Greek, 'moon-force' (p. 37)

Isobel (f.) also *Isobell*, *Isobelle*. Variants of Isabel, etc. (p. 49)

Isolda (f.) also *Isolde*. Of unknown origin

Israel (m.) Hebrew, 'may God show his strength' or 'may God reign' (p. 11)
Ita (f.) Irish, 'thirst' (p. 69)
Ithel (m.) Welsh, 'generous lord'
Ithiel (m.) Hebrew, 'God is with me'
Iva (f.) feminine form of Ivan
Ivan (m.) Russian form of John
Ivo (m.) Germanic, 'yew wood'
Ivor (m.) Old Norse variant of Ingvar
Ivory (m., f.) the word used as a name (p. 14)
Ivy (f.) the plant name (p. 30)
Iwan (m.) variant of Ifan (p. 71)
Izaak (m.) variant of Isaac
Izzy (m.) pet form of Isidore

J

Jabal (m.) Hebrew, 'guide'
Jabez (m.) Hebrew, 'distress'
Jacinta (f.) variant of Hyacinth
Jacinthe (f.) French form of Jacinta
Jack (m.) pet form of John (via Jankin, Jackin), influenced by French Jacques (pp. 35, 71)
Jackie (m.) diminutive of Jack
Jackie (f.) pet form of Jacqueline
Jackson (m.) family name, 'son of Jack'
Jacob (m.) Hebrew, linked with words meaning 'heel' and 'to supplant', but explained by authorities as a form of an Arabic phrase, 'let

God protect' (pp. 30, 33)

Jacobina (f.) Scottish feminine of Jacob

Jacqueline (f.) French feminine diminutive of Jacques (James)

Jacquelyn (f.) modern variant of Jacqueline

Jacques (m.) French form of James or Jacob

Jade (f.) the word used as a name (pp. 14, 15)

Jael (f.) Hebrew, 'antelope' (p. 5)

Jago (m.) Cornish form of James

Jaguar (m.) the word used as a name (suggested by the car) (p. 3)

Jaime (m., f.) Spanish/Portuguese form of James but also used as variant of Jamie

Jaine (f.) variant of Jane

Jake (m.) pet form of Jacob

Jaleesa (f.) also *Jalisa*, *Jaleisa*, etc. Fanciful variants of Lisa

Jamaica (f.) the place name (p. 11)

Jamal (m.) Arabic, 'handsome'

James (m.) Latin form of Jacob (p. 45)

Jamesina (f.) feminine form of James

Jamie (m.,f.) Scottish pet form of James, used in modern times as a feminine form

Jan (m.) form of John in several European languages

Jan (f.) pet form of Janet

Jana (f.) form of Jane in several European languages

Jancis (f.) a name invented by Mary Webb, perhaps a blend of Jane and Frances (p. 17)

Jane (f.) English form of Johanna, feminine of Johannes (John) (pp. 17, 41, 44, 53, 64)

Janelle (f.) also *Janel, Janell.* Diminutives of Jane

Janene (f.) variant of Janine

Janet (f.) diminutive of Jane (pp. 9, 49, 70)

Janetta (f.) Latinized form of Janet

Janette (f.) variant of Janet influenced by French Jeanette

Janey (f.) variant of Janie

Janice (f.) diminutive of Jane introduced by Paul Leicester Ford in his novel *Janice Meredith* (1899)

Janie (f.) pet form of Jane

Janine (f.) variant of Jeannine

Janis (f.) variant of Janice

Janita (f.) variant of Juanita

Jannetta (f.) variant of Janetta. Similarly Janice, Jannine, etc., occur for Janice, Janine

Januetta (f.) January adapted to first name use (p. 9)

Janus (f.) Greek, 'door, entrance' (p. 37)

Japheth (m.) Hebrew, 'may he extend'

Jaqueline (f.) variant of Jacqueline

Jarrad (m.) variant of Jared

Jared (m.) Assyrian, 'servant'

Jarvis (m.) family name linked with Gervase

Jasmine (f.) the flower name (p. 54)

Jason (m.) Greek form of Jesus or Joshua (pp. 37, 50, 52, 56)

Jasper (m.) possibly Persian, 'treasure holder'

Jay (m., f.) for the letter J or the bird (pp. 12, 32, 61)

Jayme (f.) also *Jaymie, Jaymee*. Variants of Jamie

Jayne (f.) variant of Jane

Jayson (m.) variant of Jason

Jean (f.) French Jehane, from Latin Johanna, feminine of Johannes (John)

Jeanette (f.) mainly Scottish diminutive of Jean (p. 70)

Jeanie (f.) pet form of Jean

Jeanne (f.) French feminine form of Jean (John)

Jeannette (f.) variant of Jeanette

Jeannie (f.) variant of Jeanie

Jeannine (f.) French diminutive of Jeanne

Jean-Paul (m.) a typical French blend of Jean (John) and Paul (p. 22)

Jedaiah (m.) Hebrew, 'Jehovah knows'

Jedidiah (m.) Hebrew, 'loved by Jehovah'

Jeff (m.) pet form of Geoffrey or Jeffrey

Jefferson (m.) family name, 'son of Geoffrey/Jeffrey'

Jeffrey (m.) mainly US variant of Geoffrey (p. 55)

Jehiel (m.) Hebrew, 'may God live'

Jehoram (m.) Hebrew, 'Jehovah is high'
Jehoshaphat (m.) Hebrew, 'Jehovah judges' (p. 33)
Jehu (m.) Hebrew, 'it is he, Jehovah'
Jekamiah (m.) Hebrew, 'may Jehovah establish'
Jem (m.) pet form of James
Jemima (f.) Hebrew, 'dove'
Jemma (f.) variant of Gemma
Jenet (f.) also *Jenette*. Variants of Jeanette
Jenifer (f.) Cornish variant of Jennifer
Jenkin (m.) family name, 'little John'
Jenna (f.) Latinized form of Jennie/Jenny
Jennette (f.) variant of Jeanette (p. 44)
Jennie (f.) also *Jenny*. Formerly pet forms of Janet, now of Jennifer
Jennifer (f.) Welsh, 'fair and yielding' (pp. 21, 55)
Jenniphine (f.) blend of Jennifer and Josephine (p. 21)
Jenny (f.) variant of Jennie
Jephthah (m.) Hebrew, 'whom God rescues'
Jerald (m.) modern variant of Gerald
Jeremiah (m.) Hebrew, 'Jehovah raises up'
Jeremy (m.) English form of Jeremiah (pp. 52, 55)
Jeri (f.) variant of Gerry
Jermaine (m.) variant of French Germain, 'German' (p. 55)

Jerold (m.) modern variant of Gerald

Jerome (m.) Greek, 'sacred name'

Jerrold (m.) family name linked with Gerald

Jerry (m.) pet form of Jeremiah or variant of Gerry (p. 71)

Jerry (f.) variant of Gerry

Jervis (m.) variant of Jarvis

Jess (m.) pet form of Jesse, Jessie

Jess (f.) pet form of Jessica or, in Scotland, of Janet

Jessamine (f.) variant of Jasmine

Jesse (m.) Hebrew, 'man of Jehovah'

Jessica (f.) Shakespearian form of Iscah, Hebrew, 'he beholds'

Jessie (f.) pet form of Jessica, Janet (p. 70)

Jestina (f.) Welsh form of Justina

Jesus (m.) Hebrew, 'Jehovah is generous' or 'Jehovah saves' (p. 56)

Jesus-Christ-came-into-the-world-to-save (m.) a Puritan slogan name (p. 49)

Jethro (m.) Hebrew, 'pre-eminence' (p. 33)

Jewel (f.) the word used as a name

Jezebel (f.) Hebrew, 'control, domination' (p. 34)

Jill (f.) modern variant of Gill (p. 71)

Jillian (f.) also *Jillianne*. Variants of Gillian, Gilliane

Jim (m.) pet form of James

Jimmy (m.) also *Jimmie*. Pet forms of James

Jinny (f.) pet form of Jane, Virginia or a variant

of Jenny

Jo (f.) pet form of Josephine, Joanna, etc

Joab (m.) Hebrew, 'Jehovah is Father'

Joah (m.) Hebrew, 'Jehovah is brother'

Joan (f.) contraction of Johanna (p. 73)

Joanna (f.) contracted form of Johanna

Joanne (f.) French form of Joanna (p. 50)

Job (m.) Hebrew, perhaps 'the persecuted one, man treated as an enemy' (p. 33)

Job-raked-out-of-the-ashes (m.) a Puritan slogan name (p. 49)

Jocelyn (m., f.) also *Jocelin, Joceline, Joclyn.* Germanic, of unknown meaning

Jock (m.) Pet form of John (via Jonkin, Jokin)

Jodie (f.) also *Jodi, Jody.* Pet forms of Judith

Jody (m.) apparently a pet form of Joseph or Jude

Joe (m.) pet form of Joseph

Joel (m.) Hebrew, 'Jehovah is God' (p. 33)

Joella (f.) also *Joelle.* Feminine forms of Joel

Joellen (f.) apparently a blend of Jo and Ellen

Joey (m.) diminutive of Joe

Johan (m.) short form of Latin Johannes (John)

John (m.) English form of Hebrew Yohanan, 'Jehovah has shown favour' (pp. 31, 32, 49, 57, 72)

Johnny (m., f.) also *Johnnie.* Pet form of John now frequently used for girls (p. 65)

Johnson (m.) family name, 'son of John'

Joi (f.) variant of Joy influenced by French *joie*, 'joy'

Jolene (f.) also *Jolean*. Modern blend of fashionable name elements

Jolie (f.) French, 'pretty'

Jolly (m.) pet form of Jolyon or the word used as a name (pp. 30, 65)

Jolyon (m.) variant of Julian

Jon (m.) variant of John influenced by Jonathan

Jonah (m.) Hebrew, 'dove' (p. 33, 61)

Jonas (m.) Latin form of Jonah

Jonathan (m.) Hebrew, 'Jehovah has given' (p. 33)

Joni (f.) modern feminine form of Jon

Jonquil (f.) the flower name (p. 54)

Jordan (m.) from the River Jordan, which probably means 'to descend' (pp. 11, 60)

José (m.) Spanish form of Joseph

Joseph (m.) Hebrew, 'may God add' (p. 69)

Josephine (f.) feminine form of Joseph (pp. 13, 21)

Josette (f.) French feminine form of Joseph

Joshua (m.) Latin form of Jesus (pp. 33, 52, 55, 56)

Josiah (m.) Hebrew, 'Jehovah supports'

Josie (f.) pet form of Josephine

Jotham (m.) Hebrew, 'Jehovah is perfect'

Joy (f.) the word used as a name (p. 30, 72)

Joyce (m., f.) Celtic name identified with Latin Jocosa, 'merry' (pp. 30, 73)

Juan (m.) Spanish form of John

Juanita (f.) Spanish diminutive of Juana, feminine of Juan

Jubal (m.) Hebrew, 'horn, trumpet' (p. 34)

Judas (m.) Greek form of Jude

Jude (m.) also *Judah*. Hebrew, '[God be] praised'

Judith (f.) Hebrew, 'Jewess'

Judy (f.) also *Judi, Judie*. Pet forms of Judith

Julia (f.) Latin feminine form of Julius (pp. 73, 74)

Julian (m.) derivative of Julius via Julianus

Juliana (f.) Latin feminine form of Julianus

Julianne (f.) also *Julie-Ann, Julie-Anne, Julieanne*. Blends of Julie and Ann(e)

Julie (f.) French form of Julia (pp. 8, 50, 55)

Julien (m.) French form of Julian

Julienne (f.) French feminine form of Julien

Juliet (f.) English form of Italian Giuletta, diminutive of Giulia (Julia) (pp. 8, 13, 18, 71)

Juliette (f.) also *Julietta*. French and Latinized forms of Juliet

Julio (m.) Spanish form of Julius

Julius (m.) Roman clan name traditionally interpreted as Greek, 'downy bearded' but probably 'descended from Jove'

June (f.) the name of the month. As a male name a pet form of Junior (pp. 8, 16, 55)

Junior (m.) the word used as a name (p. 16)

Junita (f.) simplified form of Juanita or diminutive of June

Jupiter (m.) Greek, 'Father sky' (p. 37)

Justice (m., f.) the word used as a name (by the Puritans) (p. 62)

Justin (m.) Latin, 'just'

Justina (f.) feminine form of Justin

Justine (f.) French form of Justina

K

Kai (f.) variant of Kay, though it has been linked with the Hawaiian word for 'sea-water'

Kane (m.) Welsh, 'beautiful' or Celtic, 'warrior'

Kanisha (f.) variant of Tanisha

Kara (f.) variant of Cara

Karel (m.) Dutch form of Charles

Karen (f.) Danish pet form of Katarina (Catherine) (pp. 50, 65)

Karenza (f.) variant of Kerensa

Karin (f.) Swedish form of Karen

Karina (f.) shortened form of Katarina (Catherine)

Karl (m.) variant of Carl (p. 53)

Karla (f.) variant of Carla

Karlene (f.) also *Karleen, Karline, Karli, Karlie.* Variants of Carlene, etc.

Karol (m.) Polish form of Charles

Karrie (f.) variant of Carrie

Karyn (f.) modern variant of Karen

Katarina (f.) form of Catherine or Katherine in several countries, e.g. Sweden

Kate (f.) pet form of Catherine/Katherine (pp. 53, 71)

Katey (f.) variant of Katie

Katharine (f.) variant of Katherine/Catherine (pp. 18, 20, 36, 44, 45)

Katherine (f.) normal American spelling of Catherine

Katheryn (f.) modern variant of Katherine

Kathleen (f.) English form of Irish Caitlin (Catherine) (p. 12, 55, 69)

Kathlyn (f.) modern variant of Kathleen

Kathrine (f.) modern variant of Katherine/ Catherine

Kathryn (f.) variant of Katherine/Catherine introduced by the American actress Kathryn Grayson

Kathy (f.) pet form of Katherine/Catherine

Katie (f.) diminutive of Kate (p. 20)

Katina (f.) short form of Katarina (p. 55)

Katrina (f.) modern variant of Catriona

Katrine (f.) name of a Scottish loch (p. 70)

Katy (f.) variant of Katie

Kay (f.) also *Kaye*. Pet form of names beginning with K– (p. 12)

Kayla (f.) short form of Michaela

Keeley (f.) also *Kayleigh*, *Kealey*, *Kealy*, *Keelie*, *Keellie*, *Keely*, *Keighley*. Family names, variants of Kelly

Keir (m.) Gaelic, 'swarthy' (p. 70)

Keira (f.) feminine form of Keir or Kieran

Keiran (m.) variant of Kieran

Keisha (f.) also *Keesha*, *Kesha*, *Keshia*, *Keysha*, *Kiesha*, *Kisha*. Apparently a back-formation from Lakeisha, etc, as used by black American families. Perhaps ultimately from Aisha (p. 55)

Keith (m.) Scottish place name/family name possibly meaning 'wood' (p. 56)

Kelley (f.) also *Kellie*. Variants of Kelly

Kelly (f.) Irish family name, 'strife' or 'the warlike one'. Probably suggested as a first name by Grace Kelly, the American actress who became Princess Grace of Monaco (pp. 39, 50, 55)

Kelly-Ann (f.) also *Kelly-Anne*. Popular blends of Kelly and Ann(e)

Kelsey (m., f.) also *Kelsie*, *Kelcey*. Place name/family name, 'Ceol's island'

Kelvin (m.) Scottish river name of uncertain origin (p. 55)

Ken (m.) also *Kenn*. Pet forms of Kenneth

Kendall (m.) also *Kendal*. Place name/family name, 'valley of the river Kent'

Kendra (f.) apparently a blend of Kenneth and Alexandra or Sandra

Kendrick (m.) variant of Kenrick

Kenelm (m.) Old English, 'brave-helmet'

Kennedy (m.) Irish family name, 'ugly head'

Kennet (m.) river name (p. 60)

Kenneth (m.) Gaelic, 'fair one' or fire-sprung' (pp. 55, 64)

Kenny (m.) pet form of Kenneth. Kennie is used as a feminine form (p. 64)

Kenrick (m.) Welsh, 'chief hero'

Kent (m.) place name/family name. Also a river name (pp. 38, 60)

Kentigern (m.) Celtic, 'chief lord'

Kenton (m.) place name/family name

Kenwyn (m.) river name (p. 60)

Kenya (f.) place name (pp. 11, 55)

Keren (f.) short form of Kerenhappuch

Kerenhappuch (f.) Hebrew, 'mascara'

Kerensa (f.) also *Kerenza*. Cornish, 'love, affection' (p. 37)

Keri (f.) also *Kerie*. Variants of Kerry

Kermit (m.) variant of Dermot

Kerr (m.) Scottish place name/family name

Kerri (f.) also *Kerrie*. Variants of Kerry

Kerrick (m.) variant of Kenrick

Kerry (m., f.) Irish place name. In some parts of US seen as variant of Carrie (p. 50)

Kerry-Ann (f.) also *Kerri-Ann*, *Kerrianne*, *Kerryann*, *Kerry-Anne*. Popular modern blends of Kerry and Ann(e)

Kersti (f.) also *Kerstie*. Variants of Kirsty

Kerwin (m.) Irish, 'dark, black' (p. 14)

Kester (m.) early form of Christopher

Keturah (f.) Hebrew, 'incense' (p. 13)

Kevan (m.) variant of Kevin or a Scottish family name

Kevin (m.) Irish, 'handsome at birth' (pp. 55, 69)

Keziah (f.) Hebrew, 'cassia' (a fragrant shrub) (pp. 13, 34)

Kia (f.) pet form of Kiana

Kiana (f.) also *Quiana*, *Quianna*. Apparently Anna with a prefix fashionable amongst black American families in the 1980s

Kiera (f.) feminine form of Kieran

Kieran (m.) Irish, 'little dark one', (pp. 14, 69)

Killan (m.) Irish, 'strife'

Kim (m., f.) pet form of Kimberley, Kimberly or Kimball, though in Edna Ferber's *Showboat* it derives from the initial letters of Kentucky, Illinois and Missouri (p. 8)

Kimball (m.) Irish family name (p. 8)

Kimberley (m., f.) South African place name (p. 26)

Kimberly (f.) modern form of Kimberley (p. 55)

King (m.) family name (p. 5)

Kingsley (m.) place name/family name, 'king's wood or clearing'

Kirk (m.) Old Norse, 'church' (pp. 45, 70)

Kirsten (f.) Scandinavian form of Christine (p. 70)

Kirstie (f.) variant of Kirsty (p. 70)

Kirstin (f.) variant of Kirsten

Kirsty (f.) Scottish pet form of Christine

Kirstyn (f.) modern variant of Kirsten

Kish (m.) Hebrew, 'gift' (p. 33)

Kissie (f.) pet form of Keziah

Kit (m.) early pet form of Christopher (p. 34)

Kitty (f.) pet form of Katherine, Kathleen (p. 5)

Kizzy (f.) pet form of Keziah, though Alex Haley explained it in *Roots* as 'you stay put' in Mandinka

Klaus (m.) German pet form of Nikolaus (Nicholas)

Knola (f.) fanciful variant of Nola (p. 44)

Korina (f.) variant of Corinne

Kris (m.) pet form of Kristian or Kristofer

Krista (f.) variant of Christa, and a form of Christine in languages such as Czech

Kristen (f.) US variant of Kirsten

Kristi (f.) also *Kristie*. Variants of Kristy

Kristian (m.) Danish form of Christian

Kristin (f.) shortened form of Kristina

Kristine (f.) form of Christine in several languages, e.g. Norwegian (p. 55)

Kristopher (m.) form of Christopher influenced by Kristofer

Kristy (f.) pet form of Kristen, Kristina, etc.

Krystina (f.) Czech form of Christine

Kurt (m.) German pet form of Konrad

Kyla (f.) apparently a feminine form of Kyle

Kyle (m.) Scottish place name/family name, 'narrow piece of land'. Sometimes used as a feminine name, perhaps confused with Kylie

Kylie (f.) Aboriginal, 'curled stick, boomerang' (p. 29)

Kym (m., f.) variant of Kim

Kyra (f.) Greek feminine of Cyril

Kyran (m.) variant of Kieran

L

Laban (m.) Hebrew, 'white' (p. 14)

Labor Day (m.) for a child born on Labor Day (p. 51)

Lacey (m.) also *Lacy*. French place name/family name

Lachlan (m.) also *Lachlann*. Gaelic, 'fjord-land' (p. 70)

Lacy (m.) variant of Lacey

Laddie (m.) 'Lad' adapted to first name use (p. 53)

Ladonna (f.) Donna with La- prefix, the latter being very fashionable amongst black American families in the 1980s

Lady (f.) the word used as a name. Lady Bird also occurs (pp. 28, 54)

Ladysmith (f.) the place name (p. 26)

Laetitia (f.) variant of Letitia (p. 66)

Lafayette (m.) family name (of a general in Washington's army). Used only in the US as a first name

Laila (f.) variant of Leila

Lakeisha (f.) also *Lakisha*. Appears to be Aisha with fashionable prefix. *See* Ladonna

Lala (f.) the note in the musical scale reduplicated (p. 35)

Lalage (f.) Greek, 'to babble'

Lallie (f.) also *Lally*. Pet forms of Lalage

Lambert (m.) Germanic, 'land-bright' (p. 47)

Lamentation (m., f.) the word used as a name (by the Puritans) (p. 62)

Lamont (m.) family name, 'lawman' (p. 55)

Lana (f.) short form of Alana or Latin, 'wool' (p. 9)

Lance (m.) pet form of Lancelot

Lancelot (m.) French, 'the servant'

Lancia (f.) Italian family name linked with car company (p. 3)

Lane (m.) also *Layne*. Family name indicating someone who lived near or in a lane

Lara (f.) name of a Roman nymph linked with 'to chatter' or pet form of Larissa (p. 37)

Laraine (f.) perhaps a feminine form of Leroy, i.e. French 'the queen' (p. 6)

Larissa (f.) also *Larisa*. Latin, 'cheerful'

Lark (f.) the bird name. Also the name of a river (pp. 60, 61, 62)

Larraine (f.) variant of Laraine

Larry (m.) pet form of Laurence or Lawrence (p. 64)

Lars (m.) Swedish form of Laurens (Laurence)

Latasha (f.) Tasha with the La- prefix. *See* Ladonna

Latisha (f.) modern variant of Letitia

Latonia (f.) also *Latona*. Variants of Latonya

Latonya (f.) Tonya with La- prefix. *See* Ladonna (p. 55)

Latoya (f.) appears to be a simplified form of Latonya

Latrice (f.) a blend of the fashionable prefix La- with Trice, probably from Patrice, Patricia. *See* Ladonna

Launcelot (m.) variant of Lancelot

Laura (f.) Latin, 'laurel' (pp. 41, 55)

Lauraine (f.) variant of Lorraine

Laurance (m.) variant of Laurence

Laureen (f.) also *Laurene*, *Laurine*. Modern diminutives of Laura

Laurel (f.) name of the tree (p. 54)

Lauren (f.) short form of Laurena

Laurena (f.) variant of Laurina

Laurence (m.) Latin, 'of Laurentium' (a city south of Rome)

Lauretta (f.) diminutive of Laura

Laurette (f.) French diminutive of Laure (Laura)

Lauri (f., m.) pet form of Laura, occasionally of Laurence

Lauriane (f.) French diminutive of Laure (Laura)

Laurice (f.) variant of Loris

Laurie (m., f.) pet form of Laurence, more recently of Laura

Laurina (f.) Roman feminine form of Laurentius (Laurence)

Laurinda (f.) modern diminutive of Laura

Laurine (f.) variant of Laureen

Laurraine (f.) variant of Lorraine

Lavender (f.) the flower name (p. 54)

Lavenia (f.) also *Lavena*. Variants of Lavinia

Laverna (f.) Latin 'to lie hidden' (p. 37)

Laverne (f.) Californian place name, intended to mean 'the green place' in Spanish. Occasionally used for males

Lavinia (f.) Roman place name of uncertain origin (p. 37)

Law (m.) the word used as a name (p. 33)

Lawrence (m.) popular variant of Laurence

Lawrie (m.) Scottish pet form of Lawrence

Lawson (m.) family name, 'son of Laurence'

Lawton (m.) place name/family name, 'settlement on a hill'

Layne (m.) variant of Lane

Layton (m.) place name/family name

Lazarus (m.) Hebrew, 'God has given help'

Lea (f.) variant of Lee or feminine form of Leo (pp. 25, 60)

Leah (f.) Hebrew, 'wild cow' (p. 34)

Leanda (f.) feminine form of Leander

Leander (m.) Greek, 'lion man' (p. 37)

Leandra (f.) feminine form of Leander

Leanne (f.) variant of Lianne

Leantha (f.) variant of Leandra (p. 44)

Lear (m.) variant of Llyr, name of the sea-god of the ancient Britons (p. 18)

Learn-wisdom (m., f.) Puritan slogan name (p. 49)

Leda (f.) Cretan, 'lady' (p. 37)

Lee (m., f.) place name/family name, 'wood, meadow' (pp. xi, 20, 39, 50)

Leeann (f.) also *Lee Ann*, *Leeanne*, *Lee Anne*. Variants of Lianne

Leesa (f.) variant of Lisa

Leigh (m., f.) mainly a feminine variant of Lee

Leighton (m.) variant of Layton

Leila (f.) Arabic, 'dark as night'

Lela (f.) variant of Lelia

Leland (m.) American place name/family name

Lelia (f.) feminine form of Laelius, a Roman family name

LeMans (f.) French place name linked with motor racing (p. 3)

Lemmy (m.) pet form of Lemuel

Lemuel (m.) Hebrew, 'who belongs to God' (p. 33)

Len (m.) pet form of Leonard (p. 60)

Lena (f.) pet form of Helena, Selena, etc.

Lenda (f.) feminine form of Leonard

Lennard (m.) variant of Leonard

Lennox (m.) also *Lenox*. Scottish place name/family name linked with 'elm trees'

Lenny (m.) also *Lennie*. Pet forms of Leonard

Lenora (f.) Russian form of Eleanor

Lenore (f.) Germanic variant of Eleanor

Leo (m.) Latin, 'lion' (p. 5)

Leon (m.) Greek, 'lion' (p. 72)

Leona (f.) feminine form of Leon

Leonard (m.) Germanic, 'strong as a lion' (p. 5)

Leonie (f.) French feminine form of Leon

Leonora (f.) short form of Eleonora, Italian form of Eleanora

Leopold (m.) Germanic, 'people-bold'

Leroy (m.) also *Leroi.* French, 'the king' (pp. 5, 6)

Les (m.) pet form of Leslie, Lesley or Lester

Lesley (f.) feminine form of Leslie

Leslie (m., f.) Scottish place name/family name of uncertain meaning (pp. xi, 9, 32, 39)

Lester (m.) from the place name Leicester

Leta (f.) Latin, 'glad'

Letitia (f.) Latin, 'gladness'

Lettice (f.) variant of Letitia (p. 66)

Lettie (f.) variant of Letty

Lettuce (f.) early variant of Letitia (p. 66)

Letty (f.) pet form of Letitia or Violette (p. 66)

Levi (m.) Hebrew, 'united to, joined'

Levy (m.) family name, 'beloved warrior' or a variant of Levi

Lewin (m.) Old English, 'beloved friend'

Lewis (m.) variant of Louis

Lex (m.) pet form of Alex

Leyland (m.) place name/family name, 'untilled land'

Leyton (m.) variant of Layton

Lia (f.) Italian form of Leah

Liam (m.) Irish pet form of William (p. 69)

Lian (f.) pet form of Gillian

Liana (f.) pet form of Juliana, Liliana, etc.

Lianne (f.) pet form of Julianne but re-interpreted as Lee plus Ann in modern times

Libby (f.) also *Libbie*. Pet forms of Elizabeth (p. 44)

Liberty (m., f.) the word used as a name

Libya (f.) Greek, 'rain', name of a character in Greek mythology who gave her name to the country (p. 37)

Liesa (f.) also *Liese*. German pet forms of Elisabeth

Liesl (f.) also *Liesel, Lisel*. Diminutive forms of Liesa

Lila (f.) variant of Leila

Lilac (f.) the flower name (p. 54)

Lilia (f.) Latin, 'lilies'

Lilian (f.) short form of Italian Liliana (Lily)

Lilias (f.) Gaelic form of Lilian

Lilla (f.) pet form of Elizabeth

Lilli (f.) German pet form of Elisabeth

Lillian (f.) variant of Lilian

Lillias (f.) variant of Lilias

Lily (f.) also *Lilly, Lillie*. The name of the flower, or a pet form of Elizabeth (p. 54)

Lincoln (m.) place name/family name, 'Roman colony at the pool' (pp. 3, 9)

Linda (f.) pet form of Belinda, Malinda, etc. Also Spanish 'pretty'. Earliest meaning was Germanic, 'serpent' (pp. 10, 57)

Lindon (m.) variant of Lyndon

Lindsay (m., f.) Scottish place name/family name

Lindsey (f.) variant of Lindsay, usually feminine

Lindy (f.) pet form of Linda

Linnet (f.) the bird name (p. 61)

Linette (f.) variant of Lynette

Linnie (f.) pet form of Caroline, Pauline, etc.

Linsay (f.) also *Linsey*. Variants of Lindsay

Linton (m.) variant of Lynton

Linus (m.) Greek, 'flax' (p. 37)

Lionel (m.) Latin, 'little lion' (p. 5)

Lisa (f.) pet form of Elisabeth (pp. 28, 50)

Lisanne (f.) variant of Lizanne

Lisbeth (f.) pet form of Elisabeth

Lisa-Jane (f.) also *Lisa-Marie*. Popular modern blends of Lisa and Jane, Marie

Lisette (f.) French pet form of Elisabeth

Lister (m.) occupational family name, 'dyer'

Lita (f.) pet form of Roselita, Lolita, etc.

Livingston (m.) also *Livingstone*. Place name/family name (p. 63)

Liz (f.) pet form of Elizabeth

Liza (f.) pet form of Elizabeth

Lizanne (f.) modern blend of Liz (Elizabeth) and Anne

Lizbeth (f.) short form of Elizabeth

Lizzie (f.) also *Lizzey*, *Lizzy*. Pet forms of Elizabeth

Llewellyn (m.) Welsh, based on a word for 'leader'

Llinos (f.) Welsh, 'linnet' (pp. 61, 71)

Lloyd (m.) Welsh, 'grey, holy'

Llyr (m.) Welsh form of Lear (p. 71)

Lois (f.) presumed to be a Greek name but of unknown meaning

Lola (f.) pet form of Dolores

Lolita (f.) diminutive of Lola (Dolores)

Lona (f.) Welsh pet form of Maelona, 'princess' (p. 71)

London (f.) The place name (p. 74)

Lonnie (m.) pet form of Alonzo (p. 65)

Lora (f.) variant of Laura (p. 71)

Loraine (f.) variant of Lorraine

Lord (m.) family name or the word used as a name

Loreen (f.) variant of Laureen

Loren (m.) short form of German Lorenz (Laurence)

Lorena (f.) variant of Laurena, Laurina

Lorene (f.) variant of Laureen

Lorenza (f.) German feminine form of Lorenz (Laurence)

Lorenzo (m.) Spanish/Italian form of Laurence

Loretta (f.) variant of Lauretta, possibly linked with the place name Loretto in Italy

Lorette (f.) variant of Laurette

Lori (f.) pet form of Laura

Lorin (m.) variant of Loren

Lorinda (f.) variant of Laurinda

Loris (f.) form of Lauricia, Roman feminine form of Laurence

Lorna (f.) based on Scottish place name Lorn, which also occurs in Scotland as a first name (p. 18)

Lorraine (f.) French place name, family name

Lot (m.) Hebrew, 'covering' (p. 33)

Lottie (f.) pet form of Charlotte, Charlotta

Lou (m.) pet form of Louis

Lou (f.) pet form of Louise, Louisa

Louann (f.) also *Louanne*. Modern blend of Lou and Ann(e)

Louella (f.) modern blend of Louise and Ella

Louis (m.) French form of Ludwig, a German name 'famous in battle' (pp. 26, 36)

Louisa (f.) Latinized feminine form of Louis (p. 26)

Louise (f.) French feminine form of Louis (pp. 26, 32, 41, 53)

Love (m., f.) the word used as a name or the family name (p. 37)

Loveday (m.) also *Lovie*, *Lovey*. Family names (p. 37)

Lovell (m.) French family name, 'wolf-cub' (p. 5)

Love-well (m., f.) Puritan slogan name (p. 49)

Lowri (f.) Welsh form of Laura (p. 71)

Lucas (m.) short form of Latin Lucanus, 'man from Lucania' (in southern Italy)

Lucetta (f.) also *Lucette*. Diminutives of Lucy

Lucia (f.) Latin feminine of Lucius

Lucian (m.) short form of Latin Lucianus (Lucius)

Lucie (f.) French form of Lucy

Lucien (m.) French form of Lucian

Lucille (f.) French form of Latin Lucilla, diminutive of Lucia (p. 35)

Lucinda (f.) diminutive of Lucia

Lucius (m.) Latin, 'light'

Lucky (f.) also *Luckie, Luck*. The words used as names (pp. 51, 67)

Lucy (f.) English form of Lucia

Ludovic (m.) Latinized form of Ludwig (Louis) (p. 70)

Luke (m.) English form of Lucas (p. ix)

Lulu (f.) pet form of Luçy, Louisa, Louise

Luna (f.) Latin, 'moon' (p. 37)

Lusitania (f.) name of a Roman province (Portugal) and a famous ship (p. 27)

Luther (m.) family name, 'people army'

Lycus (m.) Greek, 'wolf' (p. 37)

Lydia (f.) Greek, 'woman of Lydia' (a region of Asia (p. 49)

Lyle (m.) place name/family name, 'one who lived on an island'

Lyn (f.) variant of Lynne

Lynda (f.) variant of Linda

Lyndon (m.) place name/family name, 'hill with lime trees' (p. 26)

Lyndsay (m., f.) variant of Lindsay

Lynette (f.) French form of Welsh Eiluned, 'idol, icon'

Lynne (f.) also *Lynn*. Pet forms of Carolyn, Marilyn, etc.

Lynsey (f.) variant of Lindsay

Lynwen (f.) Welsh, 'fair image'

M

Mabel (f.) short form of Amabel

Mabelle (f.) French, 'my beautiful one' or variant of Mabel

Mable (f.) variant of Mabel

Macbeth (m.) Gaelic, 'son of Life' (p. 18)

Macon (m.) family name, 'stone-mason' (p. 3)

Madaline (f.) variant of Madeleine

Madeleine (f.) French form of Magdalene

Madeline (f.) English form of Madeleine

Madge (f.) pet form of Margaret

Madine (f.) also *Madyben*. Adaptations of family name Mady (p. 22)

Mae (f.) variant of May

Magdalene (f.) Hebrew, 'woman from Magdala', a town named for its 'tower'
Maggie (f.) pet form of Margaret
Magnolia (f.) the plant name (p. 54)
Magnus (m.) Latin, 'great' (p. 70)
Mahala (f.) also *Mahalia*. Hebrew, 'tenderness'
Mai (f.) Welsh form of May (p. 71)
Maia (f.) Greek, 'mother, midwife' (p. 37)
Maidie (f.) 'Maid' adapted to name use (p. 10)
Mair (f.) Welsh form of Mary (p. 71)
Mairead (f.) Irish form of Margaret (p. 69)
Mairi (f.) Gaelic form of Mary (p. 70)
Mairwen (f.) Welsh, 'beautiful Mary'
Maisie (f.) Scottish pet form of Margery
Maitland (m.) place name/family name
Majella (f.) a reference to St Gerard Majella (p. 69)
Major (m.) the word used as a name, or a use of the family name or military title
Makepeace (m.) Puritan slogan name (p. 4)
Malcolm (m.) Gaelic, 'servant of St Columba' (pp. 36, 70)
Malinda (f.) variant of Melinda
Malvina (f.) Gaelic, 'smooth brow' (p. 70)
Man (m.) the word used as a name (p. 53)
Mandy (f.) also *Mandi, Mandie*. Pet forms of Amanda, Miranda
Manfred (m.) Germanic, 'man-peace' (p. 4)

Manly (m.) English form of Andrew (p. 28)

Manuel (m.) Spanish pet form of Emanuel, Immanuel

Manuela (f.) feminine form of Manuel

Maralyn (f.) variant of Marilyn

Marathon (m.) Greek place name where 'fennel' grew (p. 37)

Marba (m.) the family name Abram spelt backwards (p. 25)

Marc (m.) French form of Mark

Marcel (m.) French form of Latin Marcellus, diminutive of Marcus

Marcella (f.) also *Marcelle*. Feminine forms of Marcellus (Marcus)

Marci (f.) also *Marcie*. Variants of Marcy

Marcia (f.) Latin feminine form of Marcius, a Roman name related to Marcus (p. 8)

Marco (m.) Italian form of Mark

Marcus (m.) Roman name linked with Mars, Roman god of war (p. 8)

Marcy (f.) pet form of Marcia

Mardi (f.) French, 'Tuesday' (p. 50)

Maree (f.) modern variant of Marie

Margaret (f.) Greek, 'pearl' (pp. 14, 15, 36)

Margaretta (f.) variant of Margaret

Margarita (f.) also *Margareta*. Spanish and German forms of Margaret

Margaux (f.) French place name associated with wine (p. 3)

Margery (f.) early form of Margaret

Margot (f.) also *Margo,* which indicates the usual pronunciation of this French form of Margaret (p. 4)

Marguerite (f.) also *Marguerita,* its Latinized form. Flower name or a French form of Margaret

Maria (f.) Latin form of Mary

Marian (f.) English form of Marion

Marianne (f.) French blend of Marie and Anne

Marie (f.) French form of Mary

Marigold (f.) the flower name (p. 54)

Marilyn (f.) probably a blend of Mary and Ellen

Marina (f.) traditionally associated with a Latin word for 'the sea' but probably feminine form of Marinus, itself from Marius (pp. 18, 27)

Mario (m.) Italian form of Marius

Marion (f., m.) French diminutive of Mary (pp. 31, 64)

Marise (f.) also *Marisa, Maris, Marissa.* Latin, 'of the sea' (p. 27)

Marita (f.) Latin, 'married'

Marius (m.) a Roman clan name linked with Mars, god of war

Marjoram (f.) the herb name (p. 12)

Marjorie (f.) spoken form of Marguerite, Margaret

Mark (m.) English form of Marcus (p. 8)

Marlene (f.) also *Marlena*, *Marleen*, *Marline*. Marlene was a blend of Maria and Magdalene in the case of Marlene Dietrich (p. 9)

Marlon (m.) family name (pp. 16, 55)

Marmaduke (m.) Irish, 'servant of St Maedoc' (p. 27)

Marna (f.) also *Marni*, *Marnie*. Forms of Marina

Marquis (m.) title of a nobleman

Mars (m.) Greek, 'to fight'. Name of the Roman god of war (pp. 8, 37)

Marsha (f.) modern form of Marcia

Marshall (m.) also *Marshal*. Family name, 'horse-servant'

Martha (f.) Aramaic, 'mistress of the household' (p. 34)

Martin (m.) Latin diminutive of Mars, god of war

Martina (f.) Latin feminine form of Martin

Martine (f.) French form of Martina

Marty (m.,f.) pet form of Martin or Martha

Martyn (m.) modern variant of Martin

Marvel (m.) the word used as a name (p. 74)

Mary (f.) English form of Maria, itself the Greek form of Miriam

Mary-Ann (f.) also *Mary-Anne*. Popular modern blends of Mary and Ann(e)

Marybeth (f.) also *Maryjan*, *Marykay*, *Marylynn*, *Marypat*, *Maryrose*, *Marysue*. Series of blended names used by the same family (p. 42)

Mason (m.) occupational family name, 'stone mason'

Matilda (f.) Germanic, 'mighty in battle' (p. 26)

Matthew (m.) also *Mathew*. Hebrew, 'Jehovah has given' (p. 55)

Matthias (m.) Greek and Latin form of Matthew

Maud (f.) also *Maude*. Short forms of Matilda (pp. 30, 53)

Maura (f.) variant of Moira (p. 69)

Maureen (f.) Irish diminutive of Mary (p. 9)

Maurice (m.) Latin, 'Moorish, dark-skinned' (p. 14)

Mavis (f.) poetical word for the song-thrush (p. 61)

Max (m.) pet form of Maximillian (p. 64)

Maxine (f.) also *Maxene*, *Maxeen*, *Maxina*, *Maxena*. Modern feminine forms of Max, and not to be confused with Maxime, a male name used in France

Maxwell (m.) Scottish place name/family name, 'Maccus's well' (p. 70)

May (f.) pet form of Mary, Margaret, etc. or the name of the month (pp. 8, 64, 72)

Meagan (f.) also *Meaghan*. US variants of Megan

Meda (f.) also *Medea*. Greek, 'cunning' (p. 37)

Medi (f.) Welsh, 'September' (p. 71)

Medina (f.) river name (p. 60)

Meg (f.) pet form of Margaret

Megan (f.) Welsh pet form of Margaret (pp. 55, 70, 71)

Meghan (f.) variant of Megan, apparently used to give it an Irish look

Meironwen (f.) also *Meirionwen*. Welsh, 'white dairymaid' (p. 71)

Mel (m., f.) pet forms of names beginning with Mel-

Melanie (f.) Greek, 'black, dark-complexioned' (pp. 9, 14, 18)

Melech (m.) Hebrew, 'king' (p. 6)

Melfyn (m.) Welsh variant of Mervyn (p. 71)

Melia (f.) pet form of Amelia, or Greek, 'ash tree' (p. 37)

Melina (f.) Greek, 'honey', or pet form of Emmelina (p. 24)

Melinda (f.) Latin, 'honey', plus a diminutive ending (p. 24)

Melissa (f.) Greek, 'bee' (pp. 24, 54, 72)

Melita (f.) Greek, 'honey', or Latin, 'island of Malta' (p. 24)

Melody (f.) also *Melodie*. The word used as a name (p. 40)

Melonie (f.) also *Melony*. Variants of Melanie

Melville (m.) French place name/family name

Melvin (m.) also *Melvyn*. Scottish place name/family name

Menna (f.) ancient Welsh name of unknown meaning (p. 71)

Mentor (m.) Greek, 'to stay, abide' (p. 37)

Mercedes (f.) Spanish, 'mercies' (p. 3)

Mercury (m.) Latin, 'reward, payment' (p. 37)

Mercy (f.) the word used as a name (pp. 15, 30, 62)

Meredith (m., f.) Welsh, 'great chief'

Mererid (f.) Welsh form of Margaret (p. 71)

Meriel (f.) variant of Muriel (p. 71)

Merle (f.) French, 'blackbird' (pp. 9, 61)

Merlin (m., f.) the bird name or variant of Mervyn (p. 61)

Merrick (m.) Welsh form of Maurice

Merry (f.) pet form of Mercy or the word used as a name or a use of the family name (pp. 30, 35)

Mervyn (m.) also *Mervin*. Welsh, 'from Carmarthen'

Meryl (f.) also *Merrill*. Variants of Muriel

Meshach (m.) a biblical name of unknown meaning (p. 16)

Mestor (m.) Greek, 'counsellor' (p. 37)

Metis (f.) Greek, 'thought, counsel' (p. 37)

Mia (f.) Spanish/Italian, 'my' as used in phrases like *Cara mia* 'my dear'

Michael (m.) Hebrew, 'who is like God' (pp. 31, 32, 49)

Michaela (f.) feminine form of Michael

Michaelmas (m.) a name given to boys born on 29 September (p. 51)

Michèle (f.) French feminine form of Michel (Michael)

Michelle (f.) variant of Michèle (p. 41)

Mick (m.) pet form of Michael

Midas (m.) possibly Greek, 'seed' (p. 37)

Miguel (m.) Spanish form of Michael

Mike (m.) pet form of Michael

Milcah (f.) Hebrew, 'queen' (p. 6)

Mildred (f.) Old English, 'mild-strength'

Miles (m.) perhaps Germanic, 'generous', or pet form of Emile

Millard (m.) occupational family name, 'mill-keeper' (p. 44)

Millicent (f.) Germanic, 'noble-strength'

Millie (f.) also *Milly*. Pet forms of Mildred, Millicent, Amelia, Emily

Milo (m.) form of Miles used in Ireland

Milton (m.) place name/family name, 'settlement near a mill'

Mimi (f.) pet form of Mary and other names beginning with M- (p. 35)

Mimosa (f.) the flower name (p. 54)

Minerva (f.) Latin, 'mind', name of Roman goddess of wisdom (p. 37)

Mink (f.) the word used as a name (p. 40)

Minnie (f.) pet form of Wilhelmina (p. 36)

Mira (f.) variant of Myra

Mirabel (f.) Latin, 'wonderful'

Miranda (f.) Latin, 'fit to be admired' (p. 18)

Miriam (f.) Hebrew, of disputed origin, perhaps 'seeress' or 'lady' (p. 34)

Misty (f.) the word used as a name (p. 59)

Mitchell (m.) family name linked with Michael

Mitzi (f.) German pet form of Maria

Modesty (f.) the word used as a name

Modestine (f.) also *Modestina*. Diminutives of Latin Modesta, itself the feminine of Modestus, 'modest'

Mohammed (m.) Arabic, 'greatly praised'

Moira (f.) phonetic form of Irish Maire (Mary)

Molly (f.) also *Mollie*. Pet forms of Mary (p. 64)

Momus (m.) Greek, 'blame, censure' (p. 37)

Mona (f.) Irish, 'noble' or pet form of Monica (p. 28)

Monday (f.) the day name (p. 50)

Monica (f.) language of origin and meaning unknown

Monique (f.) French form of Monica (p. 55)

Monsieur (m.) French, 'Mister' (p. 74)

Montague (m.) French place name/family name

Monty (m.) pet form of Montagu(e), though associated with Field Marshal Lord Montgomery

Morag (f.) Gaelic, 'great' (p. 70)

Moreen (f.) variant of Maureen

Morgan (m.) Welsh, 'great and bright' (pp. 3, 71)

Morleena (f.) a name invented by Charles Dickens (p. 21)

Morna (f.) Gaelic, 'beloved' (p. 70)

Morris (m.) variant of Maurice (p. 3)

Mortimer (m.) French place name/family name, 'dead water' (p. 39)

Morton (m.) place name/family name, 'village on a moor'

Morven (f.) Gaelic, 'big mountain peak' (p. 70)

Morwenna (f.) Welsh, 'maiden'

Moses (m.) Egyptian, 'son' (p. 33)

Mousie (f.) 'little mouse' (p. 5)

Muirne (f.) Irish form of Morna (p. 69)

Mungo (m.) Gaelic, 'amiable' (p. 70)

Murdoch (m.) also *Murdo*. Gaelic, 'mariner, sea-warrior' (pp. 27, 70)

Muriel (f.) Irish, 'sea-bright' (pp. 27, 50)

Murray (m.) Scottish place name/family name, 'from Moray' (p. 70)

Myfanwy (f.) Welsh, 'my fine one' (p. 71)

Myles (m.) common variant of Miles. In Greek mythology derived from Greek, 'mill' (p. 37)

Myra (f.) probably a feminine form of Myron (p. 13)

Myrna (f.) Gaelic, 'beloved, gentle' (p. 9)

Myron (m.) Greek, 'sweet-smelling oil' (p. 13)

Myrtle (f.) the plant name (p. 54)

Mystic (m.) the word used as a name (p. 74)

N

Nadia (f.) also *Nada*. Russian, 'hope' (p. 62)

Nadine (f.) French diminutive of Nadia

Naiogabui (f.) Fijian, 'she who smells sweetly' (p. 13)

Nan (f.) pet form of Ann(e)

Nancy (f.) also *Nanci*, *Nancie*. Pet forms of Ann(e) (p. 64)

Nanette (f.) diminutive of Nan

Naomi (f.) Hebrew, 'my gracious one, my sweetness' (p. 34)

Narcissus (m.) Greek, 'benumbed' (p. 37)

Narelle (f.) appears to be a trade name (of a perfume). Used almost exclusively in Australia

Nat (m.) pet form of Nathan, Nathaniel

Natalie (f.) Latin, 'birth' [of the Lord, i.e. Christmas Day] (p. 44)

Natasha (f.) Russian form of Natalie (p. 44)

Nathalie (f.) French form of Natalie

Nathan (m.) Hebrew, 'Jehovah has given' (p. 44)

Nathaniel (m.) also *Nathanael.* Hebrew, 'God has given' (p. 33)

Neal (m.) also *Neale.* Variants of Neil

Nebuchadnezzar (m.) Accadian, 'Nabu, protect the son!' (p. 33)

Ned (m.) pet form of Edward, Edmond, etc.

Neil (m.) Irish, 'champion'

Neilson (m.) family name 'son of Neil'

Nell (f.) pet form of Helen, Eleanor (p. 36)

Nellie (f.) also *Nelly.* Diminutives of Nell

Nelson (m.) family name, 'son of Neil' (p. 27)

Nereus (m.) Greek, 'the watery one' (p. 37)

Nerissa (f.) Greek, 'sea nymph'

Nerys (f.) Welsh feminine of 'lord' (pp. 28, 71)

Nessie (f.) pet form of Agnes (p. 69)

Nesta (f.) Welsh pet form of Agnes (p. 71)

Nestor (m.) Greek, 'he who brings back safely' (p. 37)

Nevada (f.) Spanish, 'snowed upon', but usually from the US state (p. 59)

Neville (m.) also *Nevil.* Norman place name/family name, 'new town' (p. 39)

Newman (m.) family name, 'newcomer to a district'

Newton (m.) place name/family name, 'new settlement' (p. 64)

Nia (f.) a legendary name of unknown meaning (p. 71)

Niall (m.) Irish form of Neil (p. 69)

Niamh (f.) Irish, 'bright' (p. 69)

Nichola (f.) variant of Nicola

Nicholas (m.) Greek, 'victorious people' (p. 48)

Nick (m.) pet form of Nicholas

Nicki (f.) also *Nickie*. Pet forms of Nicole, Nicola

Nickolas (m.) modern variant of Nicholas

Nicky (f.) variant of Nicki

Nicodemus (m.) Greek, 'victorious people' (p. 48)

Nicol (m.) early form of Nicholas

Nicola (f.) Italian form of Nicholas, used as a feminine name in Britain (p. 48)

Nicole (f.) French feminine form of Nicholas (p. 48)

Nicoletta (f.) Italian diminutive of Nicola

Nicolette (f.) French form of Nicoletta

Niel (m.) variant of Neil

Nigel (m.) diminutive of Latin form of Neil i.e. Nigellus (p. 14)

Nigella (f.) the flower name (p. 54)

Nikki (f.) pet form of Nicola, Nicole

Nikola (f.) variant of Nicola

Nina (f.) pet form of Antonina, Janina, etc.

Ninel (m.) 'Lenin' spelt backwards (p. 58)

Ninette (f.) also *Ninetta*. Diminutive forms of Nina

Ninian (m.) Scottish saint's name of unknown meaning (p. 20)

Ninny (m.) pet form of Ninian (p. 20)

Niobe (f.) Greek, 'young' (p. 37)

Nita (f.) pet form of Anita, Juanita, Benita, etc.

Noah (m.) Hebrew, 'rest' (p. 33)

Noble (m.) the word or family name used as a first name (p. 28)

Nocturna (f.) feminine of Latin Nocturnus, 'night' (p. 52)

Noel (m.) French, 'Christmas' (pp. 44, 72)

Noelle (f.) also *Noella*. French and Latin feminine forms of Noel (p. 44)

Nola (f.) pet form of Finola

Nolan (m.) Irish, 'famous'

Nona (f.) feminine of Latin *nonus*, 'ninth' (p. 43)

Nora (f.) also *Norah*. Pet forms of Eleanora, Honora, etc. (p. 53)

Norbert (m.) Germanic, 'famous in the north'

Noreen (f.) diminutive of Nora

Norma (f.) Latin, 'pattern, model'

Norman (m.) Old English, 'Norwegian'

Norrie (m.) pet form of Norman, Norris

Norris (m.) family name, 'Northerner' or 'nurse' (p. 27)

Nova (f.) Latin, 'new' (p. 9)

Nuala (f.) pet form of Irish Fionnuala, 'white shoulder' (p. 69)

Nye (m.) pet form of Aneurin

Nyree (f.) phonetic form of Maori Ngaire, of unknown meaning.

Nyx (f.) Greek, 'night' (p. 37)

O

Obedience (m., f.) the word used as a name (by the Puritans) (p. 62)

Oberon (m.) variant of Auberon

Ocean (m.) also Latin *Oceanus*. The word used as a name for a child born at sea (p. 27)

Octave (m., f.) French male form of Octavius, but used for girls (p. 42)

Octavia (f.) Latin feminine of Octavius (pp. 9, 35, 42, 43)

Octavius (m.) famous Roman clan name based on Latin *octavus* 'eighth' (p. 43)

Odalia (f.) also *Odelia*. Variants of Odile (p. 42)

Odelin (m.) Germanic, 'richness' (p. 42)

Odell (m.) place name/family name, 'woad hill'

Odette (f.) French feminine of Odo

Odile (f.) French feminine diminutive of Odo (p. 42)

Odo (m.) variant of Otto

Oedipus (m.) Greek, 'swollen foot' (p. 37)

Ogden (m.) place name/family name, 'oak valley'

Olaf (m.) also *Olave*. Old Norse, 'forefather, ancestor'

Olevia (f.) variant of Olivia (p. 44)

Olga (f.) Russian, 'holy'

Olite (f.) pet form of Carmelite, Carmelita (p. 42)

Olive (f.) the tree name, also symbolic of 'peace' (pp. 4, 14, 26, 42)

Oliver (m.) possibly a variant of Olave or Germanic, 'elf-host' (p. 42)

Olivia (f.) Italian form of Olive (pp. 4, 9, 17, 18, 26, 42)

Olivier (m.) French form of Oliver

Olus (m.) Greek, 'sleep-destroying' (p. 37)

Olwen (f.) Welsh, 'white footprint' (p. 71)

Omar (m.) Hebrew, 'eloquent'

Omega (f.) last letter of Greek alphabet, symbolically 'the end' (p. 68)

Omra (f.) name of a ship (p. 27)

Ona (f.) pet form of Leona, Ilona, Mona, etc.

Onesia (f.) an invented name with no particular meaning (p. 42)

Onyx (m.) the precious stone (p. 16)

Oonagh (f.) Irish form of Una

Opal (f.) the jewel name (pp. 15, 25)

Ophelia (f.) Greek, 'help, aid' (pp. 18, 42, 53)

Opta (f.) short form of Optata, a saint's name, possibly Latin 'wished for' (p. 42)

Ora (f.) pet form of Cora, Dora, Nora or Latin, 'pray'

Oran (m.) Irish, 'green' (p. 14)

Orange (m.) the word used as a name (p. 7)

Orchard (f.) English form of Carmel (p. 25)

Oriana (f.) Latin, 'sunrise' (p. 51)

Oriel (f.) probably Germanic, 'fire-strife'

Orion (m.) Greek, 'mountain' (p. 37)

Orla (f.) Irish, 'golden lady' (p. 69)

Orlando (m.) Italian form of Roland

Ormes (m.) family name linked with 'snake, dragon' (p. 42)

Ormonde (m.) Irish family name, 'red' (p. 14)

Orpheus (m.) Greek, 'darkness, night' (p. 37)

Orson (m.) French, 'bear' (p. 5)

Orwell (m.) place name/family name and river name (p. 60)

Osbert (m.) Old English, 'god-bright'

Osborn (m.) also *Osborne*. Old English, 'god-bear'

Oscar (m.) Old English, 'god-spear' (p. 29)

Osla (f.) Old Norse, 'god consecrated' (p. 70)

Osmond (m.) Old English, 'god-protector'

Oswald (m.) Old English, 'god-power'

Othello (m.) a name invented by Shakespeare (p. 18)

Otho (m.) variant of Otto

Otis (m.) family name linked with Otto

Otto (m.) Germanic, 'possessions' (pp. 24, 25, 42)

Ovide (f.) Latin, 'sheep' (p. 42)

Owain (m.) Welsh form of Owen (p. 71)

Owen (m.) ultimately from Greek *eugenes*, 'well-born'

P

Packard (m.) French family name, 'peasant' (p. 3)

Paddy (m.) pet form of Patrick

Padraig (m.) Irish form of Patrick (p. 69)

Paige (f.) also *Page*. Family name indicating one who was a 'page'

Pallas (m.) Greek, 'young man' (p. 37)

Palm (f.) for a child born on Palm Sunday (p. 44)

Pamela (f.) probably Greek, 'all honey or sweetness' (p. 24)

Pan (m.) Greek, 'all' (p. 37)

Pandarus (m.) Greek, 'he who flays all' (p. 37)

Pandora (f.) Greek, 'all giving' (p. 37)

Pansy (f.) the flower name (p. 54)

Paris (m.) family name, usually linked with Patrice (Patrick) (p. 37)

Parker (m.) occupational family name, 'keeper of a park'

Parry (m.) Welsh family name, 'son of Harry'

Parthenia (f.) Greek, 'maid' (p. 46)

Parthenope (f.) Greek, 'maiden face' (p. 38)

Pascal (m.) French, 'Easter child' (p. 44)

Pascale (f.) French feminine form of Pascal (p. 44)

Passion (f.) the word (in its religious sense) used as a name (p. 74)

Pat (m, f.) pet form of Patrick, Patricia (p. 32)

Patience (f.) the word used as a name (p. 62)

Patina (f.) blend of Patricia and Tina (p. 21)

Patrice (f.) French form of Patricia (p. 55)

Patricia (f.) Latin feminine of Patricius, 'noble' (p. 21)

Patrick (m.) English form of Latin Patricius, 'noble' (p. 69)

Patsy (f.) pet form of Patricia

Patti (f.) pet form of Patricia

Paul (m.) Latin, 'small' (p. 72)

Paula (f.) Latin feminine of Paulus, 'small'

Paulette (f.) French diminutive of Paul

Paulina (f.) Latin feminine of Paulinus, diminutive of Paulus (Paul)

Pauline (f.) French form of Paulina

Peace (f.) also *Peaceable*. The words used as names (p. 4)

Peach (f.) the word used as a name (p. 7)

Pearce (m.) family name linked with Peter

Pearl (f.) the word used as a name (p. 15)

Pearline (f.) diminutive of Pearl

Pedro (m.) Spanish form of Peter

Peggy (f.) also *Peggie*. Pet forms of Margaret via Meggy, Meggie

Pelham (m.) place name/family name, 'Peola's residence'

Penelope (f.) Greek, 'bobbin' (pp. 19, 37, 44, 64)

Penny (f.) also *Pennie*. Pet forms of Penelope (pp. 19, 64)

Pepita (f.) diminutive of Italian Giuseppa (Josephine)

Percival (m.) French, perhaps 'one who pierces the vale [i.e. breaks through into the valley]'

Percy (m.) Norman place name/family name (p. 39)

Perdita (f.) Latin, 'lost' (p. 18)

Peregrine (m.) Latin, 'traveller, stranger, pilgrim' (p. 3)

Perry (m.) pet form of Peregrine or the family name, 'one who lived near a pear tree' (pp. 3, 60)

Persephone (f.) Greek, 'bringer of death' (p. 37)

Perseus (m.) Greek, 'I will destroy' (p. 37)

Perseverance (f.) the word used as a name (by the Puritans) (p. 62)

Peta (f.) modern feminine form of Peter

Pete (m.) pet form of Peter (p. 71)

Peter (m.) Greek, 'stone, rock' (pp. 28, 55)

Petra (f.) Latin feminine of Peter

Petrice (f.) also *Petrina*. Modern feminine forms of Peter

Petronella (f.) Latin feminine of Petronius, a Roman clan name

Petula (f.) Latin, 'sauciness' (p. 22)

Phaedra (f.) Greek, 'bright' (p. 37)

Pheasant (f.) the bird name (p. 61)

Phelan (m.) Irish family name, 'wolf' (p. 5)

Phil (m.) pet form of Philip

Philip (m.) Greek, 'fond of horses' (pp. 5, 14)

Philippa (f.) feminine form of Philip (p. 5)

Philippe (m.) French form of Philip

Phillip (m.) also *Phillippa (f.)*. Common variants of Philip and Philippa

Phillis (f.) variant of Phyllis

Philomela (f.) Greek, 'sweet song' (p. 37)

Philomena (f.) Greek, 'beloved'

Phineas (m.) Hebrew form of an Egyptian name, 'the black one' (p. 33)

Phineus (m.) variant of Phineas (p. 37)

Phocas (m.) Greek, 'seal' (p. 57)

Phoebe (f.) Greek, 'pure, bright' (pp. 18, 37, 64)

Phoenix (m.) Greek, 'blood red' (p. 37)

Phyllida (f.) variant of Phyllis

Phyllis (f.) Greek, 'foliage, leafy branch' (p. 37)

Pi (f.) Greek letter used as mathematical symbol (p. 68)

Pierce (m.) family name linked with Peter

Pierre (m.) French form of Peter

Piers (m.) early form of Peter (English form of French Pierre)

Piety (f.) the word used as a name (p. 63)

Piper (f.) occupational family name (p. 34)

Pippa (f.) pet form of Philippa

Pixie (f.) the word used as a name

Placido (m.) Spanish, 'peaceful' (p. 4)

Pleasance (f.) also *Pleasant*. The words used as names (p. 15)

Pluto (m.) Greek, 'wealth' (p. 37)

Polly (f.) pet form of Mary *via* Mally (p. 60)

Pomona (f.) Latin, 'fruit, apple' (p. 7)

Poppy (f.) the flower name (p. 54)

Portia (f.) Latin feminine of Porcius, a Roman clan name of unknown meaning (pp. 3, 18)

Precious (m., f.) the word used as a name (p. 15)

Preston (m.) place name/family name, 'priest's settlement'

Priam (m.) Greek, 'I buy' (p. 37)

Price (m.) Welsh family name, 'son of Rhys'

Prima (f.) also *Primitiva*, feminine of Primitivus. Latin, 'first' (p. 43)

Primrose (f.) the flower name or family name (p. 54)

Primula (f.) the flower name (pp. 43, 54)

Primus (m.) Latin, 'first' (p. 43)

Prince (m.) the word or family name used as a first name (p. 6)

Princess (f.) the word used as a name (p. 6)

Princeton (m.) American place name (p. 52)

Priscilla (f.) Latin feminine diminutive of *priscus*, 'old, primitive'

Providence (m., f.) the word used as a name (by the Puritans) (p. 63)

Prudence (f.) the word used as a name (p. 62)

Prue (f.) pet form of Prudence, Prunella

Prunella (f.) Latin, 'little plum'

Pryce (m.) variant of Price

Pyramus (m.) possibly Greek, meaning a kind of cake (p. 37)

Q

Quartina (f.) Latin feminine of Quartinus, 'fourth' (p. 43)

Quasimodo (m.) for a child born on Quasimodo Sunday (p. 44)

Queen (f.) the word used as a name. Also adapted as *Queena*, *Queenette* (p. 6)

Queenie (f.) the word 'queen' adapted to first name use (p. 6)

Quentin (m.) variant of Quintin

Quiana (f.) variant of Kiana

Quince (f.) the fruit name (p. 53)

Quincy (m., f.) French place name/family name,

'estate belonging to Quintus' (p. 44)

Quinta (f.) Latin feminine of Quintus 'fifth child' (p. 43)

Quintin (m.) Latin diminutive of Quintus, 'fifth'

Qupid (m.) fanciful variant of Cupid (p. 74)

R

Rab (m.) Scottish pet form of Robert

Rabbie (m.) diminutive of Rab

Rachel (f.) Hebrew, 'sheep' (pp. 5, 34, 73)

Rachelle (f.) modern variant of Rachel

Rae (f.) pet form of Rachel

Raelene (f.) Australian diminutive of Rae

Raina (f.) Russian form of Regina (pp. 6, 58)

Rainbow (f.) the word used as a name (p. 59)

Raine (f.) variant of Raina (p. 58)

Ralph (m.) Old Norse, 'wolf-counsel' (p. 5)

Ralphina (f.) also *Ralphine*. Feminine forms of Ralph

Ralston (m.) place name/family name, 'Hroaldr's settlement'

Ramon (m.) Spanish form of Raymond

Ramona (f.) feminine form of Ramon

Ramsay (m.) place name/family name (p. 70)

Ramsden (m.) place name/family name, 'valley with rams'

Randal (m.) also *Randall*. Family name linked with Randolph (p. 55)

Randi (f.) pet form of Miranda used in US only
Randolph (m.) Old English, 'shield-wolf' (p. 5)
Randy (m.) pet form of Randolph, Randal(l)
Raoul (m.) French form of Ralph
Raper (m.) family name, a variant of Roper, 'rope-maker/seller' (p. 74)
Raquel (f.) Spanish form of Rachel
Rashida (f.) Turkish, 'rightly guided'
Raul (m.) Spanish form of Ralph
Raven (f.) the bird name
Rawdon (m.) place name/family name, 'rough hill'
Ray (m.) pet form of Raymond (p. 60)
Raye (f.) variant of Rae
Raymond (m.) Germanic, 'counsel-protection' (p.55)
Raymonde (f.) French feminine form of Raymond
Rayner (m.) family name, Germanic, 'mighty army'
Rea (f.) pet form of Andrea
Rebecca (f.) Hebrew 'cow' (pp. 20, 34, 53, 55, 74)
Rebekah (f.) form of Rebecca used in Authorized Version of the Bible
Reece (m.) variant of Rhys
Rees (m.) also *Reese*. Variants of Rhys
Reg (m.) pet form of Reginald
Regan (m.) Irish family name, 'descendant of

the little king'. Shakespeare has a female character of this name (p. 18)

Reggie (m.) diminutive of Reg

Regina (f.) Latin, 'queen' (pp. 6, 58)

Reginald (f.) Old English, 'counsel-power' (p. 55)

Regine (f.) French form of Regina (p. 6)

Reid (m.) variant of Reed

Reine (f.) French, 'queen' (p. 6)

Remus (m.) Latin, 'of Rome' (p. 37)

Rena (f.) pet form of Irena, Serena, etc.

Renata (f.) Latin, 're-born'

Rene (f.) pet form of Irene

René (m.) French, 're-born'

Renée (f.) feminine form of René

Repeat (m.) the word used as a name (for a twin brother of Pete) (p. 71)

Repentance (m., f.) the word used as a name (by the Puritans) (p. 62)

Rere (f.) the note in the musical scale reduplicated (p. 35)

Reuben (m.) Hebrew, 'He has seen my misery' (p. 33)

Revilo (m.) 'Oliver', spelt backwards (p. 25)

Rex (m.) Latin, 'king' (p. 5)

Reynold (m.) early form of Reginald

Rhea (f.) Greek, 'earth' (p. 37)

Rhian (f.) also *Rhiain*. Welsh, 'maiden' (pp. 10, 71)

Rhiannon (f.) Welsh, 'nymph, goddess' (p. 71)

Rhoda (f.) Greek, 'rose' (p. 54)
Rhodri (m.) Welsh, 'circle-ruler' (p. 71)
Rhona (f.) Scottish place name, 'rough isle' (p. 70)
Rhonda (f.) Welsh river and place name
Rhonwen (f.) Welsh, 'fair lance'
Rhydian (m.) early Welsh saint's name of unknown meaning (p. 71)
Rhys (m.) Welsh, 'ardour' (p. 71)
Ria (f.) pet form of Maria, Victoria, etc.
Rica (f.) pet form of Erica
Ricardo (m.) Spanish form of Richard
Richard (m.) Germanic, 'ruler-hard' (p. 36)
Richie (m.) Scottish pet form of Richard
Richmond (m.) French place name/family name, 'hill richly covered in vegetation'
Rick (m.) pet form of Richard or Derrick
Ricki (f.) also *Rickie, Rikki, Rikky*. Pet forms of Erica, Frederica, etc.
Ricky (m.) pet form of Richard or Derrick
Rika (f.) pet form of Erica/Erika
Riley (m.) Irish family name, 'valiant' (p. 3)
Rita (f.) pet form of Margarita, Dorita, etc.
Roald (m.) Scandinavian, 'fame-power'
Rob (m.) also *Robb*. Pet forms of Robert (p. 47)
Robbie (m.) Scottish diminutive of Rob(b)
Robbin (f.) variant of Robin
Robena (f.) variant of Robina (p. 61)

Robert (m.) Old English, 'fame-bright' (pp. 20, 47, 61, 63, 65)

Roberta (f.) feminine form of Robert (p. 13)

Roberto (m.) Spanish/Italian form of Robert

Robin (m., f.) pet form of Robert or the name of the bird (pp. 32, 50, 61)

Robina (f.) also *Robinetta*. Diminutives of Robin, emphasizing that it is a girl's name (p. 61)

Robinson (m.) family name, 'son of Robert'

Robson (m.) variant of Robinson

Robyn (f.) variant of Robin (p. 61)

Rocco (m.) Italian form of Germanic name, 'repose'

Rochelle (f.) place name, 'little rock' (p. 16)

Rock (m.) also *Rocky*. The words used as names (p. 28)

Rod (m.) also *Roddy*. Pet forms of Rodney, Roderick

Roderick (m.) Germanic, 'fame-rule' (p. 70)

Rodger (m.) family name linked with Roger

Rodney (m.) place name/family name (p. 27)

Rodrigo (m.) Spanish form of Roderick

Roger (m.) Germanic, 'fame-spear' (p. 29)

Rohan (m.) Irish family name, 'red'

Róisín (f.) Irish diminutive of Rois (Rose) (p. 69)

Roland (m.) Germanic, 'famous land'

Rolf (m.) Scandinavian form of Rudolph

Rollo (m.) pet form of Roland, Rudolph or Ralph
Roma (f.) Italian place name (Rome)
Romany (m.) name of the gypsy language
Romeo (m.) Latin, 'pilgrim to Rome' (pp. 8, 18, 71)
Romy (f.) pet form of Rosemarie
Ron (m.) pet form of Ronald
Ronaele (f.) 'Eleanor' spelt backwards (p. 58)
Ronald (m.) Old Norse, 'counsel-power' (pp. 14, 56)
Ronan (m.) Irish, 'little seal' (pp 65, 69)
Ronnie (m.) pet form of Ronald (p. 65)
Ronnoc (m.) 'Connor' spelt backwards (p. 25)
Roosevelt (m.) family name, 'one who lived near a rose-field' (p. 55)
Rory (m.) Gaelic, 'red' (pp. 14, 70)
Rosa (f.) Latin, 'rose'
Rosabella (f.) Latin, 'beautiful rose'
Rosalee (f.) variants of Rosalie
Rosaleen (f.) Irish diminutive of Rosa
Rosalie (f.) French form of Latin Rosalia, diminutive of Rosa
Rosalind (f.) fanciful variant of Rosa (p. 18)
Rosaline (f.) variant of Rosalind
Rosalyn (f.) modern variant of Rosaline
Rosamond (f.) US variant of Rosamund
Rosamund (f.) possibly Germanic, 'fame-protection' but normally interpreted as Latin, 'rose of the world'

Rosanna (f.) also *Rosana*. Blend of Rose and Anna

Rosanne (f.) also *Roseann*, *Roseanne*. Often written Rose Ann, Rose Anne, and a blend of those two names

Rose (f.) the flower name (pp. 42, 54, 63)

Rosemary (f.) also *Rosemarie*. Identified with the flower, but probably from Latin *ros marinus*, 'dew of the sea' (pp. 12, 54)

Rosetta (f.) 'little rose' (p. 34)

Rosheen (f.) English form of Irish Róisín

Roshelle (f.) variant of Rochelle

Rosie (f.) pet form of Rose or Rosa

Rosina (f.) Italian diminutive of Rosa

Rosita (f.) Spanish diminutive of Rosa

Roslyn (f.) modern variant of Rosaline

Ross (m.) Scottish place name/family name, 'cape, promontory' (p. 70)

Rossini (m.) family name of the Italian composer linked with 'red' (p. 34)

Rosslyn (f.) Scottish place name

Rowan (m.) Irish, 'red' (pp. 14, 70)

Rowena (f.) probably a variant of Rhonwen

Rowland (m.) variant of Roland

Roxana (f.) Latin form of a Persian name, 'dawn' (p. 51)

Roy (m.) Gaelic, 'red', or pet form of Elroy, Leroy where it means 'king' (pp 5, 14)

Royal (m.) the word or family name used as a

first name (p. 7)

Royalyn (f.) also Royalene. 'Royal' adapted to name use (p. 7)

Royston (m.) place name/family name

Rubina (f.) feminine form of Reuben or diminutive of Ruby

Ruby (f.) the word used as a name (pp. 14, 15, 31)

Rudi (m.) pet form of Rudolph

Rudolph (m.) also *Rudolf*. Germanic, 'fame-wolf' (p. 5)

Rufus (m.) Latin, 'red-haired' (p. 14)

Rupert (m.) Germanic form of Robert (p. 47)

Russell (m.) also *Russel*. French family name, 'man with red face or hair' (pp. 14, 39)

Rusty (m.) the word used as a name, usually for someone with red hair

Ruth (f.) Hebrew, 'friend, companion' (pp. 14, 34, 44)

Ruthie (f.) pet form of Ruth

Ryan (m.) Irish family name of unknown meaning

S

S (m.) the letter used as a name (p. 12)

Sabrina (f.) Roman name of the River Severn (p. 60)

Sacha (m.) Russian pet form of Alexander

Sadie (f.) pet form of Sarah

Saffron (f.) the flower name (p. 54)

Sally (f.) also *Sallie*. Pet forms of Sarah

Sally-Ann (f.) also *Sally-Anne*. Blends of Sally and Ann(e)

Salmon (m.) Hebrew, possibly 'garment' (p. 65)

Salome (f.) Hebrew, 'peace' (pp. 4, 34)

Salvatore (m.) Latin, 'one who saves'

Sam (m.) pet form of Samuel

Samantha (f.) feminine form of Samuel (p. 9)

Same (m.) possibly Sam(my) was meant, or the word used as a name (p. 74)

Sammy (m.) pet form of Samuel

Samson (m.) also *Sampson*. Hebrew, 'sun' (p. 59)

Samuel (m.) Hebrew, 'name of God'

Sandie (f.) pet form of Sandra

Sandra (f.) pet form of Italian Alessandra (Alexandra)

Sandy (m., f.) pet form of Alexander or Sandra

Sapphire (f.) the jewel name (p. 14)

Sara (f.) variant of Sarah (p. 6)

Sarah (f.) Hebrew, 'princess' (pp 6, 34, 44, 73)

Sarah-Jane (f.) popular modern blend of Sarah and Jane

Sardina (f.) Italian, 'sardine' (p. 65)

Sasha (m.) variant of Sacha

Saul (m.) Hebrew, 'asked for (from God)' (p. 33)

Saundra (f.) US variant of Sandra

Saxon (m., f.) family name

Scarlet (f.) also *Scarlett*. Family name, 'maker of scarlet cloth' (p. 14)

Scott (m.) also *Scot*. Family name, 'a Scot' (pp. 11, 50, 55)

Seaborne (m.) for a child born at sea, though in this form the name means 'carried by the sea' (p. 27)

Seamus (m.) Irish form of James (p. 69)

Sean (m.) Irish form of John (p. 69)

Search-the-Scriptures (m.) Puritan slogan name (p. 49)

Sebastian (m.) Latin, 'man from Sebastia (a city in Asia Minor)'

Sebert (m.) Old English, 'sea-bright'

Secunda (f.) Latin feminine of Secundus, 'second child' (p. 43)

Sefton (m.) place name/family name, 'settlement in the rushes'

Selena (f.) also *Selina*. Variants of Selene

Selene (f.) Greek, 'bright light', name of a moon goddess (p. 37)

Selma (f.) pet form of Anselma

Selwyn (m.) English form of Latin Silvanus, 'of the woods, savage, wild'

Senga (f.) Agnes spelt backwards (pp. 57, 70)

Seonaid (f.) Gaelic form of Janet

September (f.) the name of the month

Septima (f.) Latin feminine of Septimus, 'seventh child' (p. 43)

Serena (f.) Latin, 'calm' (p. 67)

Serge (m.) also *Sergio*, *Sergei*. French, Italian and Russian forms of Latin Sergius, a Roman clan name, 'servant'

Seth (m.) Hebrew, 'God has raised up' (p. 33)

Seumas (m.) variant of Seamus

Seward (m.) family name, 'sea-guardian' or 'sea victory' (p. 27)

Sexta (f.) Latin feminine of Sextus, 'sixth child' (p. 43)

Seymour (m.) place name/family name

Shadrach (m.) biblical name of unknown meaning

Shafaye (f.) also *Shalinda*, *Shalisa*, *Shalyn*, etc. Names which make use of a fashionable Sha-prefix, much favoured by black American families in the 1980s

Shamus (m.) variant of Seamus

Shan (f.) English form of Welsh Sian. Shan- is also a popular prefix for newly invented names used by black American families

Shane (m.) English form of Irish Sean (p. 50, 69)

Shanell (f.) also *Shanel*, *Shanelle*, *Shannel*. Variants of Chanel (p. 13)

Shanita (f.) also *Shani*, *Shanika*. Apparently

newly invented names making use of a popular prefix. *See* Shan

Shanna (f.) pet form of Shannon

Shannon (m., f.) Celtic river name (p. 60)

Shanta (f.) also *Shante*. Pet forms of Chantal

Shantel (f.) also *Shantele, Shantell, Shantelle*. Variants of Chantal

Shara (f.) also *Shari*. Pet forms of Sharon

Sharon (f.) Hebrew, 'flat country' (pp. 50, 55, 65)

Shaun (m.) English form of Irish Sean

Shauna (f.) feminine form of Shaun

Shavon (f.) also *Shavonne*. English forms of Irish Siobhan (p. 36)

Shawn (m.) US variant of Sean

Shayne (m.) variant of Shane

Sheelagh (f.) variant of Sheila

Sheena (f.) English form of Gaelic Sine (Jean or Jane) (p. 70)

Shelia (f.) English form of Irish Sile (Celia) (p. 69)

Shelah (m.) Hebrew, 'request'

Shelley (m., f.) place name/family name, 'meadow on a slope'

Shena (f.) also *Sheona*. Variants of Sheena

Sheralyn (f.) variant of Cherylyn

Sheree (f.) also *Sherree*. Variants of Cherie

Shereen (f.) also *Sherene, Sherena, Sherina*. Diminutives of Sheree

Sheri (f.) also *Sherie*. Variants of Cherie

Sherilyn (f.) variant of Cherilyn

Sherry (f.) variant of Cherie or the name of the drink (pp. 3, 55)

Sheryl (f.) variant of Cheryl

Shevon (f.) also *Shevonne*. Variants of Shavon(ne)

Shiny (m.) the word used as a name (p. 74)

Shiona (f.) variant of Sheena

Shirley (f.) place name/family name, 'bright clearing' (pp. 9, 32)

Shona (f.) English short form of Gaelic Seonaid, a feminine form of John (p. 70)

Shoshana (f.) also *Shoshanna, Shushana*. Hebrew forms of Susannah (p. 20)

Sian (f.) Welsh form of Jane (p. 71)

Sibyl (f.) Greek, 'prophetess'

Sibylla (f.) Greek, possibly 'counsel of Zeus' (p. 37)

Sid (m.) pet form of Sidney (p. 60)

Sidney (m.) place name/family name, 'St Denis' or 'wide well-watered land' (p. 39)

Sierra (f.) Spanish, 'mountain range'

Sigmund (m.) Germanic, 'victory-shield' (p. 48)

Silas (m.) Greek form of Latin Silvanus

Sile (f.) Irish form of Celia, Cecilia but usually anglicized as Sheila, Sheelagh

Silence (f.) the word used as a name (by the Puritans) (p. 7)

Silvanus (m.) Latin, 'living in a wood'

Silvester (m.) Latin, 'woody, rural' (p. 26)

Silvia (f.) Latin feminine of Silvius, 'wood' (p. 26)

Simeon (m.) Hebrew, 'Jehovah has heard'

Simon (m.) New Testament variant of Simeon (p. 36)

Simone (f.) also *Simona*. French and Latin feminine forms of Simon

Sinclair (m.) place name/family name, 'St Clair'

Sinéad (f.) Irish form of Janet (p. 69)

Sinnie (f.) Old Norse, 'new victory' (p. 70)

Siobhán (f.) Irish form of Joan (pp. 36, 69)

Sioned (f.) Welsh form of Janet (p. 71)

Sir (m.) the word used as a name (p. 28)

Sisi (f.) the note of the musical scale reduplicated (p. 35)

Skye (f.) 'Sky' adapted to name use (p. 47)

Slosh (f.) pet form of Shoshana (p. 20)

Smith (m.) occupational family name (p. 63)

Snowdrop (f.) the flower name (p. 54)

Sofia (f.) variant of Sophia

Solomon (m.) Hebrew, 'the peaceful' (pp. 4, 5, 33)

Sonia (f.) Russian diminutive of Sophia

Sonny (m.) the word 'son' converted to name use (p. 59)

Sophia (f.) Greek, 'wisdom'

Sophie (f.) French form of Sophia (p. 35)

Sophronia (f.) Greek, 'prudent, self-controlled' (p. 19)

Sophy (f.) pet form of Sophia (p. 19)

Sorcha (f.) Irish, 'bright' (p. 69)

Sorrel (f.) the plant name (p. 54)

Sorry-for-sin (m., f.) Puritan slogan name (p. 49)

Soso (m.) the note in the musical scale reduplicated (p. 35)

Sparkle (f.) the word used as a name (p. 74)

Spencer (m.) occupational family name, 'dispenser of provisions' (p. 40)

Squire (m.) the word or family name used as a first name (p. 28)

Stacey (m., f.) family name linked with Eustace or pet form of Anastasia when feminine

Staci (f.) also *Stacie*, *Stacy*. Variants of Stacey (pp. 19, 55)

Stafford (m.) place name/family name, 'ford near a landing-place'

Stand-fast-on-high (m.) Puritan slogan name (p. 49)

Stanford (m.) place name/family name, 'stony ford' (p. 52)

Stanley (m.) place name/family name, 'stony clearing' (p. 3)

Star (f.) the word used as a name (p. 51)

Starkey (m.) family name, 'firm, tough' (p. 53)

Starling (f.) the bird name (p. 61)

Stella (f.) Latin, 'star' (pp. 51, 64)

Stephanie (f.) French feminine form of Stéphane (Stephen) (p. 55)

Stephen (m.) Greek, 'crown' (p. 36)

Sterling (m.) the word meaning 'of excellent quality' used as a name (p. 20)

Steve (m.) pet form of Stephen, Steven

Steveland (m.) family name (p. 39)

Steven (m.) modern variant of Stephen (p. 36)

Stevie (f.) pet form of Stephanie. Occasionally used for boys, a pet form of Stephen, Steven (p. 39)

Stewart (m.) variant of Stuart

Storm (f.) also *Stormy*. The words used as names (p. 58)

Streaker (m.) family name, 'strong, violent' (p. 74)

Stuart (m.) Old English, 'steward, keeper of the household' (p. 70)

Sue (f.) pet form of Susan (p. 14)

Sultan (m.) the word used as a name (p. 74)

Sunday (f.) the day name (p. 50)

Sunny (m.) also *Sunset (f.)*. The words used as names (pp. 51, 59)

Surprise (f.) the word used as a name (p. 33)
Susan (f.) short form of Susannah (pp. 31, 50, 55)
Susannah (f.) also *Susanna*. Hebrew, 'lily' (p. 54)
Susanne (f.) German variant of Susannah
Susie (f.) also *Susy*. Pet forms of Susan
Suzanne (f.) French form of Susannah
Suzette (f.) French diminutive of Suzanne
Swan (f.) the bird name (p. 61)
Sybil (f.) variant of Sibyl
Sydney (m.) variant of Sidney
Sylvester (m.) variant of Silvester (p. 26)
Sylvia (f.) popular variant of Silvia
Syringa (f.) the flower name (p. 54)

T

Tabitha (f.) Aramaic, 'gazelle' (p. 5)
Tacey (f.) also *Tacy*. Latin, 'Be silent!' (p. 7)
Talitha (f.) Aramaic, 'little girl' (p. 10)
Tallulah (f.) American Indian place name, 'running water'
Tamar (f.) Hebrew, 'palm tree' (pp. 26, 34, 60)
Tamara (f.) Russian form of Tamar
Tameka (f.) also *Tamika*, *Tomika*, etc. Appears to be a feminine form of Thomas (p. 55)
Tamesa (f.) Latin form of Thames, the river name (p. 60)

Tammie (m., f.) also *Tammy*. Originally Scottish pet form of Thomas, now pet form of Tamsin, Tamara, etc. (p. 46)

Tamsin (f.) contracted form of Thomasin, feminine of Thomas (p. 71)

Tanga (f.) blend of 'tango' and 'rumba' used by parents who were keen dancers (p. 21)

Tania (f.) variant of Tanya

Tanisha (f.) possibly a Hausa day-name, 'born on Monday'

Tansy (f.) the flower name (p. 54)

Tanya (f.) short form of Russian Tatiana, feminine form of a Roman name of unknown meaning

Tara (f.) Irish, 'hill'

Tarquin (m.) English form of Tarquinius, name of two legendary kings of Rome (p. 18)

Tasha (f.) pet form of Natasha (p. 55)

Taylor (f.) family name, tailor

Ted (m.) pet form of Edward

Temperance (m.,f.) the word used as a name (by the Puritans) (p. 62)

Tempest (m.) the family name (p. 58)

Ten (m.) the word used as a name (p. 43)

Tequila (f.) a Mexican place name and liquor (p. 4)

Terena (f.) apparently a feminine form of Terence

Terence (m.) Roman clan name of unknown meaning (p. 11)

Teresa (f.) Greek, 'woman of Therasia (an island)' or 'summer, harvest' (pp. 19, 53, 69)

Terrance (m.) US variant of Terence

Terrence (m.) modern variant of Terence

Terri (f.) pet form of Teresa (pp. 19, 55)

Terry (m.) pet form of Terence, Terrence, Terrance (pp. 11, 32)

Tertia (f.) Latin feminine of Tertius, 'third child' (p. 43)

Tessa (f.) also *Tess*, *Tessy*. Pet forms of Teresa (p. 58)

Tex (m.) short form of Texas or Texan (p. 32)

Thaddeus (m.) Aramaic, 'the courageous one'

Thalassa (f.) Greek, 'the sea' (p. 27)

Thanksgiving (m.) the word used as a name for a child born on the fourth Thursday in November (in the US) (p. 51)

Thea (f.) pet form of Dorothea (p. 37)

Thelma (f.) Greek, 'will' (pp. 19, 44)

Theo (m.) pet form of Theodore

Theodora (f.) feminine form of Theodore

Theodore (m.) Greek, 'God's gift' (p. 31)

Theresa (f.) variant of Teresa, influenced by Thérèse

Thérèse (f.) French form of Teresa

Theseus (m.) Greek, 'civilizer' (p. 37)

Theta (f.) the eighth letter of the Greek alphabet used as a name (p. 68)

Thetis (f.) Greek, 'to dispose' (p. 37)

Thirza (f.) Hebrew, 'pleasure'

Thomas (m.) Aramaic, 'twin' (pp. 50, 63, 71)

Thomasina (f.) also *Thomasin*, *Thomasine*. Feminine forms of Thomas

Thora (f.) Scandinavian, 'Thor-battle' (p. 70)

Thornton (m.) place name/family name, 'settlement among thorns'

Thyme (f.) the herb name (p. 12)

Ti (m). 'It' spelt backwards (p. 58)

Tia (f.) pet form of Tiana, or of names like Ignatia, Lucretia, Florentia, Laurentia, Vinzentia

Tiara (f.) jewelled ornament

Tierra (f.) variant of Tiara

Tiffany (f.) English form of Theophania, Greek, 'manifestation of God' (p. 51)

Tim (m.) also *Timmy*. Pet forms of Timothy

Timothy (m.) Greek, 'honouring God'

Tina (f.) pet form of Christina, Martina, etc. (pp. 21, 70)

Tish (f.) also *Tisha*. Pet forms of Letitia (p. 66)

Toban (m.) a short form of 'Manitoban' (p. 38)

Tobias (m.) Greek form of Hebrew Tobiah, 'Jehovah is good'

Toby (m.) pet form of Tobias

Todd (m.) family name, 'fox hunter' (pp. 5, 55)

Tom (m.) pet form of Thomas

Tomasina (f.) also *Tomasine*. Variants of Thomasina, Thomasine

Tommie (m., f.) also *Tommy*. Pet forms of Thomas, Thomasina, Thomasine, etc. (p. 55)

Tomorrow (f.) the word used as a name (p. 74)

Toni (f.) also *Tonia*, *Tonie*. Pet forms of Antonia

Tony (m.) pet form of Antony, Anthony

Tonya (f.) modern variant of Tonia

Torquil (m.) Old Norse name of uncertain meaning (pp. 49, 70)

Tory (m.) family name (p. 74)

Tota (m.) Hindi, 'parrot' (p. 60)

Toya (f.) short form of Latoya (p. 55)

Tracy (m., f.) also *Tracey*, *Tracie*. Place name/family name, used originally for males, usually explained as a pet form of Teresa when used for girls (pp. 9, 32, 50, 55)

Tram (m.) appears to be the word used as a name (p. 74)

Travis (m.) family name, 'toll-collector'

Treasure (f.) the word used as a name (p. 35)

Trefor (m.) Welsh form of Trevor

Tremendous (m.) transferred from the name of a ship (p. 27)

Trent (m.) river name, place name/family name

Trevor (m.) place name, 'great' or 'sea homestead'

Tribulation (m., f.) the word used as a name (by the Puritans) (p. 62)

Tricia (f.) pet form of Patricia

Trilby (f.) a name invented by George du Maurier for the heroine of his novel *Trilby* (p. 46)

Trisha (f.) variant of Tricia

Tristan (m.) usually linked with French, *triste*, 'sad'

Tristram (m.) English form of Tristan

Trixie (f.) pet form of Beatrix (Beatrice)

Troilus (m.) Greek,'Trojan' (p. 37)

Troy (m.) name of an ancient city in Asia Minor

Trudy (f.) also *Trudi, Tridie*. Pet forms of Gertrude, Ermintrude (p. 64)

Tubervill (m.) place name/family name (p. 63)

Tudor (m.) also *Tudur*. Welsh forms of Theodore (p. 71)

Tuesday (f.) the day name (p. 50)

Tulane (m.) name of an American university (in New Orleans) (p. 52)

Tyler (m.) family name, 'tiler'

Tyrone (m.) Irish place name, 'Owen's country' (p. 55)

U

Ulrick (m.) Old English, 'wolf-powerful' (p. 5)

Ultimus (m.) Latin, 'last child' (p. 43)

Ulysis (f.) modern feminine form of Ulysses (p. 53)

Ulysses (m.) possibly Greek, 'wounded in the thigh' (pp. 37, 44)

Una (f.) an ancient Irish name of unknown meaning but linked with Latin, 'one' since the seventeenth century (pp. 51, 69)

Undecima (f.) Latin, 'eleventh child' (p. 43)

Unity (f.) the word used as a name (by the Puritans) (p. 62)

Upton (m.) place name/family name

Urban (m.) Latin, 'of the city, courteous'

Uriah (m.) Hebrew, 'Jehovah is my light'

Ursula (f.) Latin, 'little bear' (pp. 5, 18)

V

Val (m., f.) pet form of Valentine or Valerie

Valentina (f.) feminine form of Valentine

Valentine (m., f.) Latin, 'to be strong' (pp. 29, 56)

Valerie (f.) Latin feminine of Valerius, a Roman clan name, 'to be strong' (pp. 25, 29)

Van (m.) pet form of Evan

Vance (m.) family name, 'one who lived near a marsh'

Vanda (f.) variant of Wanda

Vanessa (f.) invented by Jonathan Swift with reference to Esther Vanhomrigh (p. 17)

Vanya (m., f.) also *Vania.* Russian pet form of Ivan (John) now also used for girls

Vashti (f.) Persian, 'the most beautiful' (pp. 10, 34)

Vaughan (m.) Welsh, 'little' used in the same way as Junior, to distinguish father and son with the same name

Vaughn (m.) usual US form of Vaughan

Velma (f.) probably a pet form of Wilhelmina

Venetia (f.) Latin form of Venice

Venice (f.) the Italian place name or a variant of Venus

Venson (m.) family name (p. 44)

Venus (f.) Latin, 'desire, sexual love'. The name of the goddess of beauty and love (pp. 37, 53)

Vera (f.) Slavic, 'faith' but long associated with Latin, 'true' (p. 62)

Verena (f.) Latin, 'true'

Verity (f.) the word used as a name (p. 62)

Verna (f.) also *Vernal.* Latin, 'spring' (p. 45)

Vernetta (f.) diminutive of Verna

Vernon (m.) place name/family name, 'alder tree' (pp. 26, 27)

Verona (f.) German short form of Veronika (Veronica)

Veronica (f.) Latin, 'true image'. Also a flower name (p. 54)

Vesta (f.) Greek, 'hearth of a house' (p. 37)

Vicesimus (m.) Latin, 'twentieth child' (p. 43)

Vicki (f.) also *Vickie*, *Vicky*, *Vikki*. Modern pet forms of Victoria

Victor (m.) Latin, 'conqueror' (pp. 48, 50)

Victoria (f.) Latin, 'victory' (pp. 6, 48, 49, 67)

Vida (f.) pet form of Davida. On rare occasions a male name, a form of Guy (Guido) or Vitus, Vitalis, 'vital' (p. 16)

Vikki (f.) variant of Vicki

Vilma (f.) variant of Wilma

Vince (m.) pet form of Vincent

Vincent (m.) Latin, 'to conquer' (p. 48)

Vinch (m.) family name (p. 64)

Viola (f.) Latin, 'violet' (pp. 18, 34)

Violet (f.) the flower name (p. 14)

Violetta (f.) also *Violette*. Italian and French forms of Violet

Virgil (m.) English form of the Roman clan name Vergilius (later written Virgilius). Meaning unknown

Virginia (f.) originally a feminine form of Virgil but long associated with Latin, 'maiden, virgin' (pp. 10, 46)

Virtue (m., f.) the word used as a name (by the Puritans) (p. 63)

Viva (f.) Latin, 'alive, living'

Vivian (m., f.) Roman family name Vibius, but associated with Latin *vivus*, 'living, alive' (p.32

Vivien (f.) feminine form of Vivian influenced by Vivienne (p. 9)

Vivienne (f.) French feminine form of Vivian

Vulcan (m.) Cretan, 'god of fire' (p. 37)

W

Wade (m.) place name/family name, 'ford'

Waldo (m.) Germanic, 'rule, power'

Wallace (m.) Scottish family name, 'Celt, Welshman' (pp. 11, 70)

Wallis (f.) variant of Wallace

Wally (m.) pet form of Walter, Wallace

Walt (m.) pet form of Walter

Walter (m.) Germanic, 'ruling people'

Wanda (f.) Slavic, 'Vandal [name of a Germanic tribe]' (p. 55)

Warren (m.) place name/family name (p. 60)

Warwick (m.) place name/family name, 'dwelling near a weir'

Washington (m.) place name/family name (p. 39)

Wayne (m.) occupational family name, 'maker of wagons' or 'wagon-driver' (p. 50)

Webster (m.) occupational family name, 'female weaver'

Welthy (f.) 'Wealthy' adapted to name use (p. 20)

Wembley (m.) place name, strongly associated with sport (pp. 11, 12)

Wendy (f.) also *Wendie*, *Wendi*. Invented by J. M. Barrie in *Peter Pan*, based on 'friendy-wendy' (p. 50)

Wentworth (m.) place name/family name (p. 36)

Wesley (m.) place name/family name, 'west meadow' (p. 39)

Westray (f.) place name/family name (p. 26)

*What-God-will (m.,f.)*Puritan slogan name (p. 49)

Whitney (f.) English place name/family name, 'white island'

Wilbert (m.) Old English, 'will-bright' (p. 47)

Wilbur (m.) family name linked with Wilburg, Germanic feminine name, 'beloved stronghold'

Wilfred (m.) Old English, 'will-peace' (p. 4)

Wilfrid (m.) mainly Roman Catholic form of Wilfred

Wilhelmina (f.) German feminine form of Wilhelm (William)

Will (m.) pet form of William

Willa (f.) pet form of Wilhelmina

Willard (m.) Old English, 'bold resolve'

William (m.) Germanic, 'will-helmet' (pp. 55, 72)

Williamina (f.) Scottish feminine form of William

Willie (m.) pet form of William (p. 55)

Willis (m.) family name linked with William

Willow (f.) the tree name (p. 26)

Wilma (f.) pet form of Wilhelmina

Wilmer (m.) Germanic, 'will-fame'

Wilson (m.) family name, 'son of Will' (p. 44)

Windsor (m.) place name, 'river bank with a winch'

Winfred (f.) Old English, 'peace-friend' (p. 4)

Winifred (f.) Welsh, 'blessed reconciliation (p. 53)

Winnie (f.) pet form of Winifred, Edwina, etc.

Winston (m.) place name/family name, 'Wine's settlement'

Winwaloe (m.) name of an obscure saint (p. 57)

Wisdom (m., f.) the family name or the word used as a name

Wolf (m.) the word used as a name (p. 5)

Woodrow (m.) place name/family name, 'row of cottages in a wood'

Woody (m.) English form of Silvester (p. 26)

Wyn (m.) also *Wynn*, *Wynne*. Welsh, 'white, pure' (pp. 14, 71)

Wyndham (m.) place name/family name, 'Wyman's settlement'

Wynford (m.) place name/family name, 'white torrent'

X

X *(m.)* the letter used as a name (p. 12)

Xana (f.) pet form of Roxana (p. 44)

Xanthe (f.) Greek, 'yellow' (p. 14)

Xavier (m.) Basque place name, 'new house'

Xenophone (f.) Greek, 'foreign voice'. Adaptation of Xenophon, name of a famous Greek writer (p. 53)

Y

Yale (m.) place name/family name, 'fertile upland' (p. 35)

Yasmine (f.) the flower name (p. 54)

Yehudi (m.) Hebrew, 'Jew'

Yetty (f.) family name (p. 53)

Yolanda (f.) also *Yolande*. French form of Greek Iolanthe, 'violet flower' (p. 55)

Yon (m.) short form of Yonathan, Yehonathan (Jonathan) (p. 44)

Yootha (f.) Maori, 'goddess of luck' (p. 67)

Ysanne (f.) blend of Isabel and Ann

Yul (m.) Mongolian, 'beyond the horizon'

Yvonne (f.) also *Yvette*. French feminine forms of Ivo, 'yew wood'

Z

Zaccheus (m.) Hebrew, 'pure' (p. 46)

Zachariah (m.) also *Zechariah*. Hebrew, 'Jehovah remembers'

Zak (m.) pet form of Zachariah or Isaac

Zale (m.) family name (p. 42)

Zandra (f.) pet form of Alexandra

Zane (m.) family name, usually linked with John (p. 42)

Zara (f.) Arabic, 'splendour, brightness of the east' (p. 6)

Zarnell (m.) presumably a family name (p. 42)

Zatha (f.) an invented name of no particular meaning (p. 42)

Zealandia (f.) ship name, referring to Zealand, part of Denmark (p. 27)

Zeal-of-the-land (m.) Puritan slogan name (p. 49)

Zechariah (m.) variant of Zachariah

Zed (m.) also *Zee*. The letter of the alphabet used as a name (p. 12)

Zelda (f.) pet form of Griselda

Zella (f.) pet form of German Marzella (Marcelle) (p. 42)

Zellum (m.) perhaps Greek, 'zeal' (p. 42)

Zelma (f.) pet form of Anselma

Zelpha (f.) an invented name of no particular meaning (p. 42)

Zena (f.) pet form of Rosina or variant of Xenia, Greek, 'hospitable'

Zeno (m., f.) short form of Greek Zenodotos, 'gift of Zeus' (p. 53)

Zerrill (m.) family name (p. 42)

Zeta (f.) sixth letter of the Greek alphabet used as a name (p. 68)

Zetus (m.) Greek, 'to blow' (p. 37)

Zeus (m.) Indo-European, 'sky, day' (p. 37)

Zillah (f.) Hebrew, 'shadow, protection'

Zilpah (f.) Arabic, 'with a little nose' (p. 30)

Zinnia (f.) the flower name (p. 54)

Zippor (m.) Hebrew, 'bird' (p. 61)

Zipporah (f.) feminine of Zippor (pp. 34, 61)

Zirckle (m.) family name (p. 44)

Zita (f.) Greek, 'to seek'

Zoë (f.) Greek, 'life, lively'

Zoey (f.) also *Zowie*, *Zoee*, etc. Modern variants of Zoë

Zola (f.) family name, 'clod of earth'

Zolund (m.) an invented name of no known meaning (p. 42)

Zorah (f.) biblical place name, a town near Jerusalem

Zorin (m.) Arabic, 'morning star' (p. 42)

Zorina (f.) feminine of Zorin (p. 42)

Zowie (f.) modern variant of Zoë

Zuba (f.) pet form of Azubah

The top fifty first names

Boys, England and Wales

1900

1 William
2 John
3 George
4 Thomas
5 Charles
6 Frederick
7 Arthur
8 James
9 Albert
10 Ernest
11 Robert
12 Henry
13 Alfred
14 Sidney
15 Joseph
16 Harold
Harry
18 Frank
19 Walter
20 Herbert
21 Edward
22 Percy
23 Richard
24 Samuel
25 Leonard
26 Stanley
27 Reginald
28 Francis
29 Fred
30 Cecil
31 Wilfred
32 Horace
33 Cyril
34 David
Norman
36 Eric
37 Victor
38 Edgar
39 Leslie
40 Bertie
Edwin
42 Donald
43 Benjamin
Hector
Jack
Percival
47 Clifford
48 Alexander
Baden
50 Bernard
Redvers

1925

1 John
2 William
3 George
4 James
5 Ronald
6 Robert
7 Kenneth
8 Frederick
9 Thomas
10 Albert
11 Eric
12 Edward
13 Arthur
14 Charles
15 Leslie
16 Sidney
17 Frank
18 Peter
19 Dennis
20 Joseph
21 Alan
22 Stanley
23 Ernest
24 Harold
25 Norman
26 Raymond
27 Leonard
28 Alfred
Harry
30 Donald
Reginald
32 Roy
33 Derek
34 Henry
35 Geoffrey
36 David
Gordon
Herbert
Walter
40 Cyril
41 Jack
42 Richard
43 Douglas
44 Maurice
45 Bernard
Gerald
47 Brian
48 Victor
Wilfred
50 Francis

Boys, England and Wales

1950

1 David
2 John
3 Peter
4 Michael
5 Alan
6 Robert
7 Stephen
8 Paul
9 Brian
10 Graham
11 Philip
12 Anthony
13 Colin
14 Christopher
15 Geoffrey
16 William
17 James
18 Keith
Terence
20 Barry
Malcolm
Richard
23 Ian
24 Derek
25 Roger
26 Raymond
27 Kenneth
28 Andrew
29 Trevor
30 Martin
31 Kevin
32 Ronald
33 Leslie
34 Charles
George
36 Thomas
37 Nigel
Stuart
39 Edward
40 Gordon
41 Roy
42 Dennis
43 Neil
44 Laurence
45 Clive
Eric
47 Frederick
Patrick
Robin
50 Donald
Joseph

1975

1 Stephen
2 Mark
3 Paul
4 Andrew
5 David
6 Richard
7 Matthew
8 Daniel
9 Christopher
10 Darren
11 Michael
12 James
13 Robert
14 Simon
15 Jason
16 Stuart
17 Neil
18 Lee
19 Jonathan
20 Ian
Nicholas
22 Gary
23 Craig
24 Martin
25 John
26 Carl
27 Philip
28 Kevin
29 Benjamin
30 Peter
31 Wayne
32 Adam
33 Anthony
34 Alan
35 Graham
36 Adrian
37 Colin
Scott
39 Timothy
40 Barry
41 William
42 Dean
Jamie
44 Nathan
45 Justin
46 Damian
Thomas
48 Joseph
49 Alexander
Alistair
Nigel
Shaun

1985

1 Christopher
2 Matthew
3 David
4 James
5 Daniel
6 Andrew
7 Steven
8 Michael
9 Mark
10 Paul
11 Richard
12 Adam
13 Robert
14 Lee
15 Craig
16 Benjamin
Thomas
18 Peter
19 Anthony
20 Shaun
21 Gary
22 Stuart
23 Jonathan
Simon
25 Philip
26 Darren
27 Carl
28 Martin
Nicholas
30 John
31 Luke
32 Neil
33 Jason
34 Alexander
Kevin
36 Dean
37 Ian
Jamie
39 Ryan
40 Stacey
Timothy
Wayne
43 Alan
Graham
Oliver
46 William
47 Joseph
48 Gavin
Nathan
50 Ben
Edward
Gareth

1993

1 Daniel
2 Matthew
3 James
4 Christopher
5 Thomas
6 Joshua
7 Adam
8 Michael
9 Luke
10 Andrew
11 Benjamin
12 Samuel
13 Stephen
14 Robert
15 Jamie
16 Aaron
17 Jonathan
18 Alexander
19 Joseph
20 Ryan
21 David
22 Liam
23 Jack
24 Richard
25 William
26 Jordan
27 Craig
28 Mark
29 Nicholas
30 Ashley
31 Nathan
32 Lee
33 Oliver
34 Shaun
35 Scott
36 Callum
37 Lewis
38 Paul
39 Ben
40 John
41 Edward
42 Anthony
43 Jake
44 Charles
45 Martin
46 Philip
47 Carl
48 Bradley
49 Kieran
50 Simon

Girls, England and Wales

1900

1 Florence
2 Mary
3 Alice
4 Annie
5 Elsie
6 Edith
7 Elizabeth
8 Doris
9 Dorothy
Ethel
11 Gladys
12 Lilian
13 Hilda
14 Margaret
15 Winifred
16 Lily
17 Ellen
18 Ada
19 Emily
20 Violet
21 Rose
Sarah
23 Nellie
24 May
25 Beatrice
26 Gertrude
Ivy
28 Mabel
29 Jessie
30 Maud
31 Eva
32 Agnes
Jane
34 Evelyn
35 Frances
Kathleen
37 Clara
38 Olive
39 Amy
40 Catherine
41 Grace
42 Emma
43 Nora
44 Louisa
Minnie
46 Lucy
47 Daisy
Eliza
49 Phyllis
Ann

1925

1 Joan
2 Mary
3 Joyce
4 Margaret
5 Dorothy
6 Doris
7 Kathleen
8 Irene
9 Betty
10 Eileen
11 Doreen
12 Lilian
Vera
14 Jean
15 Marjorie
16 Barbara
17 Edna
18 Gladys
19 Audrey
20 Elsie
21 Florence
Hilda
Winifred
24 Olive
25 Violet
26 Elizabeth
27 Edith
28 Ivy
29 Peggy
Phyllis
31 Evelyn
32 Iris
33 Annie
Rose
35 Beryl
Lily
Muriel
Sheila
39 Ethel
40 Alice
41 Constance
Ellen
43 Gwendoline
Patricia
45 Sylvia
46 Nora
Pamela
48 Grace
49 Jessie
50 Mabel

1950

1 Susan
2 Linda
3 Christine
4 Margaret
5 Carol
6 Jennifer
7 Janet
8 Patricia
9 Barbara
10 Ann
11 Sandra
12 Pamela
Pauline
14 Jean
15 Jacqueline
16 Kathleen
17 Sheila
18 Valerie
19 Maureen
20 Gillian
21 Marilyn
Mary
23 Elizabeth
24 Lesley
25 Catherine
26 Brenda
27 Wendy
28 Angela
29 Rosemary
30 Shirley
31 Diane
Joan
33 Jane
Lynne
35 Irene
36 Janice
37 Elaine
Heather
Marion
40 June
41 Eileen
42 Denise
Doreen
Judith
Sylvia
46 Helen
Yvonne
48 Hilary
Joyce
Julia
Teresa

1975

1 Claire
2 Sarah
3 Nicola
4 Emma
5 Joanne
6 Helen
7 Rachel
8 Lisa
9 Rebecca
10 Karen
Michelle
12 Victoria
13 Catherine
14 Amanda
15 Trac(e)y
16 Samantha
17 Kelly
18 Deborah
19 Julie
Louise
21 Sharon
22 Donna
23 Kerry
24 Zoe
25 Melanie
26 Alison
27 Caroline
28 Lynsey
29 Jennifer
30 Angela
31 Susan
32 Hayley
33 Dawn
Joanna
Lucy
36 Natalie
37 Charlotte
38 Andrea
Laura
40 Paula
41 Marie
42 Teresa
43 Elizabeth
Suzanne
45 Kirsty
Sally
Tina
48 Jane
49 Anne(e)
Jacqueline

Girls, England and Wales

1985

1 Sarah
2 Claire
3 Emma
4 Laura
5 Rebecca
6 Gemma
7 Rachel
8 Kelly
9 Victoria
10 Katharine
11 Katie
Nicola
13 Jennifer
Natalie
15 Hayley
Michelle
17 Amy
Lisa
19 Lindsay
20 Samantha
21 Joanne
22 Louise
23 Leanne
24 Helen
25 Joanna
26 Hannah
27 Jodie
28 Charlotte
29 Kirsty
30 Lucy
31 Caroline
32 Elizabeth
33 Ashley
Stephanie
35 Jessica
36 Emily
37 Kerry
Tracey
39 Charlene
Danielle
Zoë
42 Kate
Lauren
44 Amanda
45 Alison
Anna
Carla
Carly
Marie
50 Alexandra
Melissa

1993

1 Rebecca
2 Charlotte
3 Laura
4 Amy
5 Emma
6 Jessica
7 Lauren
8 Sarah
9 Rachel
10 Catherine
11 Hannah
12 Katie
13 Emily
14 Sophie
15 Victoria
16 Stacey
17 Natalie
18 Jade
19 Stephanie
20 Lucy
21 Danielle
22 Kirsty
23 Samantha
24 Gemma
25 Abigail
26 Chloë
27 Holly
28 Claire
29 Hayley
30 Zoë
31 Jodie
32 Elizabeth
33 Kelly
34 Kimberley
35 Natasha
36 Alexandra
37 Nicola
38 Kerry
39 Chelsea
40 Eleanor
41 Jennifer
42 Leanne
43 Melissa
44 Alice
45 Louise
46 Harriet
47 Lisa
48 Kayleigh
49 Megan
50 Naomi

Boys, USA

1900

1	John	19	Frank		Stanley
2	William	20	Raymond	38	Donald
3	Charles	21	Francis		Earl
4	Robert	22	Frederick		Elmer
5	Joseph	23	Albert	41	Leon
6	James		Benjamin		Nathan
7	George	25	David	43	Eugene
8	Samuel	26	Harold		Floyd
9	Thomas	27	Howard		Ray
10	Arthur	28	Fred		Roy
11	Harry		Richard		Sydney
12	Edward	30	Clarence	48	Abraham
13	Henry		Herbert		Edwin
14	Walter	32	Jacob		Lawrence
15	Louis	33	Ernest		Leonard
16	Paul		Jack		Norman
17	Ralph	35	Herman		Russell
18	Carl		Philip		

1925

1	Robert	18	Kenneth	35	Fred
2	John	19	Walter	36	Earl
3	William	20	Raymond		Philip
4	James	21	Carl		Stanley
5	Charles	22	Albert	39	Daniel
6	Richard	23	Henry	40	Leonard
7	George	24	Harry		Marvin
8	Donald	25	Francis	42	Frederick
9	Joseph	26	Ralph	43	Anthony
10	Edward	27	Eugene		Samuel
11	Thomas	28	Howard	45	Bernard
12	David	29	Lawrence		Edwin
13	Frank	30	Louis	47	Alfred
14	Harold	31	Alan	48	Russell
15	Arthur	32	Norman		Warren
16	Jack	33	Gerald	50	Ernest
17	Paul	34	Herbert		

Boys, USA

1950

1 Robert
2 Michael
3 James
4 John
5 David
6 William
7 Thomas
8 Richard
9 Gary
10 Charles
11 Ronald
12 Dennis
13 Steven
14 Kenneth
15 Joseph
16 Mark
17 Daniel
18 Paul
19 Donald
20 Gregory
21 Larry
22 Lawrence
23 Timothy
24 Alan
25 Edward
26 Gerald
27 Douglas
28 George
29 Frank
30 Patrick
31 Anthony
32 Philip
33 Raymond
34 Bruce
35 Jeffrey
36 Brian
37 Peter
38 Frederick
39 Roger
40 Carl
41 Dale
Walter
43 Christopher
44 Martin
45 Craig
46 Arthur
47 Andrew
48 Jerome
49 Leonard
50 Henry

1984 *Whites*

1 Michael
2 Christopher
3 Matthew
4 Joshua
5 David
6 Daniel
7 Ryan
8 Andrew
9 Brian
10 John
11 James
12 Justin
13 Jason
14 Joseph
15 Adam
16 Nicholas
17 Robert
18 Steven
19 Eric
20 Brandon
21 Jeffrey
22 Jonathan
23 William
24 Timothy
25 Sean
26 Aaron
27 Kyle
28 Benjamin
29 Anthony
30 Thomas
31 Mark
32 Zachary
33 Jacob
34 Tyler
35 Jeremy
36 Nathan
37 Dustin
38 Kevin
39 Travis
40 Scott
41 Patrick
42 Richard
43 Derek
44 Jared
45 Jesse
46 Paul
47 Charles
48 Bradley
49 Gregory
50 Chad

1984 *Non-whites*

1 Michael
2 Christopher
3 Brandon
4 Anthony
5 James
6 Robert
7 Marcus
8 David
9 Brian
10 Jason
11 Charles
William
13 John
14 Eric
15 Antonio
16 Steven
17 Kevin
18 Darryl
19 Joseph
20 Jonathan
21 Antoine
Kenneth
23 André
24 Terrance
25 Aaron
26 Justin
27 Derrick
28 Shawn
29 Corey
30 Mark
31 Timothy
32 DeAndre
33 Joshua
34 Daniel
35 Ronald
36 Ryan
37 Richard
Terrell
39 Larry
40 Jermaine
41 Maurice
42 Gregory
Matthew
44 Keith
45 Thomas
46 Demetrius
47 Curtis
Jeffrey
Jerome
50 Andrew

1993 *Whites*

1 Michael
2 Christopher
3 Matthew
4 Joshua
5 Andrew
6 James
7 John
8 Nicholas
9 Justin
10 David
11 Daniel
12 Ryan
13 Steven
14 Robert
15 Joseph
16 Zachary
17 Jonathan
18 William
19 Kyle
20 Tyler
21 Jacob
22 Brian
23 Brandon
24 Eric
25 Sean
26 Cody
27 Anthony
28 Thomas
29 Kevin
30 Alexander
31 Jordan
32 Timothy
33 Benjamin
34 Corey
35 Adam
36 Jeffrey
37 Aaron
38 Richard
39 Nathan
40 Travis
41 Charles
42 Derek
43 Patrick
44 Mark
45 Jeremy
46 Jason
47 Jesse
48 Samuel
49 Jared
50 Dustin

1993 Non-whites

1 Michael	18 Antonio	35 Andrew
2 Christopher	19 Jeremy	36 Ryan
3 Brandon	20 Derrick	37 Jordan
4 Anthony	21 Joseph	38 Travis
5 James	22 Darius	39 Jeffrey
6 Joshua	23 Sean	40 Richard
7 Jonathan	24 Darryl	41 Jamal
8 Robert	25 Charles	42 Gregory
9 Eric	26 Corey	43 André
10 David	27 Daniel	44 Dominique
11 Justin	28 Terrance	45 Willie
12 Marcus	29 Kenneth	46 Thomas
13 Brian	30 Aaron	47 Antoine
14 Steven	31 Timothy	48 Donte
15 Kevin	32 Devin	49 Marquis
16 William	33 Matthew	50 Mark
17 John	34 Nicholas	

Girls USA

1900

1 Mary	19 Edith	37 Beatrice
2 Ruth	Lucy	Gertrude
3 Helen	21 Clara	39 Alma
4 Margaret	Doris	Mabel
5 Elizabeth	23 Marjorie	Minnie
6 Dorothy	24 Annie	Pauline
7 Catherine	25 Louise	Rose
8 Mildred	Martha	44 Fanny
9 Frances	27 Ann(e)	45 Agnes
10 Alice	Blanche	Carrie
Marion	Eleanor	Edna
12 Anna	Emma	Evelyn
13 Sarah	Hazel	Harriet
14 Gladys	32 Esther	Ida
15 Grace	Ethel	Irene
Lillian	Laura	Miriam
17 Florence	Marie	
Virginia	36 Julia	

1925

1 Mary
2 Barbara
3 Dorothy
4 Betty
5 Ruth
6 Margaret
7 Helen
8 Elizabeth
9 Jean
10 Ann(e)
11 Patricia
12 Shirley
13 Virginia
14 Nancy
15 Joan
16 Martha
17 Marion
18 Doris
19 Frances
Marjorie
21 Marilyn
22 Alice
23 Eleanor
Catherine
25 Lois
26 Jane
27 Phyllis
28 Florence
Mildred
30 Carol(e)
31 Carolyn
Marie
Norma
34 Anna
Louise
36 Beverly
Janet
38 Sarah
39 Evelyn
40 Edith
Jacqueline
Lorraine
43 Grace
44 Ethel
Gloria
Laura
47 Audrey
Esther
Joanne
Sally

1950

1 Linda
2 Mary
3 Patricia
4 Susan
5 Deborah
6 Kathleen
7 Barbara
8 Nancy
9 Sharon
10 Karen
11 Carol(e)
12 Sandra
13 Diane
14 Catherine
15 Christine
16 Cynthia
17 Donna
18 Judith
19 Margaret
20 Janice
21 Janet
22 Pamela
23 Gail
24 Cheryl
25 Suzanne
26 Marilyn
27 Brenda
28 Beverly
Carolyn
30 Ann(e)
31 Shirley
32 Jacqueline
33 Joanne
34 Lynn(e)
Marcia
36 Denise
37 Gloria
38 Joyce
39 Kathy
40 Elizabeth
41 Laura
42 Darlene
43 Theresa
44 Joan
45 Elaine
46 Michelle
47 Judy
48 Diana
49 Frances
Maureen
Phyllis
Ruth

Girls, USA

1984 *Whites*

1 Jennifer
2 Sarah
3 Jessica
4 Ashley
5 Amanda
6 Megan
7 Nicole
8 Katherine
9 Lindsey
10 Stephanie
11 Heather
12 Rachel
13 Elizabeth
14 Amy
15 Melissa
16 Crystal
17 Christina
18 Amber
19 Rebecca
20 Emily
21 Kristin
22 Danielle
23 Jamie
24 Michelle
25 Laura
26 Erin
27 Kelly
28 Lauren
29 Kimberly
30 Angela
31 Andrea
32 Tiffany
33 Brittany
34 Stacy
35 Lisa
36 Katie
37 Brandy
38 Mary
39 Allison
40 Erica
41 Shannon
42 Samantha
43 Tara
44 Alicia
45 Courtney
46 Chelsea
47 Julie
48 Christine
49 Kristy
50 Holly

1984 *Non-whites*

1 Tiffany
2 Ashley
3 Latoya
4 Crystal
5 Erica
6 Danielle
7 Jennifer
8 Ebony
9 Jessica
10 Candice
11 Nicole
12 Michelle
13 Kimberly
14 Brandi
15 Alicia
Christina
17 Tamika
18 Latasha
Stephanie
20 Andrea
21 Kelly
22 Jasmine
23 Monique
24 Rachel
25 Natasha
26 Brittany
27 Amber
April
29 Angela
30 Aisha
31 Lakeisha
32 Lauren
33 Amanda
Jacqueline
35 Sheena
Tanisha
37 Angel
Kiana
39 Dominique
Victoria
41 Sherise
42 Katrina
Melissa
44 Shana
45 Marquita
Shannon
Tierra
48 Chanel
49 Alexis
50 Courtney
Latrice
Theresa

1993 *Whites*

1 Brittany
2 Ashley
3 Jessica
4 Amanda
5 Sarah
6 Megan
7 Caitlin
8 Samantha
9 Stephanie
10 Katherine
11 Emily
12 Lauren
13 Kayla
14 Rachel
15 Nicole
16 Jennifer
17 Elizabeth
18 Chelsea
19 Courtney
20 Rebecca
21 Amber
22 Christina
23 Kristen
24 Heather
25 Lindsey
26 Danielle
27 Melissa
28 Tiffany
29 Kelsey
30 Kelly
31 Michelle
32 Alyssa
33 Hannah
34 Allison
35 Erica
36 Alicia
37 Amy
38 Crystal
39 Jamie
40 Kimberley
41 Laura
42 Erin
43 Alexandra
44 Mary
45 Katie
46 Cassandra
47 Anna
48 Casey
49 Victoria
50 Taylor

1993 *Non-whites*

1 Brittany
2 Jasmine
3 Ashley
4 Jessica
5 Tiffany
6 Courtney
7 Erica
8 Briana
9 Crystal
10 Amber
11 Danielle
12 Sierra
13 Alicia
14 Michelle
15 Christina
16 Kiara
17 Ebony
18 Stephanie
19 Kanisha
20 Jennifer
21 Alexis
22 Nichole
23 Bianca
24 Tanisha
25 Amanda
26 Kimberly
27 Victoria
28 Kierra
29 Candice
30 Kayla
31 Dominique
32 Samantha
33 Whitney
34 Tiara
35 Andrea
36 Chelsea
37 Latoya
38 Shaniqua
39 Raven
40 Monique
41 Lauren
42 Kiana
43 Jalisa
44 Tierra
45 Iesha
46 Breanna
47 Kristen
48 Natasha
49 Sarah
50 Lakeisha

Boys and Girls, Australia

1993

1 Matthew
2 James
3 Thomas
4 Joshua
5 Benjamin
6 Daniel
7 Samuel
8 Nicholas
9 Alexander
10 Michael
11 Jake
12 Luke
13 Christopher
14 Dylan
15 Andrew
16 Ryan
17 Jack
18 Bradley
19 David
Jordan
21 Nathan
22 Scott
23 Adam
Jarrad
25 Cameron
26 William
27 Mitchell
28 Lachlan
Steven
30 Timothy
31 Anthony
32 Rhys
33 Sean
34 Patrick
35 John
36 Alex
Jacob
38 Aaron
Jonathan
40 Angus
41 Jason
42 Henry
43 Simon
44 Sam
45 Jesse
Mark
47 Peter
48 Kieran
49 Hayden
50 Justin

1993

1 Jessica
2 Sarah
3 Emily
4 Rebecca
5 Emma
6 Hannah
7 Stephanie
8 Amy
9 Caitlin
10 Lauren
11 Laura
12 Ashleigh
13 Nicole
Rachel
15 Kate
16 Samantha
17 Madeleine
18 Alexandra
19 Melissa
20 Alicia
Katherine
22 Georgia
23 Hayley
24 Megan
Olivia
Sophie
27 Danielle
28 Alana
Chloë
Kelly
31 Claire
32 Victoria
33 Alice
Lucy
35 Courtney
Elise
37 Erin
38 Brooke
39 Brittany
Chelsea
41 Bianca
Jasmine
43 Georgina
44 Jade
Taylor
46 Cassandra
Elizabeth
Kayla
49 Kimberley
Natalie
Natasha
Rhiannon
Shannon

Final Quiz

When you think you've found a suitable first name (and any middle names) for your child, it's worth making an objective evaluation before making a final decision. I suggest that you write down the full name that your child is likely to bear – first name, middle name(s), family name – and then answer the following questions:

1. Will the first name distinguish your child as an individual? (It won't if it's high in the popularity charts. Many contemporaries will bear the same name.)
2. Will the first name you've chosen 'date' your child later in life? (It almost certainly will if it's currently in the top ten, especially if you're naming a daughter.)
3. Will the first name balance your family name? (It will if you've chosen a fairly common first name to balance an uncommon family name, or vice versa.)
4. Will the first name, middle name and family name create an embarrassing set of initials? (If they do they will lead to an unpleasant nickname later in life.)
5. Is the initial letter of the first name shared by someone else in the immediate family circle? (If so, it may cause inconvenience, especially if the other person is of the same sex.)
6. Will everyone know how to pronounce the first name? (Some names create problems – see page 39.)
7. Will the first name make the sex of your child immediately apparent? (Names which are used for both sexes can be inconvenient.)
8. Will everyone be able to spell the first name?

(Avoid 'variant' spellings. Use the most usual forms.)

9. Do the first name and family name sound pleasant when spoken together? (Be careful to avoid combinations such as Ida Lydiatt, Isla White, Rick O' Shea.)

10. Are you intending to give your child at least one middle name? (One middle name is normal, two or three are acceptable, more than three cause inconvenience when it comes to filling in forms. Those without a middle name may feel cheated. They have no alternative name to turn to if they don't happen to like their first name.)

11. Does the first name have an acceptable meaning? (A correspondent tells me that she suffered agonies during her school days when it became known that her name meant 'white breast'. Another was not pleased to discover that she was a 'sheep'.)

12. Is the first name you have in mind a name in its own right, or is it the pet form of another name? (Avoid pet forms – see page 20.)

13. Are the short forms and pet forms of the name you've chosen acceptable to you? (The child's friends will certainly use them, even though you may not.)

14. Is the first name so unusual that it will constantly attract attention? (Children can be very severe critics of any child with an 'odd' name. They assume that the child who bears the name must be 'odd'. There is some evidence that the name-bearer eventually comes to share that view.)

15. Is the first name acceptable at all social levels? (If you're in doubt, ask people of different social classes for their reactions.)

16. Does the first name reflect a very strong parental interest? (If the name is suitable in other

ways, it may not matter whether it does or not, but the child's interests come first, not the parents'.)

It's always possible to find a name which is both practical and sensible while being highly personal in its associations for the parents. It can reflect family tradition, nationality and religion if the parents want it to do so, while still being suitable for both baby and adult. The name you choose will become part of your child's identity, and it's important to get it right. If the questions asked above raise serious doubts of any kind, then think again. If they don't, then congratulations, you've found your name.